Rough Collies of Distinction

A PICTORIAL RECORD OF INFLUENTIAL BRITISH ROUGH COLLIES FROM THE 1860'S TO THE PRESENT DAY

Iris Combe, Dareen Bridge and Pat Hutchinson

Published by Iris Combe, Dareen Bridge and Pat Hutchinson

ISBN 0 9540257 0 9

First published in 2001 by Iris Combe, Dareen Bridge and Pat Hutchinson

"This useful and intelligent animal is one of the most placid, obedient, serene, and graceful members of the canine race. He is ever alive to the slightest indication of his master's wishes, prompt and gratified to execute them; and he seems to enjoy the greatest delight when employed to any kind of useful service. Formed by nature with an instinctive propensity to industry, he is never more pleased than in exerting his talents for the benefit of man, and in giving constant proofs of his inviolable attachment."

(Eulogy on the Rough Collie from the early eighteenth century, by Captain Thomas Brown F L S, a keen observer of canine character).

Designed by Mark Howlett
Printed in Great Britain by Piggott Printers Ltd. of Cambridge

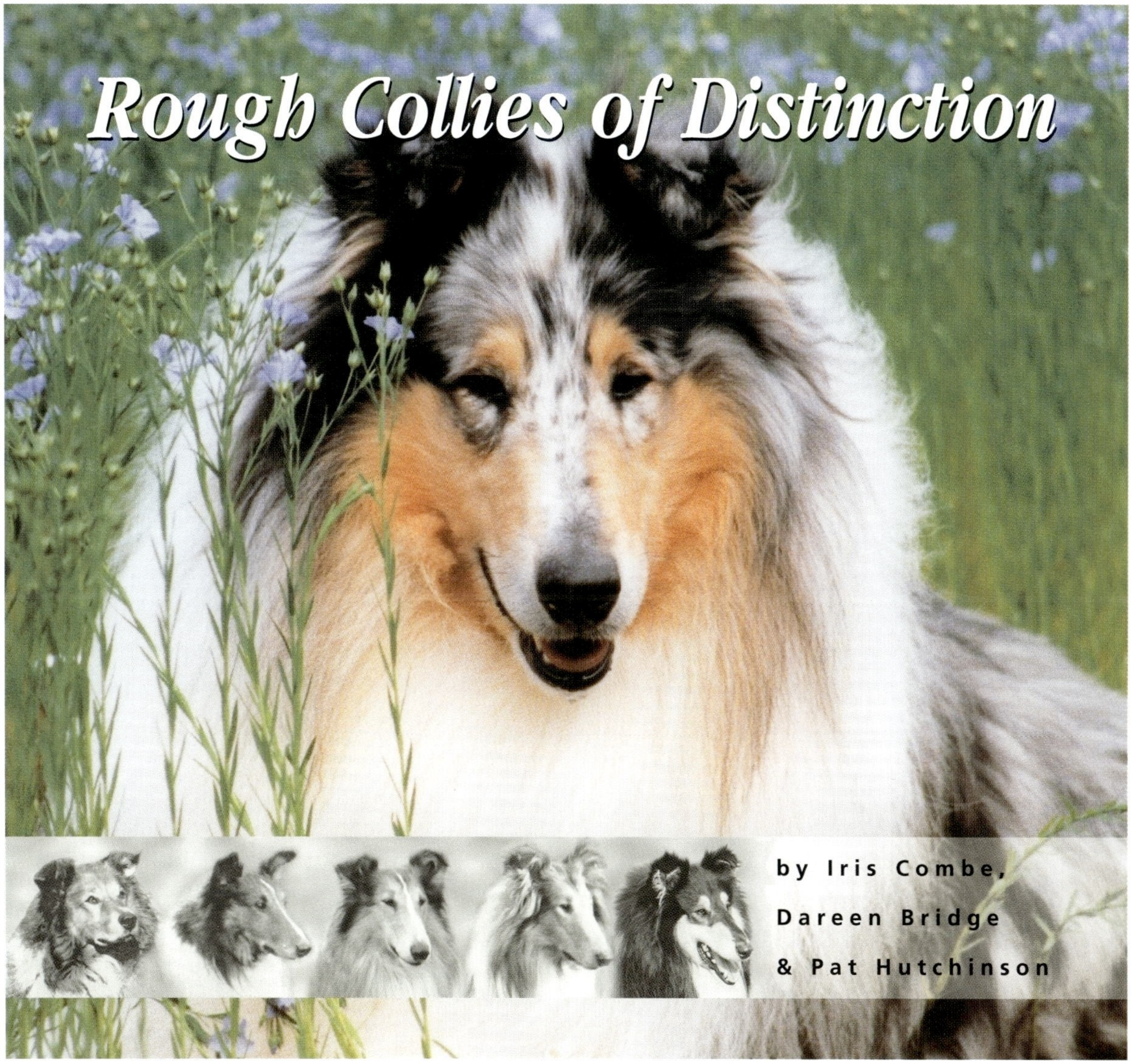
Rough Collies of Distinction
by Iris Combe,
Dareen Bridge
& Pat Hutchinson

Acknowledgements

We extend our grateful thanks to those organisations and individuals, too numerous to mention individually, who have loaned photographs and supplied information on the Rough Collies included within these pages. We hope they feel the results of rummaging in attics, boxes, albums and art collections have been worthwhile and we are most appreciative of their support.

Special mention must be made of John Hamshere (Hamshere Gallery) for his knowledge and help with locating many of the paintings of early Collies; John Baguley who, with his photographic skills, has brought some of the fragile scraps of Collie memorabilia to life; Mark Howlett whose responsibility has been for the design of the book and scanning the photographs and, although this was his first attempt at a specialist canine subject, interpreted our requirements so promptly; Don Hutchinson who volunteered to proof-read the draft; and numerous others, many of whom are unconnected with the show world, who provided valuable information.

We regret any errors that may have crept in but have relied on the accuracy of Kennel Club Stud Book Records together with information received, in good faith, from various sources.

Iris, Dareen & Pat.

Frontispiece photographs:

Champion Phreelancer Phrosty Moon Over Corydon *Present day*

Working Collie *1850's*

Seedley Superior *1920's*

Champion & Irish Champion Lochinvar of Ladypark *1940's*

Dazzler of Dunsinane *1960's*

Champion Karava Kornishman *1980's*

Preface

Rough Collies of Distinction is a tribute to those British Collies, their breeders and owners who have exerted influence over the breed's global development. Presented as a unique pictorial record this book traces the evolution of the Collie, from the nineteenth Century rough-coated farm dog to the instantly recognisable and registered breed that we all admire.

The book is compiled by Iris Combe, Collie historian and international Championship Show judge of Rough, Smooth and Border Collies; Pat Hutchinson, breeder, exhibitor and judge of Rough Collies; and breed archivist Dareen Bridge, who has been responsible for producing the principal male and female 'blood-line' charts which form an integral part of this work.

Dogs and bitches are catalogued in chronological order and include registration details, four-generation pedigrees, Kennel Club Stud Book entries and major awards, together with a brief profile of each representative. In certain cases the absence of suitable photographs has resulted in some influential Collies being incorporated into the entries of close family members.

Stud dogs have far greater potential for influencing breed type, due to the number of bitches they can serve and the numerous offspring produced during their stud careers, and because of this they tend to come under closer scrutiny. Those dogs which excel in the show ring quickly gain a reputation, which explains why it became fashionable for breeders to mate their bitches to the latest Champion. With a few notable exceptions it has therefore been the Champions who have been responsible for perpetuating blood-lines. Fortunately, discerning breeders have looked beyond show ring successes and we owe it to them that several prepotent sires have also been given opportunities to exert their influence on the breed.

Experienced breeders have always chosen their brood bitches with care, a fact which was echoed by Hugh Dalziel in 1888 with his comment in 'The Collie: Its History, Points and Breeding': *"...and a third mistake is to look for good pups from a worthless, ill-bred bitch, however good the dog she has been mated to"*. Great brood bitches, which reproduce quality progeny irrespective of the stud dog used, are a boon to any kennel. The influence of such paragons will often continue for several generations, forming the back-bone of the leading kennels of their day. History shows that, whether or not they possess show ring charisma, these bitches usually exhibit correct type and balance and should therefore be considered 'Collies of Distinction'.

A study of the 'Principal Sire and Dam Lines', in Appendices I & II, should enable readers to understand the major blood-lines more easily thereby drawing their own conclusions as to whether a particular 'Collie of Distinction' resulted from the dominance of the sire, the dam, a combination of the two, or the prepotency of one or more of the grandparents. This knowledge should be invaluable to breeders when selecting stud dogs and brood bitches to complement one another, the ultimate aim being the development, improvement and retention of essential Rough Collie characteristics for perpetuity.

No work of this nature would be complete without the inclusion of Collies who have excelled in working ability or show ring successes, and the interest generated by such ambassadors assures them a place as 'Rough Collies of Distinction'.

Editors: Iris Combe, Dareen Bridge and Pat Hutchinson.

Footnotes:
Throughout this work the editors have used name forms, breeding details and titles published in the Kennel Club Stud Books, and in some cases these may differ from those in general circulation. Reserve Challenge Certificate wins are generally omitted because they have been officially recorded only in recent years.
Successive Breed Standards refer to various alien breeds which are believed to have been incorporated by early enthusiasts in their efforts to improve the Collie's appearance and from the photographs it should become apparent how the Collie profile has altered over the years (see Appendix III).

List of Pictures

Contents

Introduction

Development of the Rough Collie as a Show Dog

The elegant and aristocratic Rough Collie seen in the show ring today, has its roots in the working farm dogs that have assisted British farming communities for many centuries. The Collie's evolution is evident in the pages that follow but here we highlight some of the events that led to this transformation.

Specialist canine breeding has been carried on for centuries and, prior to the emergence of dog shows, the emphasis was on a dog's working ability with little or no regard for appearance. The shepherds, drovers, and stockmen of yesteryear practised selective breeding as they required active, lithe, intelligent dogs with stamina and weather-proof coats to enable them to work in all conditions. Poor husbandry, infectious diseases such as hard pad and distemper, and the culling of surplus puppies, especially bitches, depleted populations ensuring only the fittest would survive. Male Collies were always the herdsman's preference whilst bitches, whose working lives were interrupted by seasons, were kept only if they proved to be either exceptional workers or broods.

The first documented dog show, held at Newcastle upon Tyne in 1859, was confined to Setters and Pointers. In December of the following year the Birmingham Dog Show Society, commonly referred to as Birmingham National, included classes for 'Non-Sporting Dogs'. The inclusion of pastoral dogs met with a degree of disapproval from country folk who considered a class for "sheepdogs, colleys, yard or keepers' dogs" to be unnecessary and demeaning of working sheepdogs. Most judges at that time were only conversant with Sporting Breeds and, in the absence of any Pastoral Breed Standards, their placings caused a great deal of criticism. The indoor arena was another bone of contention, and many exhibitors made it clear they considered it unsuitable for the judging of pastoral dogs by withdrawing their entries from this and subsequent shows.

The sketch by R H Moore provides an impression of an early show scene (circa 1860)

L'entrée d'une Exposition du *Kennel Club Anglais*

(Gravure extraite du Journal *Nederlandsche Sport.*)

A "Grand National Exhibition of Sporting and Other Dogs" was held at the Ashburnham Hall in Chelsea between 23 and 28 March 1868. This ambitious endeavour, intended to introduce dog shows to the social calendar, attracted huge crowds although arrangements for both exhibits and exhibitors invited censure.

Over the next few years interest in dog showing gradually increased and at the Birmingham Show of 1872 the committee scheduled a class for each sex, drawing an entry of twenty-four dogs and four bitches. Dog Shows at this time frequently had different management committees for each event and as each one issued its own set of rules and regulations, with profits going to the promoters, all kinds of malpractices abounded giving the sport a poor reputation. Not least amongst these was the custom of attaching a tag to the exhibit's collar which clearly advertised both dog and owner's names.

On 4 April 1873 twelve men met in London and the Kennel Club came into existence. This was largely at the instigation of Mr Sewallis Evelyn Shirley (see Appendix VII) who felt a body with the power to enforce decisions would do for dogs what the Jockey Club had done for equine affairs. The Kennel Club was formed principally for the promotion of Dog Shows, the inaugural one being held later the same year. For the first time all exhibitors had to abide by a set of ten rules designed to increase efficiency and eradicate the fraud and cheating which was then prevalent. Other show promoters, realising the advantage of better regulations, were quick in seeking permission to adopt these guidelines. During its second year the Kennel Club published its inaugural Stud Book (see Appendix V), a valuable work of reference which has been published annually ever since. This first volume detailed 4027 dogs, including seventy-seven "Sheepdogs and Scotch Colleys" (sub-headed as either "Farm Colleys" or "Sheepdogs of either coat") who had achieved class placings during the preceding fourteen years. It was not until 1895 that the Stud Book classified Collies as "Collies (Rough) and Collies (Smooth)."

For centuries herding competitions had formed part of the rural scene allowing local shepherds and stockmen to match the working ability of their collies against one another. The first official Sheepdog Trials took place in October 1873, jointly promoted by Gundog and Collie enthusiast Mr Shirley, who brought his shepherd and two dogs over from Ireland to look after the sheep, and Old English Sheepdog supporter Mr Lloyd-Price, who hosted the Trials on his Welsh Estate at Bala (see the illustration of Shamrock at the Bala Trials on page 10).The competition was attended by all classes of society and attracted much publicity as it was organised on a far grander scale than any previous event and whilst spectators were able to appreciate the worth, grace and skill of the herdsman's dogs, many were appalled at the neglected and unkempt appearance of some of them. After much discussion the organisers decided to schedule additional classes for the 'Best Conditioned Dog or Bitch', with prize money and trophies awarded to the winners.

Inspired by the success of the Bala Trials the Kennel Club ventured to organise a similar event at London's Alexandra Palace on 30 June 1876, with the advertisement clearly showing that the event scheduled a class for 'Appearance' to be judged by Messrs Shirley and Lloyd-Price. Although several Show Collies were apparently entered for the Trials it is difficult to distinguish them from the

Group of competitors at the Colley Trials, on the 30th June 1876.

working Collies illustrated here. All the prize-winners were listed as sheepdogs from Wales, including Mr E R Currie's 'Rover' who was awarded a silver cup, valued at £5, for winning the Appearance class. The event was never repeated because of the damage inflicted on Palace grounds by the forty poorly supervised Welsh mountain sheep, brought by train especially for the occasion. After this date followers of both the appearance and working disciplines travelled different roads, making the Collie the first casualty of the show/work divide.

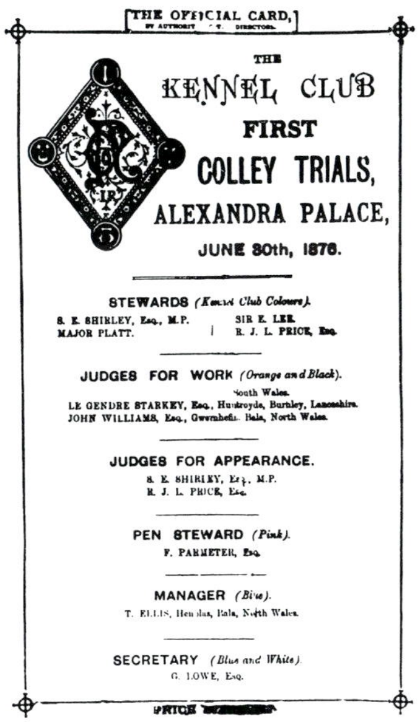

THE OFFICIAL CARD,

THE KENNEL CLUB FIRST COLLEY TRIALS, ALEXANDRA PALACE, JUNE 30th, 1876.

STEWARDS (Kennel Club Colours).
S. E. SHIRLEY, Esq., M.P. | SIR E. LEE
MAJOR PLATT. | R. J. L. PRICE, Esq.

JUDGES FOR WORK (Orange and Black).
LE GENDRE STARKEY, Esq., Huntroyde, Burnley, Lancashire.
JOHN WILLIAMS, Esq., Gwernhefin, Bala, North Wales.

JUDGES FOR APPEARANCE.
S. E. SHIRLEY, Esq., M.P.
R. J. L. PRICE, Esq.

PEN STEWARD (Pink).
F. PARMETER, Esq.

MANAGER (Blue).
T. ELLIS, Hendlas, Bala, North Wales.

SECRETARY (Blue and White).
G. LOWE, Esq.

PRICE

In 1877 the Kennel Club introduced regulations to rationalise the award of 'Champion' and this, over a twenty year period, gradually evolved to produce a close approximation to today's system of Challenge Certificates (see Appendix VI). A system of 'universal registration' for show dogs was introduced in 1880, with the twin aims of reducing the fraudulent entry of dogs under false names and improving efficiency and accuracy when compiling the annual Stud Book. These aims were bitterly opposed by many, the Birmingham Dog Show Society not least amongst these, but the Kennel Club eventually ruled the day and their transition from show promoting society to governing body was complete.

There now followed a dramatic increase in the popularity of the Collie as a show dog and, with fanciers visiting their local markets in search of good looking animals, farming communities were not slow to appreciate this new lucrative way of disposing of Collies unsuited to work. Animals acquired without pedigree appeared in show catalogues and the Kennel Club Stud Book as 'pedigree unknown'. Most of these early show Collies were 'rough-coated' and either black and white or black and tan in colour, but some were registered as black, tan and white, dull brown, brindled sable, golden sable, light sable, tortoiseshell, slate, mouse or variegated. They were commonly over-angulated, cow hocked and relatively low on the leg with unattractive feet, long backs, short necks, possessing shorter heads, a more pronounced stop and much lighter eyes than present day Collies.

The next milestone in the breed's development as a show dog came in 1881 with the formation of The Collie Club and, once again, it was the energetic Mr Shirley who provided the impetus.

Having collected together some of the breed's most prominent figures, the Collie Club's first step was the introduction of a Standard of Points, or Breed Standard (see Appendix III), thus enabling the Rough Collie to be accepted as a recognisable breed. Other Clubs took the Collie Club's lead, each issuing its own version but, by the beginning of the twentieth century, it was obvious that this situation could not continue. After a series of meetings between interested parties a new unified Breed Standard was issued jointly by all licensed Collie Clubs, and this remained in use until the Kennel Club assumed responsibility for all Breed Standards in 1950.

For the first few years of its existence the Collie Club did not hold its own Shows but supported 'special' Collie classes at 'all breed' Shows, and it was not until 2 June 1885 that the committee organised the first Collie Club Show. This was held at the Royal Aquarium, Westminster, and here we include the report taken from 'The Illustrated Sporting and Dramatic News' of 13 June 1885:

"Few dogs at the present day have risen to the height of popularity that the Collie has deservedly attained: few can boast of the intelligence that he is capable of showing under trying circumstances, as great a pet with the ladies as the fox-terrier has with the stronger sex. Alarmists effect to believe that the present training of the sheep dog is little more than a farce, that the type of the day is an overgrown, heavy, thick-coated dull-brained, timid animal, diverted from its legitimate walk in life to that of the drawing-room pet. How far they are correct in their supposition is an open question. However that may be, it would be as well to remember how uncertain and oftentimes savage in temperament was the dog taken from the care of flocks and installed as a household companion; how rarely he was trusted, how few cared for his flitting affection. Popular as he is in the present day, among all classes, it is difficult to believe that the club managed to secure little over 100 entries, liberal as was the first prize. Unaccountable circumstances have marred in numbers what is otherwise an excellent collection of first-class animals, true in type and quality, and in the favourable sable colour. Charlemagne, of whom it was his owner's proud boast that he had never been beaten until, at the late Kennel Club Show, at the Crystal Palace, Rutland snatched the palm from his grasp, was in better condition than ever, and again challenged allcomers successfully. It is to be regretted that Rutland was not present to again challenge the championship. Sly Fox, Eclipse, and Scottish Hero, of whose progeny the show was well be-sprinkled, were also in fine condition. Madge I, who won the Challenge Prize for rough-coated bitches, and Lady Help in the Challenge class for smooth-coated collies of either sex may well be looked to for fine strains. In the Open classes, Mr G Hall's Flockmaster took first, Mr S Boddington's Scotch Laddie second, and Mr W P Arkwright's Sky Blue, third prize ...."

This same article also referred to several of the winners who are featured on the adjoining illustration: *".....The following will be found among our illustrations: Mr W H Beach's Baronet, second prize; Miss Campbell's Sonsie of the Wey, commended; Mr W P Arkwright's Blue Ruin, a wonderful bitch that has a great future before her, first and special prize; Mr S T Mercier's Lowlander, first prize; Dr W A G James' Clover, commended; Mr G H Trollope's Tzar, commended; and Mr W H Ralph's champion Sly Fox."*

As interest in breeding for the show ring grew, a definite north-south divide developed amongst Rough Collie fanciers. Sheep and sheepdogs were traditionally synonymous with the hills and moorland regions of northern England, Wales, Scotland and Ireland, and this meant that the majority of unwanted Collies found their way to the markets of these regions. Not unnaturally, it was enthusiasts in these areas who were primarily attracted to the breed, customarily adopting their location as their official Kennel names such as Aughton, Parbold, Edgbaston, Wellesbourne, and Eden (which derives from the river running through Mr Fred Robson's home town of Carlisle).

The kennels of the early twentieth century were owned by either astute businessmen or the landed gentry, and were invariably run on a commercial scale, with staff employed to manage the large numbers of dogs which were often housed on more than one site. Males were still preferred, consistent winners having great potential as stud dogs, and frequently becoming 'worth their weight in gold'. Export potential was a further consideration and proven show winning stud dogs would often change hands for considerable sums. Bitches would be sent, unaccompanied, for service and they were not always mated to the dogs indicated by their owners, making pedigrees less accurate than one would wish. Young stock and brood bitches, if kept, were usually farmed out to country homes or satellite establishments in order to avoid the health problems associated with ever-changing kennel populations. The large numbers of dogs kept by many kennel owners enabled much close line-breeding and in-breeding to be undertaken. This practice quickly disclosed the best producers and aided the development of recognisable strains or families, some of which endure to this day. As several lines could be kept going within a strain, stud dogs from the home kennel were used regularly, and when no longer required would often be loaned to or exchanged with other breeders, a procedure still occasionally practised.

THE COLLIE DOG SHOW AT THE ROYAL AQUARIUM, WESTMINSTER.

Both World Wars caused many kennels to be disbanded with large numbers of Britain's best Collies crossing the Atlantic to enhance the breed in America. During the First World War the Kennel Club took the draconian step of not only suspending shows, but also limiting registration to puppies born under special licence. These difficulties were compounded by movement restrictions, imposed in response to a rabies outbreak towards the end of 1918 and followed by a universal muzzle order introduced the following June. When Championship Shows recommenced the main contenders for honours were Mr F Robson's Eden, Mr Lord's Seedley, and Mr W W Stansfield's Laund kennels, all of which had survived to dominate the early twenties. In 1920 Mr Stansfield campaigned a string of Collies to gain eighteen of the thirty-four Challenge Certificates on offer that year, making up three Champions in Laund Logic, Laird and Likeness. Indeed Logic gained eight of his ten Challenge Certificates, including the first post-war one to be awarded, during that same year.

Having gained valuable experience the first time round the Kennel Club adopted a more pragmatic approach to the Second World War. It cancelled all Championship Shows, those remaining being members-only competitions, with entries restricted to exhibitors living within a specified radius of the venue. There were no official restrictions on breeding and, although the war's duration and food shortages exerted their own constraints, several enthusiasts maintained only remnants of their original lines, whereas the likes of Mrs Newbery (Alphington), Mrs James (Mariemeau) and Mrs Nadine George (Beulah) continued something approaching serious breeding programmes. Mrs George was in a particularly strong position at the war's end, and this was reflected in the influence her dogs exerted on the successes of the immediate post-war period. Fittingly her Champion Beulah's Golden Future, the last Collie to gain its title prior to Championship Shows being suspended, sired the first post-war Challenge Certificate winner and Champion in Beulah's Golden Futureson.

Since the end of World War Two life in Britain has undergone gradual cultural and economic changes bringing increases in affluence, leisure time, and mobility, thereby enabling more people to enter the ranks of enthusiast. No longer is dog breeding restricted to the aristocracy, 'back-yard' breeder or stockman, for a new category of 'hobby exhibitor/breeder' has emerged which today forms the mainstay of the fancy. Improvements in veterinary care, particularly the introduction of immunisation against infectious diseases, nutrition, and kennel husbandry make it possible for breeders to consistently produce quality stock, albeit from a much smaller nucleus and from less frequent litters.

Rough Collies of Distinction

(1860's to the present day)

Cockie

Cockie's origins and pedigree details were never documented and one of only two known photographs, portraying him at ten years of age, is reproduced here. Despite being a typical farm-type Collie he was one of the first Collies to win in the show ring, being exhibited under the name of Cockie, Cockie Boy or Old Cockie. In farming circles 'Old' was used either as a term of endearment, or given to a dog when one of his offspring was given the same name.

Throughout the course of his fourteen years Cockie apparently changed ownership on at least three occasions but was always handled in the ring by Mr White, a livestock owner of Bleasby in Nottinghamshire. Prior to the formation of the Kennel Club in 1873, and publication of the first Stud Book in 1874, dog show results were not officially documented. However it is well known that the 1868 Birmingham Show scheduled one 'Sheepdog' class, which drew an entry of seventeen, and it was won by Mr Henshall's Old Mec, with Cockie in second place. In 1872 two 'Sheepdog' classes, one for dogs and one for bitches, drew an entry of twenty-four dogs and four bitches. Old Cockie won the dog class and Wolf the bitch class.

Mr White, Cockie's handler, regularly contributed to farming and canine journals and on 16 May 1874 he placed the following advertisement in 'The Fanciers' Gazette', making exaggerated claims about Cockie : *"The Champion Scotch Colley 'Cockie' at stud. This celebrated dog is winning upwards of thirty prizes taken at the principal shows in the North and South of England. A few of his chief performances are prizes at Birmingham four years in succession, including the Cups in 1872 and 73: first prize Maidstone and the Mayor's Cup: first prize Border Counties Show 1870, and the Open Champion Colley Cup, beating seventy four dogs (vide Mr Hetherington's letter in 'The Field' 14 March 1874) also first prize and cup for the best rough-coated Colley Nottingham 1873. Cockie is a grand, well proportioned dog, with a magnificent flag, well carried, muscular loins, and the true type of head, ears, colour and coat. Photos: 1s: large size mounted 6s each. For further particulars, stud fee etc apply owner: W.H. Johnson, High Bank House, Eccles, Manchester."*

On 18 August 1875 *"Cockie was sold at an auction at the Midland Counties Horse Repository .... there were 21 small plates engraved on his collar giving each of his wins. He was described in the catalogue as*

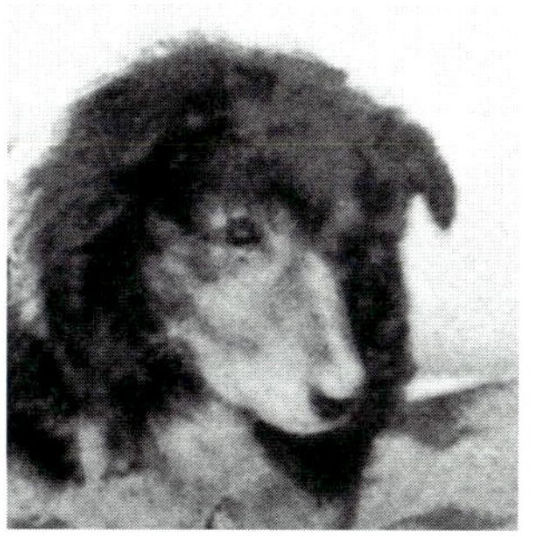

Breeder: Unknown

Owner: Mr W H Johnson

Handler: Mr White

Sable & White Dog

D.O.B. 1868

Sire: Unknown

Dam: Unknown

the best specimen ever exhibited, but he only fetched £3 that day." Following his transfer to Mr J Bissell in 1875, at the age of seven, Cockie enjoyed great success as a sire. Exhibitors were attracted to his sable and white colouring which was unusual amongst working Collies, the majority at that time being either black and white, black and tan or blue merle.

Only fourteen of Cockie's numerous progeny are entered in the Kennel Club Stud Books and they are all recorded as sable and white. This suggests that, not only was Cockie the first sable and white show Collie, he may well also have been dominant for the colour. As well as being one of the earliest Collies to win in the show ring, he was also the first Collie to establish two significant male lines, which unfortunately faded two generations later at Rob Roy MacGregor and four generations later with Caractacus, via his son Champion Wolf and grandson Champion Rutland (see page 24).

Cockie's real influence proved to be through his daughters, his most significant litter being whelped by Mr Bissell's Meg. From this litter, siblings Flirt[1] and Maude (occasionally referred to as Maud) were to exert the greatest influence on future generations. Through daughter Flirt[1], Cockie was the great grandsire of Champion Blue Ruin (see Scot, page 14), with Maude providing the greater impact by whelping siblings Flirt and Champion Charlemagne (by Trefoil). Maude's dominance was to last into the early twentieth century through such influential Collies as Champion Madge I, Champion Peggie II, Champion Eclipse (Charlemagne ex his sister Flirt), Champion Metchley Wonder and Christopher.

American fancier Dr O P Bennett asked Mr Charles H Wheeler, a knowledgeable judge and breeder of the Edgbaston Collies, to prepare a chapter on English dogs for his book 'The Collie' (1917). His description of Cockie provides one of the earliest blue prints for the rough- coated show Collie: *"In color 'Cockie' was a rich sable and white on neck, white frill, tip of tail, legs and feet; the latter slightly ticked with specks of brown. In size he was of medium order, sturdy in build and his well proportioned body was set upon legs and feet that were strong in bone and sound. He had a plentiful supply of the desirable class of coat, to the density of which a full under coat contributed. The coat was very full on neck and shoulders, forming a handsome mane and cape. Suffice to say, his head, placement of eye and expression were praiseworthy; no 'railway lines' up face with veins showing each side; but consistent in both length and shape and correct in finish of fore-face. His ears were moderate as regards size and if not carried so high as those of some of the more modern productions, were natural and carried semi-erect; a carriage which gave a more artistic finishing touch to the picture than do the tampered with pricked ears."*

Miss Margaret Osborne, in her book 'The Collie', claims that Old Cockie was not a big dog as she had read that his son, Champion Cocksie, was 'a little bigger than his sire' and it was recorded that Champion Cocksie was 21½ ins at the shoulder.

Champion Wolf, sable and white son of Cockie.
Watercolour by Arthur Wardle 1886, reproduced by kind permission of the Boddington family.
The paintings of Champions Wolf and Rutland (see page 24) were presented by the artist to Mr Samuel Boddington, in whose family they remained undiscovered until a chance meeting between his great granddaughter and one of the UK's prominent breed judges was recently brought to the editors' attention.
Photo: Ian Lott LRPS, LMPA

Footnote:
1. Cockie's daughter Flirt (ex Meg) should not be confused with his granddaughter Flirt (Trefoil ex Maude).

The first sheep dog trial (Bala, October 1873)

Shamrock

1870

Breeder: Mr Glasby

Owner: Mr S E Shirley

K.C. Stud Book No. 2897[1]

Black, Tan & White Dog

D.O.B. 1870

Sire: Shep (Mr McCall's)

Dam: Bess (Mr Glasby's)

Shamrock was one of the first rough-coated working and exhibition Collies and was fortunate to have an official, if somewhat limited, pedigree. His ancestors were descended from an ancient strain of farm dog brought to Ireland, between the fifth and first centuries B C, by migrant Celtic farming groups. The word 'Collie' or 'useful dog' is derived from their common dialect known as Q Celtic. This strain of dogs has remained pure, partly through isolation and partly by careful selection of suitable breeding stock.

When Mr Sewallis Evelyn Shirley[2] MP JP took up residence at his Lough Fea Estate in Carrickmacross he was introduced to this working strain by his shepherd Mr Smith. He admired Bess, a bitch belonging to neighbour Mr Glasby, and when Bess whelped a litter by Mr McCall's Shep, Mr Shirley purchased one of the pups and named it Shamrock. Bess was purely a working dog and, as her name does not appear in the Kennel Club Stud Book, she was presumably never exhibited. As far as we can ascertain there are no illustrations of her and the only description we have of her is taken from an extract in 'The Fanciers'Gazette' of 30 May 1874: *"….. Bess black, white and tan. When a young bitch, before she lost her feather, a handsomer one it would be hard to find, and also useful for work."* Bess' influence on the Rough Collie should not be overlooked as she was the dam of half brothers Shamrock (by Shep) and Trefoil (by Twig), and it is to these two dogs that modern day show Rough Collies can trace their ancestry.

The illustration featured here is believed to be of Shamrock. It appeared with a report in 'The Field' of the first organised Sheepdog Trials at Bala[3], North Wales in 1873. One of the organisers, Mr Shirley, brought his shepherd Mr Smith over from Ireland, together with a dog and bitch to protect the sheep for the duration of the competition. Despite being primarily a working dog Shamrock was also exhibited by Mr Shirley and he gains his place in the history books as one of the first working Rough Collies to be successful in the show ring. During the same year as the 1873 Bala Trials, Shamrock was apparently campaigned quite extensively and won first prizes in Glasgow, Fakenham and at the Kennel Club's first Show at Crystal Palace.

Previous authors have referred to Trefoil as the dog to which all show Rough Collies can be traced, but as Shamrock may well have been Trefoil's great grandsire (see Trefoil's footnote 2, page 13) his importance to the early history of the breed cannot be understated.

Sire Shep (Mr McCall's)	Dog belonging to Sir G Foster, Baronet, of Charterhouse, Louth near Carrickmacross	-	-
		-	-
	-	-	-
		-	-
Dam Bess (Mr Glasby's)	Rattler (Mr Byrne's)	-	-
		-	-
	Bess (Mr Watts')	Dog belonging to Mr J Smith (Mr Shirley's shepherd)	-
		Bitch belonging to Mr T Johnson (Steward of Longfield, Carrickmacross)	-

See 'Early Collie Male lines' in Appendix I

Footnotes:

1. *See Appendix V for Kennel Club Stud Book qualifications*
2. *See Appendix VII on Mr S E Shirley MP JP, founder member of the Kennel Club and the first Collie Club.*
3. *Details of the Bala Trials and Colley Trials can be found in 'The Development of the Rough Collie as a Show dog', page 2*

Trefoil

MR. SHIRLEY'S COLLEY DOG "TREFOIL." (see page 128).

Illustration from the 'Fanciers' Gazette', 30 May 1874

Although the Kennel Club was inaugurated in the year of **Trefoil**'s birth, detailed record keeping remained the exception rather than the norm. Mr Shirley was one of the first fanciers to understand the necessity for accurate records and so his own dogs were amongst the first to be registered with extended pedigrees. Volume I of the Kennel Club Stud Book contains extended pedigrees of Shamrock and Laddie only, and the situation was slow to improve as Volume II contains only the extended pedigrees of Trefoil and Mr Sivitel's Meggy (4531). It is interesting to note from Trefoil's breeding that he and Shamrock were half brothers, both being whelped by Bess (she originally belonged to Mr Glasby but at this stage was in Mr Shirley's ownership), but sired by different dogs.

Mr Shirley's shepherd, Mr Smith, worked Trefoil alongside Shamrock on the Shirley Estate at Lough Fea. Trefoil was a farm-type dog with cow hocks but, despite this, was a successful sire and show dog winning first prizes at Northampton and Crystal Palace. Described as *" a shapely, gay, attractive looking dog with a long coat"*, he is known to have sired dogs with frills that almost touched the ground. Hugh Dalziel in his book 'The Collie: Its History, Points and Breeding', published in 1888, described him as *"The champion of his time in good looks and genuine Collie qualities"*.

The engraving reproduced here is the only known illustration of Trefoil, and it appeared with the following extract from 'The Fanciers' Gazette' 30th May 1874:*"We were so much struck with the superiority of Mr Shirley's dog Trefoil, at the Northampton Show - the only time he has ever been exhibited and where, it will be remembered he won 1st prize- that we obtained permission to have a portrait drawn from life, which appears with these remarks. Trefoil is quite a young dog, being now just over twelve months old, and is descended from a very old pure strain that has been in Mr Shirley's possession for a considerable time. He is larger than his parents, his sire Twig being a small black and tan dog, his dam Bess black, white and tan. Trefoil himself is a dog of great intelligence, and with a most beautiful temperament. We may add that he is worked regularly with a large flock of sheep, and if the time ever comes that prizes are given for*

1873

combined looks and working sheep dogs, as for Pointers and Setters, he will prove an opponent of no ordinary pretensions".

Encouraged by Trefoil's brilliant show career Mr Shirley repeated the mating of Twig and Bess producing Tricolour[1] and the black and tan dog Tartan, and it is from these dogs that the famous Shirley strain of Irish Collies was developed. The following extract from 'The Stock Keepers' Journal' 1886 confirms this achievement: *"Nearly every winning Collie of the hour traces its pedigree back to Trefoil the pick of Mr Shirley's famous strain".*

Trefoil's sire line extends to present day Collies through his most prepotent son Champion Charlemagne and great grandson Champion Metchley Wonder (see pages 16 and 26).

Breeder/Owner: Mr S E Shirley MP JP

K.C. Stud Book No. 4523

Black, Tan & White Dog

D.O.B. 19 March 1873

Sire: Twig (Mr Shirley's)

Dam: Bess (Mr Shirley's-formerly owned by Mr Glasby)

Sire Twig (Mr Shirley's)	Old Twig	-	- -
		-	- -
	Help (see Footnote 2)	-	- -
		-	- -
Dam Bess (Mr Shirley's)	Rattler (Mr Byrne's)	-	- -
		-	- -
	Bess (Mr Watts')	Dog belonging to Mr J Smith (Mr Shirley's shepherd)	- -
		Bitch belonging to Mr T Johnson (Steward of Longfield, Carrickmacross)	- -

See 'Early Collie Male lines' in Appendix I

Footnotes:

1. *There is no colour recorded for Tricolour in the Stud Book. Dr O P Bennett suggests that, as his name implies, he was black and tan with perhaps a little white.*
2. *Most of the early Collie books do not extend Trefoil's pedigree as there appear to be discrepancies both in the parentage and sex of Help. Over the years there has been some confusion as to the sex of the Help in Trefoil's pedigree. In the first seven volumes of the Stud Books there are four Collies named Help and three of these are dogs, but all are given dates of birth that are later than Twig's dam could possibly have been. The fourth Help appears in Volume I so no sex is given, and we know only that this Collie was owned by Mr T Ashton of Cliffe Hall, Tamworth, and won a first prize at Birmingham in 1865. There are also two other Helps, without Stud Book numbers, but they appear to have no Irish connections. Additional information on the parentage of Trefoil's dam Help can be found in W.W. Thomson's Kennel Gazette article of December 1896, in which he traces Trefoil's pedigree as follows: "By Twig, ex Bess, by Byrne's Rattler, ex Watts' Bess; Twig, by Old Twig ex Help, by Shamrock, whose pedigree is interesting..." Trefoil's pedigree entry in the Kennel Club Stud Book, Volume II, reads similarly apart from the reference to Twig being "by Old Twig out of Help (see Shamrock No. 2897, Vol.I)." If we take the Stud Book and Thomson's information as correct the implication is therefore that Help was a bitch and she was sired by Shamrock. Iris Combe, however, had access to the private kennel records of the Shirley family and they maintained that Shamrock was actually the sire of Old Twig! (see Irish ancestry of the Rough Collie in the 'All Ireland Collie and Sheepdog Society's Handbook 1993', pages 41 – 45 and 'Rough Collie Records', page 24).*

Scot

Despite **Scot** being of unknown parentage and the absence of illustrations or photographic records, he is featured here as the foundation of the blue merle show Collie in Britain. Most of the merled collies at this time were smooth coated and so, when Mr Brackenbury of Thorpe Hall Farm, Downham in Norfolk introduced the heavily coated Scot onto the show scene there was a great deal of interest. Scot was quite successful in the show ring winning a third at Wigan, second at Chesterfield and firsts at Bristol and Fakenham when the judge, Hugh Dalziel, "*considered him first in a good class*'.

Mr Arkwright, a kennel owner from the Midlands, when trying to revive the blue merle Rough Collie, admired Scot describing him as *"a light silvery blue, beautifully clouded with black; white collar, frill, blaze, paws and tag; face and forelegs were bordered by bright red, and having one china eye*". Having mated Scot to his bitch Russet, who was registered as a 'red grizzle', a bitch puppy was retained and named Blue Stocking. She in turn whelped Blue Rose (by Redbreast), and when Blue Rose was mated back to her grandsire Scot she produced siblings Blue Sky and Blue Thistle on 2 April 1882. Blue Sky mated to his niece Blue Blazes produced siblings Blue Eyes and Blue Devils on 10 April 1887 (see pedigree). Blue Sky's sister, Blue Thistle, whelped two litters of great significance. In her litter to Champion Rutland (see page 24) she whelped sibling daughters Blue Blazes and Thistledown and, when mated to Donald (Carlyle ex Flirt, a daughter of Old Cockie), she produced Mr Arkwright's famous blue merle, Champion Blue Ruin in 1884, who was described as having a beautiful shape and clear blue colour. Blue Ruin became the first blue merle Champion, winning a total of eight Challenge Certificates and annexing The Collie Club's Challenge Trophy (for Best of Breed) at the Kennel Club's Show of 1888, becoming the first blue merle to do so. Two years later she was exported to the United States of America.

Among Mr Arkwright's other well known blue merles were Blue Bottle and Blue Bird, but it was Champion Blue Ruin, Blue Sky and his son Blue Devils who were to prove the most successful.

As there is no known pictorial record of Scot the portrait and pedigree of Scot's grandson, Blue Devils, are featured here.

Portrait of **Yardley Blue Devils** (formerly Blue Devils), by E Aistrop

Reproduced by kind permission of Bonhams and Brooks of London.

(The portrait was sold at auction in New York on 13 February 2001).

Sire Blue Sky	Scot	-	-
			-
		-	-
			-
	Blue Rose	Redbreast	Lynn
			Moll
		Blue Stocking	Scot
			Russett
Dam Blue Blazes	Ch Rutland	Ch Wolf	Cockie
			Lorna
		Ch Madge I	Marcus
			Ruby III
	Blue Thistle	Scot	-
			-
		Blue Rose	Redbreast
			Blue Stocking

1873

Breeder: Unknown

Owner: Mr F B Brackenbury

K.C. Stud Book No. 6495

Grey, tan, white with china eyes (Blue Merle Dog)

D.O.B. 1873

Sire: Unknown

Dam: Unknown

Mr W W Thomson, in his article 'Pillars of the Stud Book – Collies' (Kennel Gazette 1896) refers to the blue merle collie as follows: *"I must refer to a strain of Collies now again becoming popular – I mean Blue Merles. Curiously enough, for years past, there have been many good Smooths this colour, and comparatively few good Roughs. Mr W P Arkwright took great interest in these latter, and was successful in breeding some excellent specimens. Latterly, Mr Barlow has taken up the breed and I have a notion, must have some of Mr Arkwright" blood; but so far I have not been able to trace this connection. The earliest pillar of this strain, I quite believe, was Scot (6495), whose owner described him as 'grey, tan and white; china eyes'. Scot was the sire of Blue Sky, a winner on the bench, out of Blue Rose, by Redbreast ex Blue Stocking;*[1] *also by Scot. The dam of Blue Stocking was out of Lassie (4529), by Mr Waite's Scottie (4521), whelped 1870, and imported from Scotland. Lassie's dam was a Smooth bitch named Waite, bred by Wat Hotson, of Eskdale in 1867. Redbreast was by a black-and-tan dog of mine named Lynn, bred by Mr Boyle of Barnstaple, by Watch ex Trip, from a strain of collies introduced into Devonshire by Farmer John, Duke of Bedford, almost a century ago. Blue Ruin was one of the best of this colour, bred by Mr Arkwright, and she was by Donald, a black tan and white dog out of a bitch by Scot. Donald was by Carlyle, from a Cockie bitch."*

Following the disbanding of Mr Arkwright's kennels in 1890, with the subsequent export of Champion Blue Ruin[2] to the United States of America, to assist in the revival of the American merle, British interest in the colour waned for several years. Historically the blue merle was one of the most common sheepdog colours but, as farmers did not favour it, many were drowned at birth. However in his attempt at promoting new interest in blue merles Mr F Barlow obtained Blue Devils, renamed him Yardley Blue Devils, and mated him to both sable and tricolour bitches retaining only blue merle puppies. Queen Victoria and Queen Alexandra favoured the blue merle and this led to their renewed popularity. Blue specialists of the early twentieth century were Mr J Powers with Barwell Lass, Mr C White in 1906 with Princess Alice and Blue Princess Alexandra, and Mr Packwood with Billesley Bluey whose name appears behind many of the Westcarr, Ladypark, Glenmist and Rokeby Collies.

In his book of 1888 , "The Collie: Its History, Points and Breeding", Hugh Dalziel referred to the blue merle collie or Welsh Heeler as a 'mirled' or 'marbled' variety. He commented that "the animals are not peculiar to Wales, and, indeed, appear to be rather accidental productions, or freaks of Nature, than an established strain producing their like when bred inter se".

Footnotes:

1. *From information provided in the W W Thomson quotation, readers can extend Redbreast and Blue Stocking's pedigrees a further one and two generations respectively. Please note Mr Waite's Scottie (4521) was the sire of Lassie (4529) and not the sire of Blue Stocking.*
2. *The only known illustration of Champion Blue Ruin is included in the sketch of Collie exhibitors at the inaugural Collie Club Show, see page 5*

Champion Charlemagne

1879

Breeder/Owner: Mr J Bissell

K.C. Stud Book No. 10691

Sable & White Dog

D.O.B. 4 January 1879

Sire: Trefoil

Dam: Maude

WINNER OF 14 CHAMPIONS' CLASSES

WINNER OF THE COLLIE CLUB'S CHALLENGE TROPHY IN 1890

Around this time Rough Collies were becoming fashionable as companions so breeders tended to select puppies with a more aristocratic appearance rather than for their working abilities. The combination of Trefoil's Irish blood with that of Cockie's daughter Maude, produced a more elegant and refined type of Collie, epitomised by **Champion Charlemagne**[1]. Although the photograph was taken when Charlemagne was ten years old some refinement of head can still be noted . This may have come either from his dam Maude or his granddam Bess.

Charlemagne was described by Mr Packwood as having *"great grandeur, being a showily marked sable/white with a beautiful head but was inclined to carry his ears erect"*. From this remark it will be noted that, even before an official Breed Standard was in existence, the 'Show' Collie was required to have tipped ears. Charlemagne was one of the breed's earliest Champions and during his show career he was the winner of fourteen 'Champions' classes, a record that was eventually eclipsed by his son of that name. Following a win at one of the Collie Club's shows, Rawdon Lee says of Charlemagne:: *"After being kept at home for some time one was somewhat taken aback to find the old dog, - occupying the first bench in the last show of the Collie Club – Still the judge, Mr Wake-Walker, placed him over all, because he considered him best in every way excepting so far as locomotion was concerned"*.

In the Kennel Gazette article 'Pillars of the Stud Book – Collies' (December 1896) WW Thomson refers to Charlemagne as follows: *"Charlemagne's best son was undoubtedly Eclipse, who inherited his sire's wonderful coat and good ears. Maude, the dam of Charlemagne, deserves a special notice as a pillar, for in the same litter she produced Trevor, who, though not so great a winner on the bench as his illustrious brother……."*

Champion Charlemagne's most important son was Champion Eclipse (ex his litter sister Flirt[2]) and, although Eclipse (see page 22) was not a particularly important sire, he did much to popularise the Rough Collie with the general public. However Charlemagne's union with Champion Madge I exerted his greatest influence on the breed as this combination established the dominance of the Trefoil line through his prepotent grandson Champion Metchley Wonder and great grandson Christopher (see pages 26 and 28).

Sire Trefoil	Twig	'Old' Twig	-
			-
		Help *(see Trefoil, footnote 2, page*13)	-
			-
	Bess (Mr Shirley's)[3]	Rattler	-
			-
		Bess (Mr Watts')	Dog belonging to J Smith
			Bitch belonging to T Johnson
Dam Maude	Cockie	-	-
			-
		-	-
			-
	Meg	Mec	-
			-
		Clyde	-
			Bitch belonging to Mr Lacy

See 'Early Collie Male lines' in Appendix I, and '(Lacy's) Scott and Clyde-family b' in Appendix II.

Footnotes:

1. *See Appendix VI on the Development of Champion entitlement.*
2. *Maude had a sister named Flirt who should not be mistaken for her daughter Flirt, Champion Charlemagne's litter sister and dam of Champion Eclipse.*
3. *After Bess whelped Shamrock she was transferred from Mr Glasby to Mr Shirley's ownership.*

Champion Madge I

Madge's maternal great granddam Elsie, a bitch of unknown parentage, was owned by the Honourable Captain Everard Digby. She headed one of the most important breeding lines of the late nineteenth century, the most important of her female descendants being her granddaughter Ruby III, who was the dam of Champion Madge I, a granddam of Champion Peggie II (see page 20) and great granddam of siblings Christopher (see page 28) and Champion Sefton Grace respectively. In his 'Show Collies' Packwood comments: *It is a logical assumption that the Hon. Captain E Digby's Elsie, which formed the nucleus of the Rev Hans Hamilton's strain, was born of parents which were of the true type, as at this point the prevailing great feature about the Collies belonging to the latter breeder was the typical head. This valuable property was extended to both Sooty and Peggie II, and still further to that exquisite quality dog Ch Christopher."*

The following quotation is taken from an article published in the December 1896 edition of the Kennel Gazette, written by Mr W W Thomson and entitled 'Pillars of the Stud Book – Collies': *"Tricolour, brother to Trefoil from a younger litter, was through his son Tricolour II, of great service in the Rev. Hans Hamilton's kennel, as he was the sire of Ruby III, who was mated with Marcus*[1] *(a black collie, celebrated for his marvellous coat and good ears, brought from Scotland, and purchased soon after his arrival by me), and produced several prize winners, chief amongst which was Madge I, referred to in the pedigree of Metchley Wonder."*

W Baskerville, in his 'Show Collies and Shetland Sheepdogs', comments on Champion Madge I as follows:" *In 1879, at the Bristol Show, the Rev Hans Hamilton brought out a remarkably strong team, consisting of Angus (by Walker's Scott ex Charles' Lassie), Jock, Captain, Eva, and Ruby III; the latter trio being by Tricolour II, ex Nellie by Bob ex the Hon. E Digby's Elsie. His exhibits also included a litter by Marcus ex Ruby III, which contained Zulu Princess*[2]*, Donald and Madge, three famous prize winners, the last mentioned being the famous Ch Madge, the best specimen of her day; she also has had great influence in the*

1879

perfecting of the Collie, and is indeed one of the pillars of stud books. It is said that Ch Madge was the first to start the fashion of the higher ear carriage now desired."

Champion Madge I remained in the Woodmansterne Kennels, gaining her title easily by winning ten Challenge/Champions' classes in all, a feat which was later equalled by her daughter Champion Peggie II (see page 20). She is included as a 'Collie of Distinction' because of her impact on the breed as an outstanding brood bitch. Three of her offspring, each by different sires, made significant contributions to Collie history. These were Champion Peggie II (by Ruthven), Champion Rutland (by Cockie's son Champion Wolf) and Sefton (by Champion Charlemagne). Champion Peggie II was to become the dam of Christopher (see page 28); Champion Rutland was the most successful winner of his day (see page 24); and Sefton, although not of the same quality as his half sister and brother Peggie and Rutland respectively, secured his place in history as the sire of Champion Metchley Wonder.

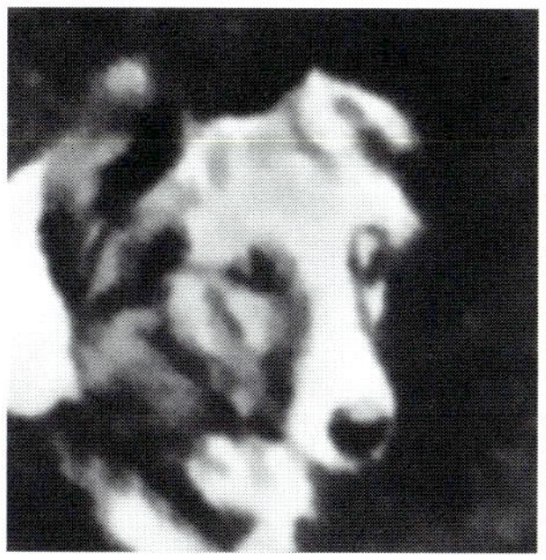

Breeder/Owner: Reverend Hans F Hamilton

K.C. Stud Book No. 10746

Tricolour Bitch

D.O.B. 10 September 1879

Sire: Marcus

Dam: Ruby III

WINNER OF 10 CHALLENGE/ CHAMPIONS' CLASSES

Sire Marcus	-	-	-
			-
		-	-
			-
	-	-	-
			-
		-	-
			-
Dam Ruby III	Tricolour II	Tricolour	Twig (Mr Shirley's)
			Bess (Mr Glasby's)
		Lorna	Tartan
			Maude (Mr Bissell's)
	Nellie	Bob (unregistered)	-
			-
		Elsie	-
			-

See '(Digby's) Elsie-family a' in Appendix II.

Footnotes:

1. *Dr O P Bennett, in 'The Collie', refers to Marcus as "a black and white, now five years of age, the winner of over twenty first prizes in England and also a Championship at Dublin. Mr Wheeler, in the forepart of this book, described him as a typical collie in every respect, but evidently age had commenced to tell for Mr Watson, who judged him often, said he had nothing wonderful and that all of his puppies, of whom he left a good many, had lop ears."*
2. *Madge's daughter Zulu Princess was exported to the Hempstead Farm Kennels, in the United States, where she joined Champion Charlemagne's sister Effie. Both bitches subsequently gained their American titles.*

Photo courtesy of the Museum of Natural History, Berne, Switzerland/Ursula Gantner[1]

Sire Ruthven	Angus (unregistered)	Scott (Mr Walker's)	Trefoil
			Waite (Smooth Collie)
		Lassie (Mr Charles')	-
			-
	Luna (unregistered)	Tricolour II	Tricolour
			Lorna (Clunny or Cluny ex Elsie)
		(see Footnote 2)	-
			-
Dam Champion Madge I	Marcus	-	-
			-
		-	-
			-
	Ruby III	Tricolour II	Tricolour
			Lorna
		Nellie	Bob (unregistered)
			Elsie

See '(Digby's) Elsie-family a' in Appendix II.

Champion Peggie II

1881

Champion Peggie II was half sister to Champion Rutland (see page 24) and the similarity of head patterns can easily be recognised from the pictures. Peggie, bred and owned by the Reverend Hans Hamilton, was a double great great granddaughter of Tricolour, full brother to Trefoil but from a later litter by Twig ex Bess. Registered with the Kennel Club as red and white she was the first sable and white in a family of black and tan or tricolour bitches.

Peggie II was the third generation of Rough Collie show bitches, a rarity in the 1880's as bitches were only occasionally exhibited. In the show ring she equalled her dam's record by winning the Challenge/Champions' classes ten times, gaining her Stud Book number in 1882 by winning the bitch class at the Kennel Club's own Show, and her title in 1884. Charles Wheeler (Edgbaston) in O P Bennett's 'The Collie' referred to Peggie as follows: *"Rev. Hans F Hamilton's 'Peggie II', winner of 1st prize and cup, bitch puppies, at the Kennel Club's show, 1882. In colour sable and white. She excelled in head, expression and Collie character, was also very shapely, and carried a coat of the desired class".*

Besides being a successful show collie Peggie excelled as a brood bitch. She whelped at least four litters, eleven of her offspring winning their way into the Kennel Club Stud Book. Several of these were well known dogs such as Christopher (by Champion Metchley Wonder), Darnley II (by Champion Charlemagne) and his half brother Oswald (by Bachelor), both owned by H M Queen Victoria.

Siblings Christopher and Grace III caused great interest at the inaugural Crufts Show in 1891, as they each won their respective Challenge classes. Later that same year Grace was transferred to the ownership of Messrs J and W Birch who changed her name to Sefton Grace. Grace's show ring successes continued, not only by gaining her title but exceeding her dam's record, by winning twenty-two Challenge/Champions' classes during a six year campaign.

It was Christopher, however, who was to go down in history as Peggie's most famous and influential son. He was to head the 'Piccolo' and 'Squire' sire lines through his two sons Edgbaston Marvel and Champion Stracathro Ralph respectively.

Breeder/Owner: Reverend Hans F Hamilton

K.C.Stud Book No. 12995

Red & White Bitch

D.O.B. 17 August 1881

Sire: Ruthven

Dam: Champion Madge I

WINNER OF 10 CHALLENGE/ CHAMPIONS' CLASSES

Footnotes:

1. *The name 'Max Fehr', a founder member of the Swiss Collie Club in 1901, is hand written on the reverse of this portrait of Peggie II. As Peggie II never left England, it is probable that Max Fehr purchased the portrait at the sale of Reverend Hamilton's personal effects, advertised in the Collie Folio following his death in 1912. The portrait of Peggie is currently owned by the Museum of Natural History in Berne, and forms part of a collection bequeathed by a Mrs Egg-Leach in 1960. The connection between Max Fehr and Mrs Egg-Leach is unknown.*
2. *Luna's sire is recorded in the Stud Book but her dam is not. On researching Tricolour II's offspring that gained Stud Book numbers, and knowing that Ruthven was bred by the Reverend Hamilton, the most likely dam of Luna is either Jessie (8532) or Nellie (daughter of Elsie, 5430). The other note of interest is that the sire of Tricolour II was Tricolour, full brother (later litter) to Trefoil.*

Painting by Frank Paton 1887, reproduced by courtesy of Christies, London

Champion Eclipse

Champion Eclipse[1], bred by Mr J Bissell, resulted from a brother to sister mating and was therefore a double grandson of Trefoil and double great grandson of Cockie. He was sold for £100 as a puppy, to Mr G R Krehl at the Birmingham Show. Eclipse was considered to be the best of Charlemagne's sons and he enjoyed a most successful show career. Between 1884 and 1888 he won a total of sixteen Champions' classes and was confirmed as the Kennel Club's first official Champion.

Champion Eclipse also helped to popularise the breed with the general public. In order to overcome the dog's shyness Mr Krehl, who lived in Hanover Square, London, used to exercise him daily in Hyde Park where he became a great favourite of the upper class ladies, their children and nannies. Eclipse's admirers followed his show career with great interest and he was photographed almost daily, often with small children. His portrait was also painted by several artists, and the picture here is taken from a Frank Paton painting of 1887.

Champion Eclipse was not especially noteworthy as a sire, but he was well used at stud, especially by American breeders who shipped bitches across the Atlantic to him, as breeders believed he was sable dominant. The following announcement found in the 'Club and Kennel Notes' of the Kennel Gazette, January 1884, proves that this was not the case:

"Mr Krehl's Collie Eclipse has had forty pups (all sable but six) born to him within three weeks. This is a very good stud form for a dog against whom it was lately insinuated in a Contemporary that he was impotent."

Sire Champion Charlemagne	Trefoil	Twig	'Old' Twig
			Help
		Bess (Mr Shirley's)	Rattler
			Bess (Mr Watts')
	Maude (Mr Bissell's)	Cockie	
		Meg	Mec
			Clyde
Dam Flirt	Trefoil	Twig	'Old' Twig
			Help
		Bess (Mr Shirley's)	Rattler
			Bess (Mr Watts')
	Maude (Mr Bissell's)	Cockie	
		Meg	Mec
			Clyde

See 'Early Collie Male lines' in Appendix I, and '(Lacy's) Scott and Clyde-family b' in Appendix II.

Breeder: Mr J Bissell

Owner: Mr G R Krehl

K.C. Stud Book No. 12949

Sable & White Dog

D.O.B. 11 January 1882

Sire: Champion Charlemagne

Dam: Flirt

WINNER OF 16 CHAMPIONS' CLASSES

WINNER OF THE COLLIE CLUB'S CHALLENGE TROPHY – 1887

Footnote:

1. *According to Kennel Club records Eclipse was the first official Champion Rough Collie. Prior to 1888 not all Champions' and Challenge classes were held under Kennel Club rules so winners were not actually entitled to be known as Champions (see Appendix VI)*

Champion Rutland

Arthur Wardle Watercolour, 1886, reproduced by kind permission of the Boddington family *Photo by Ian Lott LRPS, LMPA.*

Sire Champion Wolf	Cockie	-	-
			-
		-	-
			-
	Lorna	Tartan	Twig (Mr Shirley's)
			Bess (Mr Shirley's)
		Maude (Mr Bissell's)	Cockie
			Meg
Dam Champion Madge I	Marcus	-	-
			-
		-	-
			-
	Ruby III	Tricolour II	Tricolour
			Lorna
		Nellie	Bob (unregistered)
			Elsie

See 'Early Collie Male lines' in Appendix I, and '(Digby's) Elsie-family a' in Appendix II.

1882

At the Birmingham Show of 1879 Champion Wolf (see page 9), a shaded sable son of Cockie bred by Birmingham enthusiast Mr J Bissell, was sold to the Reverend Hans Hamilton for £50. Ten months after she gave birth to Champion Peggie II (see page 20), Champion Madge I whelped Rutland (by Champion Wolf who resulted from a grandfather to granddaughter mating). Both sides of Rutland's pedigree therefore trace back to Mr Shirley's kennels through Tricolour and Tartan, younger brothers of the celebrated Trefoil, and to Cockie through Lorna's dam Maude.

Rawdon Lee, H E Packwood and C H Wheeler have all written variable accounts of Rutland's early life and it is apparent that he was unmanageable as a puppy. Transferred into Mr Shirley's ownership he was soon passed on to Sir Charles Mordaunt as a companion. Unfortunately Rutland developed pheasant-poaching and sheep-chasing habits with the result that the gamekeeper was instructed to 'execute' him, but he escaped death by being given to a Mr Walker of Warwick in exchange for a drink and a 'noted prize winner called Staffa'. Rutland was later taken to the Birmingham Repository where he was sold to Collie exhibitor Mr Emery for £3.

In 1883 Birmingham wool merchant and Shire horse breeder, Samuel Boddington of Green Oaks, Hagley Road, Edgbaston, Birmingham, was establishing the Metchley Kennel and during this same year he purchased Wolf from Hans Hamilton and Rutland from Mr Emery at the Gloucester Show for £5. Mr Boddington then registered Rutland with the Kennel Club and campaigned him to his title before selling him two years later to Mr Megson for a reputed £250. Champion Wolf was transferred to Mr Megson's ownership in the same year.

Champion Rutland was one of the most successful show winners of his day. He won twenty one Challenge classes and six Champions' classes between 1883 and 1890, and in 1886 he was the inaugural winner of the Collie Club's Challenge Trophy[1]. Hugh Dalziel in his book 'The Collie: Its History, Points and Breeding', of 1888, wrote: *"Rutland is a splendid specimen of the breed – a black and tan in colour, of beautiful formation, and possessing all the attributes of a show-dog. He is already the sire of over twenty first-prize winners;......for prize winning dogs are given more opportunities of continuing their race than are those of less public note."*

Champion Rutland excelled at stud, siring more progeny with Stud Book entries than any other dog of his day. Mr W W Thomson, in his Kennel Gazette article of 1896, states: "*Rutland soon made his mark. By crossing Blue Thistle (one of the oldest strains in Collie history) with Rutland, Mr Arkwright bred Thistledown, and by the same sire Mr Megson bred a great winner in Vulcan.*"

Champion Rutland's influence on sire lines was negligible, fading away two generations later at Champion Caractacus, but he made his mark on posterity through several daughters. Mated to Buttercup, a great granddaughter of Mr Roberts' Fly, Rutland sired siblings Miss Rutland and Squire Rutland, who was the grandsire of Champion Portington Bar None. Another daughter, Sweet Fairy (ex Strawberry Girl), was the granddam of Edgbaston Marvel, sire of Champion Portington Bar None and grandsire of Champion Ormskirk Emerald respectively. Princess Rutland (ex Muscatelle, a granddaughter of Fly) continued her sire's influence down through Eva II and Seedley Sagacity to Denny Lively Bird where it branched into two lines through Lively Bird's daughters Eden Emily and Denny Dinah. Emily influenced many of the Eden and Ladypark Collies, and eleven generations later, via Danethorpe Laugh of Ladypark, came the Pattingham, Deloraine, Clanayre, Glenalan and Camanna Collies. In a second branch Denny Dinah influenced the Eden, Ladypark, Beulah, Faux, and Whitelea Collies.

Breeder: Reverend Hans F Hamilton

Owners: Several

K.C. Stud Book No. 13894

Black, Tan and White Dog

D.O.B. 17 June 1882

Sire: Champion Wolf

Dam: Champion Madge I

WINNER OF 21 CHALLENGE CLASSES & 6 CHAMPIONS' CLASSES

INAUGURAL WINNER OF THE COLLIE CLUB'S CHALLENGE TROPHY - 1886

The Collie Club's Challenge Trophy.

Photo courtesy of the Officers and committee of the British Collie Club

Footnotes:

1. *The Challenge Trophy was awarded for the first time at the Collie Club's second Show in 1886, when it was won by Champion Rutland.*
2. *See additional information on Champion Rutland in Appendix VIII*

Champion Metchley Wonder

Champion Metchley Wonder was a white-factored sable and white grandson of Champion Charlemagne resulting from an accidental mating between Sefton and a seven month old unregistered bitch named Minnie, owned by Mr Gold. Despite Mr C Wheeler's repeated claims that he bred Metchley Wonder, Mr Gold is officially registered as his breeder.

The following comments on Minnie and Metchley Wonder are taken from WW Thomson's paper, 'Pillars of the Stud Book – Collies', Kennel Gazette December 1896: *"Minnie, the dam of Metchley Wonder, was by Loafer, his dam by Trevor, ex Hasty, sired by Charlemagne. The dam of Minnie had for grandsire Druce, by Duncan, ex a Carlyle bitch, out of a bitch by Cockie. Druce was also the sire of Foxey, from a bitch by Cocksie, a prize-winning son of Cockie........"*

Of Metchley Wonder Mr Thomson stated *"Probably one of the best Collies ever put on the show bench was Metchley Wonder, a direct descendant of Charlemagne, his sire, Sefton, being by Charlemagne, out of Madge I. The honour of whelping Metchley Wonder belongs to Minnie, and this fairly entitles her to a place amongst 'the pillars'. Her sire, Loafer, had, through Trevor and Charlemagne, a double cross of the Bissell blood, while her dam has a pedigree dating very far back. Her breeding, indeed, is well worth studying. From Metchley Wonder the Rev. Hans Hamilton bred Christopher, who was subsequently a distinct acquisition to the now all-powerful Ormskirk Kennel."*

Champion Metchley Wonder was said to have excelled in head and ear properties, body, legs and feet. Charles Wheeler suggested that he helped to correct the weak pasterns and cow hocks that plagued the breed at that time. As well as the usual white-factoring features note his white muzzle and blaze, a popular feature at that time and included in the Scottish Breed Standard of 1885 (see Appendix III on the Breed Standards).

1886

For a time Metchley Wonder became the property of Samuel Boddington of Edgbaston, and he successfully exhibited him to win the Collie Club's Challenge Trophy whilst still a puppy, following which he was sold to Mr A H Megson, of Sale in Cheshire, an exhibitor of Rough Collies, Dalmations, St Bernards and Mastiffs, for £530. Metchley Wonder continued to excel in the show ring winning his title, a total of nineteen 'Challenge' classes, and the Challenge Trophy a further five times.

By the time Champion Metchley Wonder was six years old he had sired in excess of one hundred and fifty offspring, their details all appearing in the Kennel Club Stud Book. His most famous son was Christopher who was to continue the male lines down in two main directions – to Champion Parbold Piccolo five generations on, and to Champion Squire of Tytton eight generations on.

Sire Sefton	Ch Charlemagne	Trefoil	Twig
			Bess
		Maude	Cockie
			Meg
	Ch Madge I	Marcus	-
			-
		Ruby III	Tricolour II
			Nellie
Dam Minnie (unregistered)	Loafer	Chang	Ch Charlemagne
			Jessie
		The Lily	Trevor
			Hasty
	Catrine	Bonnie Laddie	Duncan
			Bess
		Bonnie Greta	Druce
			Lassie

See 'Early Collie Male lines' in Appendix I.

Breeder: Mr Gold

Owner: Mr S Boddington

K.C. Stud Book No. 23002

Sable & White Dog

D.O.B. 2 March 1886

Sire: Sefton

Dam: Minnie

WINNER OF 19 CHALLENGE CLASSES

WINNER OF THE COLLIE CLUB'S[1] CHALLENGE TROPHY IN 1887, 1889, 1890 (twice), 1891 & 1892.

Several interesting statistics of Champion Metchley Wonder are included in Hugh Dalziel's 'The Collie': "Mr A H Megson's Metchley Wonder: Weight, 56lb.; height at shoulder, 24in.;length from nose to stop, 4in.;length from stop to occiput, 8in.;length from occiput to set-on of tail, 29 ½ in.; length of tail, 19in.; girth of chest, 29in.; girth of head, 16 ½ in.; girth of muzzle, 9in.; girth of forearm, 8 ½ in."

Footnotes:

1. *The Collie Club's Challenge trophy was originally offered several times each year, at shows selected by the committee of the Collie Club. Champion Metchley Wonder won this trophy in 1887 at the Kennel Club's twenty-eighth Show and at it's thirty-second Show in 1889. In 1890 he won it at Manchester and Crystal Palace, and in 1891 and 1892 he won it at the Collie Club's own Shows.*
2. *Contrary to popular belief Champion Metchley Wonder was never exported to the United States but, according to Dr O P Bennett in 'The Collie', sub-heading 1892: "Mr McEwan was again very successful with an imported dog 'Metchley Wonder II' by Sefton ex Minnie, by Loafer, a sable and white brother of the noted Champion of this name and who resembled him in many respects – this dog proved a most excellent sire...." Kennel Club records, however, do not include a Metchley Wonder II!*

Christopher

Christopher is often erroneously referred to as 'Champion'[1] Christopher but there is no official record of 'Champion' Christopher in the Kennel Club Stud Book. At this stage the Kennel Club only recorded details of a Champion in the year it qualified but it is possible that he did acquire this distinction as the rules governing the title of Champion changed so frequently it is not possible to be certain.

In the December 1896 edition of the Kennel Gazette, WW Thomson's paper on 'Pillars of the Stud Book – Collies', summarises Christopher's breeding as follows: *"Christopher's dam, Peggy II, was by Ruthven, an unfashionably-bred dog, tracing his pedigree back through sire and dam to the earliest pillars. Christopher made a great name for himself on the bench, and many a good specimen owns him as sire, and perhaps the best of these was Ormskirk Amazement who, through his dam, Sweet Lassie, traces back his pedigree to Young Cockie, and Patience. Sweet Lassie's dam was by Wolf, thus possessing some of the best possible Collie blood."*

Christopher represented a major advance in Collie type, especially with regard to head properties and he was also renowned for his luxuriant coat and flashy markings. However he was said to have had pricked ears and was rather low on the leg. Initially Christopher had very little show success until Mr Tom H Stretch (Ormskirk), a breeder of Game Bantams, Turbits Owls, Magpies and Homing Pigeons, purchased him for £60 and exhibited him successfully before selling him to the Wellesbourne Kennel, owned by brothers John and William H Charles of Warwick. In 1891, following the death of John Charles, Christopher was sold for £1,000 to American breeder Mr Mitchell Harrison, who took over the Wellesbourne Kennels upon the retirement of William Charles.

The highlight of Christopher's show career was in 1891 at the inaugural Crufts Show[2], where he and his litter sister Champion Sefton Grace won their respective 'Challenge' classes from a total entry of 157 Collies. Three years later Mitchell Harrison sold the Wellesbourne Kennels and took Christopher to his

1887

Breeder: Reverend Hans F Hamilton

Owner: Mr T Stretch

K.C. Stud Book No. 25177

Sable & White Dog

D.O.B. 16 April 1887

Sire: Champion Metchley Wonder

Dam: Champion Peggie II

WINNER OF 6 CHALLENGE CLASSES, INCLUDING THE INAUGURAL CRUFTS SHOW 1891

Chestnut Hills Kennel in Philadelphia. Although Christopher never gained his American title he won Best Dog at the inaugural Collie Club of America's Specialty later that same year.

As a sire Christopher was of immense value to breeders, having inherited superb head qualities for which he was prepotent. Before he left England, Christopher sired numerous offspring and three sons in particular are worthy of note. Champion Ormskirk Charlie (see page 30) was a dual-purpose dog as, besides doing a little winning in the show ring, he had a natural ability to work and gained his title by way of his trialing wins. Christopher's two most important sons, who excelled both in the show ring and as sires of consequence, were Edgbaston Marvel, formerly known as Ormskirk Ambrose, K.C.S.B. number 27397 (ex Sweet Marie) and Champion Stracathro Ralph (ex Stracathro Fancy). They were coincidentally whelped on the same day in 1888, but to different dams, and each was to dominate the beginning of the twentieth century being responsible for two dominant sire lines from which most Rough Collies descend. Marvel's great great grandson was Champion Parbold Piccolo and, even more importantly, through Ralph's dominant sire line came his record-breaking grandson Champion Ormskirk Emerald, followed by Champion Squire of Tytton five generations later.

Of Christopher's son, Champion Edgbaston Marvel, WW Thomson (Kennel Gazette 1896) commented: *"Another of the Edgbaston kennel, whose name frequently crops up in recent pedigrees, is Marvel whose original name was Ormskirk Ambrose, sired by Christopher, and through his dam going back to the Smuggler strain; in this case, however, Rutland appearing as the grandsire of his dam with a Charlemagne bitch as grand dam."* W Baskerville commented on Marvel as follows: *"Edgbaston Marvel was not a show specimen, but he was a marvellous headed Collie. It was solely by the merit of his offspring that Mr A H Megson paid £500 to secure him, and that was when he was turned four years old".*

Sire Champion Metchley Wonder	Sefton	Ch Charlemagne	Trefoil
			Maude
		Ch Madge I	Marcus
			Ruby III
	Minnie	Loafer	Chang
			The Lily
		Catrine	Bonnie Laddie
			Bonnie Greta
Dam Champion Peggie II	Ruthven	Angus	Scott (Mr Walker's)
			Lassie (Mr Charles')
		Luna	Tricolour II
	Ch Madge I	Marcus	
		Ruby III	Tricolour II
			Nellie

See 'Early Collie Male lines' in Appendix I, and '(Digby's) Elsie-family a' in Appendix II.

Footnotes:

1. *See Appendix VI on Championship entitlement.*
2. *Charles Cruft was not interested in following his family's jewellery business and left College in 1876 to work as a travelling salesman for James Spratt, of London, a distributor of 'dog cakes'. During his travels the young Cruft visited many large estates and sporting kennels and was asked by French breeders to organise the canine section of the 1878 Paris Exhibition. In 1886 he took up the management of the Allied Terrier Club Show at the Royal Aquarium and, in 1891, he organised the Crufts inaugural Show which was held at the Agricultural Hall, Islington. Charles Cruft died in 1938 and his widow ran the show for three years before asking the Kennel Club to take over.*

Champion Ormskirk Charlie (Field Trials Title)

During the transition of the Rough Collie from a purely working dog to a show dog it is interesting to see that the working instinct is occasionally retained. In the early days this innate working ability was promoted through Sheepdog Trials, the earliest recorded public Trials being held at Bala in October 1873 (see The Development of the Rough Collie as a Show Dog, page 2). Trialing events gradually expanded to national and international gatherings and, by the 1920's, were held at Tarporley, Bingley, Buntingford, Bletchley, Tring, Llangollen, Harden Moss, Hope, Longshaw, Burnley, Silsden, Conway, Towyn, Durham, Colinsburgh, Lanark and Huntly.

An obvious feature of working sheepdogs was the absence of type but, as Charlie's photograph and pedigree show, he had obviously inherited certain prepotent show qualities, especially from his sire's side. Bred by a Mr Thornton, Charlie was sold to Mr W P Barnes who, recognising that he had strong working instincts, sold him to Nottinghamshire livestock farmer Mr R S Piggin, a one-time exhibitor and judge of Rough Collies, and pioneer of sheepdog trials.

Champion Ormskirk Charlie is noteworthy as a dual-purpose dog, distinguishing himself both at sheep-dog trials and occasionally in the show ring[1]. Charlie became Mr Piggin's principal working dog gaining his Championship title by way of his trialing achievements, as a result of which Mr Piggin would give regular demonstrations of Charlie's prowess and versatility to the general public.

In 1893 Champion Ormskirk Charlie took second place at the inaugural Wirral Trials. Five years later he won the famous Longshaw Trials, and subsequently won the Dovedale Trials twice and the Llangollen event on four successive occasions.

Champion Ormskirk Charlie was occasionally used at stud and there are records of two daughters, Pretty Lass and Rowan Mandeline, winning Stud Book numbers.

1889

Breeder: Mr Thornton

Owner: Mr R S Piggin

Colour: unknown

D.O.B. 31 May 1889

Sire: Christopher

Dam: Prim of Winmarleigh

Mr H E Packwood commented on Mr Piggin and Charlie, in his book 'Show Collies Rough and Smooth', as follows: *"As a breeder,his first principle is to breed for a perfect Collie; he has afterwards endeavoured, with success, to make his product a perfect sheepdog. It seems a good many years since I first saw Ormskirk Charlie win in the ring, and, work at the same show. It was at Belper Show, late in the 'eighties, I believe. Ch Edgbaston Fox had caused some little sensation by beating Christopher on the latter's first appearance after being sold for £1,000. Mr Piggin had done some winning, and after lunch, gave an exhibition that delighted me and fairly astounded some of the farmers present. Ormskirk Charlie's life and doings would make an interesting book. His fame has spread all over the world. He won the World's Championship, and her master's arms, hoops etc, and was no mean trickster."*

Champion Ormskirk Charlie and Mr Piggin at the Sheepdog Trials

Sire Christopher	Ch Metchley Wonder	Sefton	Chang
			The Lily
		Minnie	Loafer
			Catrine
	Ch Peggie II	Ruthven	Angus
			Luna
		Ch Madge I	Marcus
			Ruby III
Dam Prim of Winmarleigh	Bruce	Lord Elcho	Tweed
			Elcho
		Susan (unregistered)	-
			-
	Dolly	Flockmaster	Trevor
			Ling
		Susan (unregistered)	-
			-

See 'Early Collie Male lines' in Appendix I.

Footnote:

1. *Several sources suggest that Ormskirk Charlie was a show winner, with the implication that he was registered with the Kennel Club. However no details of him have been found in the Stud Book or Kennel Gazette, although omissions occasionally occurred.*

Champion Ormskirk Emerald

In his article 'Pillars of the Stud Book – Collies', featured in the December 1896 edition of the Kennel Gazette, Mr WW Thomson made the following observation on Emerald's sire: *"Heather Ralph has recently made his mark as a sire, and brought into prominence on this account his own sire, Stracathro Ralph (lately deceased), the latter being by Christopher from a Scottish-bred bitch, whose dam was by Smuggler ex Sweet Lassie. The dam of Heather Ralph goes back to Eclipse, and on the dam's side to Wolf, and a highly-bred bitch of the Rev. H Hamilton's."*

Champion Ormskirk Emerald, a big[1] upstanding sable and white grandson of Champion Stracathro Ralph and Edgbaston Marvel, was bred by Mr W P Barnes, brother-in-law of Hugo Ainscough ('Parbold').The litter was bred on the advice of Mr Ainscough and all the puppies were sold to Mr Tom H Stretch's 'Ormskirk' kennel for £25. Emerald did not do much winning as a puppy because he was difficult to handle and did not carry sufficient coat, but at thirteen months of age he won the Limit Class at Edinburgh under judge John Powers (Barwell). Tom Stretch eventually campaigned him to his title and he became a record holder winning a total of twenty-two Challenge Certificates from fourteen judges. He was awarded four of these by Hugo Ainscough and five by Tom Stretch, following his transfer to Mr A H Megson for the record price of £1,300. (It is believed that Emerald's grandsire Edgbaston Marvel was taken in part exchange). At the Birmingham Show in 1896 Emerald defeated Portington Bar None, Wellesbourne Conqueror and Southport Perfection, all of whom were considered among the best dogs of the time, and in 1899 he won the Collie Club's Challenge Trophy three times. Resulting from these accolades Champion Ormskirk Emerald was now also classed as one of the best Collies of his day.

Mr Charles Wheeler regarded Emerald as *"the most perfect specimen of his race in the annals of the show collie history. His head was an exquisite shape, perhaps the merest trifle Roman towards the end of his nose. Placement of eye and expression were admirable and so were his ears. In short, he possessed the beautiful type of head of his dam (Aughton Bessie) together with the unsurpassable body, legs, feet and coat of his sire (Heather Ralph)"*.

1894

Although Emerald enjoyed a spectacular show career he was to produce little of note other than Ormskirk Galopin (ex Champion Ormskirk Memoir, a granddaughter of Christopher). Ormskirk Galopin's son, Heacham Galopin, was exported to the Ravenswood Kennels of Mr D E Gardner in the Unites States of America after siring Champion Wishaw Clinker (see photograph on page 39), the grandsire of Champion Squire of Tytton (see page 40).

Mr Megson eventually sold Emerald to the Honourable Mrs Chetwyn who rarely showed him and so he went up for sale by auction. As no bids were received he was given to Mrs Chetwyn's former kennel manager, Mr Santo, for a nominal £2.

Breeder: Mr W P Barnes

Owner: Mr T H Stretch

K.C. Stud Book No. 40941

Sable & White Dog

D.O.B. 3 September 1894

Sire: Heather Ralph

Dam: Aughton Bessie

22 CHALLENGE CERTIFICATES[2]

WINNER OF THE COLLIE CLUB'S CHALLENGE TROPHY ON 3 OCCASIONS IN 1899

Sire Heather Ralph	Ch Stracathro Ralph	Christopher	Ch Metchley Wonder
			Ch Peggie II
		Stracathro Fancy	Scottish Hero
			Broadford Duchess
	Apple Blossom	Ch Metchley Wonder	Sefton
			Minnie
		Grove Daisy	Ch Eclipse
			Lady Clare
Dam Aughton Bessie	Edgbaston Marvel (formerly Ormskirk Ambrose)	Christopher	Ch Metchley Wonder
			Ch Peggie II
		Sweet Marie	Smuggler
			Sweet Fairy
	Wellesbourne Ada	Ch Great Alne Douglas (formerly Ch Parbold Rover)	Ch Metchley Wonder
			Sweet Fanny
		Wellesbourne Lady	Sir Gent
			Primula

See 'Early Collie Male lines' in Appendix I.

Footnotes:

1. *As an adult Emerald apparently measured 26in to the shoulder and weighed 70lbs.*
2. *Emerald was certainly the Challenge Certificate Record Holder of the nineteenth and twentieth centuries, winning twenty-two Challenge Certificates as we know them today (see Appendix VI on the 'Development of Championship Entitlement'). At some Shows, including Crufts, entries were often well in excess of one hundred dogs but, despite this, Emerald received several of his Challenge Certificates from the same judges, a practice which is not indulged today. During his reign only twenty-five sets of Challenge Certificates were available each year for Collies and occasionally these had to be shared between Roughs and Smooths. Readers could therefore argue that Emerald may have had a more difficult task winning his Challenge Certificates than we have today.*

Champion Parbold Piccolo

1899

Breeder/Owner: Mr H Ainscough

K.C. Stud Book No. 1413E

Sable & White Dog

D.O.B. 3 April 1899

Sire: Champion Wellesbourne Conqueror

Dam: Parbold Pinafore

5 CHALLENGE CERTIFICATES

Champion Parbold Piccolo was born eight generations after Champion Charlemagne, with dogs such as Champion Southport Perfection, Christopher and Champion Rutland featuring on the sire's side of his pedigree. In his "Show Collies", of 1906, Mr H E Packwood (Billesley), one of the earliest blue merle specialists, commented that *"Piccolo had a great wealth of coat, good bone, shapely body and small ears which he used to good effect. However his head properties needed refinement, being too deep through and showing too much dewlap[1] but he was typical of the collies of the day".*

Piccolo gained his title with ease and proceeded to establish a strong male line which extended into the first half of the twentieth century. Through one of his sons, Ormskirk Olympian, he influenced many of the Wishaw and Alphington Collies; through Champion Corella Starboy he influenced the Whiteleas; and through Champion Netherkeir Starboy he established dominant lines enduring to the 1940s, through dogs such as Champion Eden Diadem and some of the early Beulahs.

Piccolo's second influential son, Parbold Pierrot, heads a sire line which includes such notable Champions as Seedley Stirling, Eden Extra and Laund Lindrum (see page 48) and, despite the prediction that his third son Champion Anfield Model (see page 36) would have considerable influence on the breed, his line in the United Kingdom unfortunately extended only a further seven generations through Champion Laund Limit to Champion Ashtead Applause in 1924.

In 1904 Champion Parbold Piccolo was shipped to the United States of America, to the Bon Ami Kennels of Mr J H Behling in Milwaukee, Wisconsin. He arrived one October day and, whilst being taken for a walk by his new owner, slipped his leash and disappeared.

<table>
<tr><td rowspan="8">Sire
Champion Wellesbourne Conqueror</td><td rowspan="4">Wellesbourne Councillor</td><td rowspan="2">Ch Southport Perfection</td><td>Ch Edgbaston Marvel</td></tr>
<tr><td>Tabley Rose</td></tr>
<tr><td rowspan="2">Wellesbourne Christabel</td><td>Christopher</td></tr>
<tr><td>Barford Lady</td></tr>
<tr><td rowspan="4">Wellesbourne Beauty</td><td rowspan="2">Ch Edgbaston Marvel</td><td>Christopher</td></tr>
<tr><td>Sweet Marie</td></tr>
<tr><td rowspan="2">Ryland Jennie</td><td>Caractacus</td></tr>
<tr><td>Olton Pride</td></tr>
<tr><td rowspan="8">Dam
Parbold Pinafore</td><td rowspan="4">Ch Balgreggie Hope</td><td rowspan="2">Old Hall Blucher</td><td>Bay Regent</td></tr>
<tr><td>Old Hall Vera</td></tr>
<tr><td rowspan="2">Nell (unregistered)</td><td>Guy Mannering</td></tr>
<tr><td>Southport Matrimony</td></tr>
<tr><td rowspan="4">Parbold Prim</td><td rowspan="2">Darwen Marvel</td><td>Guy Mannering</td></tr>
<tr><td>Southport Matrimony</td></tr>
<tr><td rowspan="2">Grisdale Prim</td><td>Sefton Hero</td></tr>
<tr><td>Grisdale Witty</td></tr>
</table>

See 'Piccolo lines' in Appendix I.

Footnote:

1. Mr Packwood's reference to 'dewlap' (excess flesh under the chin) is misleading. He was obviously referring to the flews or lips, a feature more associated with Gundogs than Collies.

Champion Anfield Model

The average Collies at this time were still rather farm-like in appearance, with coarse, heavy heads or Borzoi-type receding skulls. At nine months of age Anfield Model was purchased by Hugo Ainscough, of the Parbold Collies, who believed his head '*was perfect in formation of every detail, true in type and perfect in expression.*'

The arrival of Anfield Model excited breeders who considered him '*the most perfect specimen ever produced*'. Model possessed a nervous temperament which unfortunately prevented Mr Ainscough from getting him into good show condition and so he left the Parbold Kennels, passing through several owners, before ending up with Mr W E Mason[1], the great promoter of the Southport Kennels, who campaigned him to his title.

Mr Packwood said of this dog: "*To the writer's mind the hereditary influence of this dog will be great indeed*". **Champion Anfield Model** sired numerous Champions and influential offspring such as Mr W W Stansfield's (Laund) first notable dog Master Willie (ex Sweet Mary), the great grandsire of Champion Magnet. However Champion Anfield Model's British influence did not last and his sire line only extended a further seven generations, through Champion Laund Limit to Champion Ashtead Applause in 1924.

At the age of five years Model was exported with Champion Wishaw Leader (see page 38) to the Valverde Kennels of William Ellery[2] in San Francisco, California. Mr Mason emigrated there for a short time, went into partnership with Mr Ellery and moved north to Ridgewood, New Jersey, where he opened the American branch of his Southport Kennel in 1909. Whilst not being particularly influential on this side of the Atlantic, Champion Anfield Model exerted considerable influence over American Collies, especially through his son Champion Laund Limit, grandson Laund Logic and Logic's daughter Seedley Queen.

1902

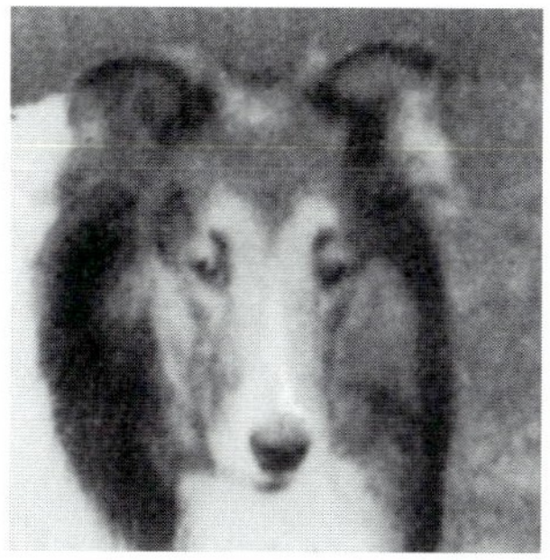

Breeder: Mr H Galt

Owner: Mr W E Mason

K. C. Stud Book No. 293H

Sable & White Dog

D.O.B. 24 June 1902

Sire: Champion Parbold Piccolo

Dam: Bellfield Beauty

5 CHALLENGE CERTIFICATES

A critique of Champion Anfield Model, found in Gayle Kaye's article from the Collie Club of America's archives, stated: *"It is universally admitted that in head, ears, eye and general Collie character, he could not be improved upon. In colour he is a rich sable with correct white markings, and he carries an abundant double coat of the right texture, every hair as straight as a rush."*

Sire Champion Parbold Piccolo	Ch Wellesbourne Conqueror	Wellesbourne Councillor	Ch Southport Perfection
			Wellesbourne Christabel
		Wellesbourne Beauty	Edgbaston Marvel
			Ryland Jennie
	Parbold Pinafore	Ch Balgreggie Hope	Old Hall Blucher
			Nell (unregistered)
		Parbold Prim	Darwen Marvel
			Grisdale Prim
Dam Bellfield Beauty	Ch Wishaw Clinker	Ch Heacham Galopin	Ormskirk Galopin
			Wishaw Dolly
		Last Rose	Parkhill Pilot
			Wishaw Rose
	Braehead Buttercup	Ormskirk Galopin	Ch Ormskirk Emerald
			Ch Ormskirk Memoir
		Bude Princess	Ollymount Print
			Hele Ninon

See 'Piccolo lines' in Appendix I.

Head study of Champion Ashtead Applause, the end of Champion Anfield Model's tail male line.

Footnote:

1. *Mr W E Mason originally edited and published 'The Collie Folio', which was freely subscribed to by both English and American fanciers. Mr Mason lived at Rose Grange in Woking, Surrey, but his publishing office was in Southport, hence his affix. The Collie Folio was later taken over by Mr W W Stansfield (Laund).*
2. *Dr O P Bennett says of William Ellery: "Mr Wm Ellery, 'Valverde Kennels', San Francisco, California- although previously interested in Collies, by his purchases at this period, assembled probably the strongest collection of Collies in the world. Unfortunately for the fancy, because of some misunderstanding with the American Kennel Club, he gave up the breeding and exhibiting of them a few years later."*

Sire Ormskirk Olympian	Ch Parbold Piccolo	Ch Wellesbourne Conqueror	Wellesbourne Councillor
			Wellesbourne Beauty
		Parbold Pinafore	Ch Balgreggie Hope
			Parbold Prim
	Ch Ormskirk Ideal	Guy Mannering	Ch Sefton Hero
			Parbold Peery
		Broadlea Belle	Union Ralph
			Lady Douglas II
Dam Hartwood Lady	Ch Wishaw Clinker	Heacham Galopin	Ormskirk Galopin
			Wisbech Dolly
		Last Rose	Parkhill Pilot
			Wishaw Rose
	Old Hall Duchess	Kirkdale Patrick	Ch Wellesbourne Conqueror
			Darwen Superba
		Old Hall Real Gem	Ch Balgreggie Hope
			Old Hall Ina

See 'Piccolo lines' in Appendix I, and '(Panmure-Gordon's) Hamish III-family d' in Appendix II.

Champion Wishaw Leader

1903

Breeder: Mr J Shields

Owner: Mr R Tait

K.C. Stud Book No. 286J

Tricolour Dog

D.O.B. 19 April 1903

Sire: Ormskirk Olympian

Dam: Hartwood Lady

15 CHALLENGE CERTIFICATES

WINNER OF THE COLLIE CLUB'S CHALLENGE TROPHY IN 1904, 1905 & 1906

WINNER OF THE NON-SPORTING GROUP AND INAUGURAL CHAMPIONS' BOWL[1] – CRUFTS 1906

Champion Wishaw Leader was bred along Christopher lines through Ormskirk Emerald on his dam's side and Parbold Piccolo on his sire's side, via Christopher's sons Edgbaston Marvel and Champion Stracathro Ralph. Leader was a grandson of Champion Parbold Piccolo and Champion Wishaw Clinker. Besides coming from a strong tail male line Champion Wishaw Leader had an equally influential tail female line behind him which ended with his dam, Hartwood Lady, the sister of Champion Balgreggie Baronet who sired Champion Squire of Tytton (see page 40).

Leader was a large, profusely coated and white-factored tricolour dog with graceful style and movement but his head was disappointing. In Mr Packwood's opinion the dog *"was too strong and deep through in head, showing a considerable amount of dewlap[2] and a straight Setter-like tail[3]."* All these features can be seen from his photograph but, despite these faults, he distinguished himself in the show ring by winning fifteen Challenge Certificates, from twelve judges in a four-year period. He also won the Collie Club's Challenge Trophy in three successive years, and the non-sporting group and Best Champion at Crufts in 1906, for which he was awarded the inaugural Champions' Bowl.

As a sire Wishaw Leader was also influential and through his great great grandson, Champion Wishaw Rival, led to Champion Netherkeir Starboy in 1928, Champion Corella Starboy in 1935, and Champion Alphington Nigger King in 1943.

He was eventually exported, along with Champion Anfield Model, to William Ellery's Valverde Kennels in San Francisco.

Champion Wishaw Clinker. According to W Baskerville he *"was an exceedingly handsome and attractive sable-and-white, with an enormous coat, good head and Collie expression, and orthodox ear carriage."* Born in 1898, he was the maternal grandsire of Champion Wishaw Leader and paternal great grandsire of Champion Squire of Tytton. Champion Wishaw Clinker won fourteen Challenge Certificates, from thirteen judges, including the Collie Club's Challenge Trophy in 1903. He was later exported to the States where he gained his American title.

Footnotes:

1. *Frank Jackson, in his book 'Crufts, The Official History', makes reference to the Champions' Bowl as follows: "It was in 1906 that a new trophy made its strangely unheralded appearance and embarked on a short and almost unnoticed career .... The Collie, Wishaw Leader, proved to be the winner, the Retriever High Legh Blarney, being Reserve. The competition still did not refer to the Best in Show winner, and still would not do so for a number of years, but it might not be unreasonable to regard the Collie, Ch Wishaw Leader,as in all but name, the first Best in Show winner." In 1915 Sonnenburgh Squire was awarded the Champions' Bowl whilst the Crufts Best in Show award, as we understand it, was not introduced until 1928.*
2. *Note the incorrect use of the term 'dewlap' when referring to lippiness or flews. (A 'dewlap' is an excessive fleshiness of the throat!)*
3. *It is interesting to note that the photographer has attempted to mask the Setter-like feathering on the tail, indicating the Setter or Gundog cross known to have occasionally taken place (see Appendix III on the Breed Standards).*

Champion Squire of Tytton

Champion Squire of Tytton was bred along Christopher lines via Champion Ormskirk Emerald on his sire's side and Champion Parbold Piccolo on his dam's side. Squire's sire, Champion Balgreggie Baronet, was litter brother to Hartwood Lady, dam of Champion Wishaw Leader (see page 38). As a puppy Squire of Tytton suffered the effects of distemper, and his first show was the Puppy class at Crufts where he created a sensation beating the previously undefeated Champion Wishaw Leader. Squire was entered at the catalogue price of £500 but Mr Mason, who missed purchasing him that day, obtained him a month later for the increased price of £800.

Squire was reportedly well known for his beautiful head, well-filled foreface, pretty eye, correct coat and excellent temperament. His most noticeable failing was reportedly his hind end, described years later by Dr Bennett as having a *"weird action"*. Despite this he was one of the biggest winners and successful sires of his day and is regarded by many as the 'corner stone' of Collie history. He was advertised by Mr Mason as '*the only unbeaten Collie in the world that has been fearlessly shown.*'

He was extremely successful as a sire, one of his most influential sons being Seedley Squire (ex Southport Sissie) who continued the tail male line down through Seedley Superior, Champion Magnet to the 'Backwoods', the sable and white 'Beulahs', Champion Eden Emerald to Champion Glenack Kingfisher and the blue merle 'Beulahs', to Eden Examine in 1944, and through Examine to most post-war show Collies.

Champion Squire of Tytton was campaigned in Britain for less than three years, and during this time he won Best in Show awards (All breeds) ten times. In 1907 he was sold for £1250, to wealthy American Attorney Samuel Untermeyer of the Greystone Kennels. Mr Mason travelled to the States with several dogs including Champion Squire of Tytton and Champion Anfield Model. Squire remained unbeaten and was campaigned to his American title as well as siring several American Champions. Most American Collies trace back to Champion Squire of Tytton through his great great great grandson Champion Magnet.

Sire Champion Balgreggie Baronet	Ch Wishaw Clinker	Heacham Galopin	Ormskirk Galopin
			Wisbech Dolly
		Last Rose	Parkhill Pilot
			Wishaw Rose
	Old Hall Duchess	Kirkdale Patrick	Ch Wellesbourne Conqueror
			Darwen Superba
		Old Hall Real Gem	Ch Balgreggie Hope
			Old Hall Ina
Dam Helle of Boston	Ch Parbold Piccolo	Ch Wellesbourne Conqueror	Wellesbourne Councillor
			Wellesbourne Beauty
		Parbold Pinafore	Ch Balgreggie Hope
			Parbold Prim
	Ellwyn Lenore	Birkie Punch (unregistered)	-
			-
		Ellwyn Fancy (unregistered)	-
			-

See 'Squire lines' in Appendix I.

1904

Breeder: Mr W T Horry

Owner: Mr W E Mason

K.C. Stud Book No. 148K

Sable & White Dog

D.O.B. 13 April 1904

Sire: Champion Balgreggie Baronet

Dam: Helle of Boston

7 CHALLENGE CERTIFICATES

Mr W W Stansfield, owner of the 'Laund' Kennels from the early twentieth century, traced the breeding of the most notable sires between 1873 and 1926. The results of blending different blood lines showed Squire of Tytton to be the most influential through Champion Magnet. Another very important line came through from Piccolo to Champion Anfield Model. Both these dogs were to be most influential in the development of American Rough Collies, and must have been a great loss to British breeders.

Painting by T D Daws, courtesy of Spratts Patent Ltd.

Sire Grimsby Squire	Ch Squire of Tytton	Ch Balgreggie Baronet	Ch Wishaw Clinker
			Old Hall Duchess
		Helle of Boston	Ch Parbold Piccolo
			Ellwyn Lenore
	Southport Sapho	Ch Anfield Model	Ch Parbold Piccolo
			Bellfield Beauty
		Southport Style (formerly Parbold Pattern)	Southport Caledonia
			Well Road Daisy
Dam Hilda of Moreton	Anfield Conqueror	Ch Wellesbourne Conqueror	Wellesbourne Councillor
			Wellesbourne Beauty
		Parbold Pinafore	Ch Balgreggie Hope
			Parbold Prim
	Seabank Dora	Kirkdale Patrick	Ch Wellesbourne Conqueror
			Darwen Superba
		Little Goldleaf	Ch Ormskirk Emerald
			Lady Curzon

See 'Squire lines' in Appendix I, and '(Lamb's) Lassie-family 7' in Appendix II.

Champion Southport Sample (formerly Grimsby Tyro)

1906

Grimsby Tyro was bred in 1906 by Captain H J Lewis[1] of the Grimsby Collies, his sire and dam having been purchased from Mr W E Mason as a potential breeding pair. He was a sable and white grandson of Champion Squire of Tytton and had several influential dogs in his tail male line, such as Champion Ormskirk Emerald, Christopher, Champion Metchley Wonder, Champion Charlemagne and Trefoil. He possessed an equally prepotent tail female line, extending back to Lady Lamb's Lassie in the 1870's.

At the age of eight and a half months Tyro attended his first show, winning every class in which he was entered. Mr Mason was quick to appreciate his potential, purchased him for £200 and changed his name to Southport Sample. Old Bob, as he was affectionately known, won his title very comfortably at three consecutive shows between 13 November and 2 December 1907. In 1908 he won seven of the nine Challenge Certificates awarded to Rough Collie males, adding a further five over the following two years. In total he was awarded fifteen Challenge Certificates, from ten judges, and won the Collie Club's Challenge Trophy at least three times.[2]

Mr Mason retired **Champion Southport Sample** from the show bench at the age of four and advertised him widely at stud. The advertisement here portrays him as the 'Champion Collie of the World' but, despite this claim, Sample could not eclipse Seedley Superior's influence on the breed. Sample was never particularly influential as a sire, most of his influence being by virtue of Champion Laund Limit's dam, Laund Lily, who was line-bred to him.

In 1910 Spratt's Dog Food Company held a competition and Sample was chosen to represent the Collie breed on a set of postcards depicting Britain's finest show dogs. The postcard of Southport Sample, reproduced here, is from an oil painting by leading canine artist F T Daws.

At the age of six years Champion Southport Sample was shipped to the American branch of Mr Mason's Southport Kennels in Ridgewood, New Jersey, to stand at stud. He sired eight American Champions but was only exhibited twice there and never did gain his American title. The American fancier, Dr O P Bennett, said of him: "*Sample was a dog of great quality, having a splendid conformation, being faultless in legs and feet, possessed a wonderful coat both as to quality and quantity, it being especially profuse about mane and frill. His ears were rather small and perfectly carried, which together with a typical head, even though it was a trifle strong yet well moulded, afforded a perfect placement of eye and true Collie expression.*"

In 1913 Mr Mason returned to England, and not wishing to place Sample in quarantine he was left in retirement at Mrs Lunt's Alstead Kennels, at Belle Mead in New Jersey. In December of that year Mr Mason placed the following advertisement in the Christmas edition of The Collie Folio (Vol.9, no.94): "*Mr W E Mason desires to announce that during his visit to England he is in a particularly good position to make selections from the most reliable Collie kennels. Old, as well as prospective clients, who require either a 'Southport' home-bred or one ear-marked with the well-known 'Southport' finish should address him at 407 Lord Street, Southport, Eng.*"

CHAMPION SOUTHPORT SAMPLE.

THE CHAMPION COLLIE OF THE WORLD.

The **only** Collie ever bred that can score the full 100 points. Winner at all the leading shows, including no less than **12 Championships**, the Collie Club's 60-Guinea Challenge Trophy four times in succession, so creating a new record. Not only is he the best Collie ever benched, but the following show bench performances against the best dogs of all breeds in Britain prove him to be one of the best dogs ever bred.

Bristol, 1907.—Cup for best dog or bitch in the Limit Classes, all varieties.
Birmingham, 1907.—Reserve for best non-sporting dog or bitch, beating many Champions.
Cardiff, 1908.—Cup for best non-sporting dog or bitch. Trophy for best of all breeds, beating over 60 Champions.
Crystal Palace.—Trophy for best non-sporting dog or bitch, beating 850 other dogs, and over 80 Champions.
Belfast.—Challenge Cup for best dog or bitch of all varieties, beating many Champions.
Birmingham, 1909.—Challenge Cup for best non-sporting: Hotel Cup for best non-sporting: joint winner of the Jubilee Stakes for best dog or bitch in the show, beating over 100 Champions.

Mr Mason was renowned for making exaggerated claims about Southport Sample and one of his many advertisements is reproduced here.

Breeder: Captain H J Lewis

Owner: Mr W E Mason

K. C. Stud Book No. 1226M

Sable & White Dog

D.O.B. 12 October 1906

Sire: Grimsby Squire

Dam: Hilda of Moreton

15 CHALLENGE CERTIFICATES

WINNER OF THE COLLIE CLUB'S CHALLENGE TROPHY IN 1907, 1908 & 1910

Footnotes:

1. *Captain H J Lewis, Southport Sample's breeder, donated the 'Grimsby Southport Sample Challenge Trophy' to the British Collie Club, and this is still awarded to the Rough Collie Best of Breed at the Club's Championship Show.*
2. *Although only three wins are recorded on the Collie Club's Challenge Trophy, Mrs Ada Bishop recorded five wins, four of them being consecutive.*

Seedley Superior

1906

Breeder/Owner: Mr R H Lord

K.C. Stud Book No. 1225M

Sable & White Dog

D.O.B. 16 October 1906

Sire: Seedley Squire

Dam: Seedley Constance

Mr R H Lord owned the Seedley Kennel at Mount Vernon, Weaste in Manchester, and employed Mr R Rudman as his kennel manager and show handler. Seedley Superior was bred in 1906 and, like Champion Southport Sample (see page 42) was also a grandson of Champion Squire of Tytton. Interestingly the paternal granddams of Superior and Sample, Southport Sissie and Southport Sapho respectively, were litter sisters.

Seedley Superior was an exceptionally sound Collie, being capable of passing on his good qualities, which he presumably inherited from his sire's side. Despite being a consistent show winner he never gained any major awards, but prior to his shipment to America in 1909, he sired Mr Horry's Champion Bayard of Tytton, winner of the Collie Club's Challenge Trophy in 1909, 1910, and 1911, and his most important son Clarksfield Superior. Through Clarksfield Superior he continued the dominance of the 'Squire Sire Lines' down through his grandson Champion Magnet and great grandson Champion Poplar Perfection (see page 46), influencing the Beulah, Backwoods, Eden and Ladypark Collies.

Seedley Superior was exported to Dr O P Bennett's Tazewell Kennels in Washington, Illinois, where Dr Bennett advertised him at stud as *"the dog with an international reputation as a sire and a bencher- fee $30."* He also made the following pronouncement about Superior: *"From the very day that Superior first saw a show bench he made many friends, whose enthusiasm advanced in fervour as the dog advanced in years. As a youngster he was of the unfurnished order. Each subsequent season has seen an improvement in stamina, coat, and body condition, until to-day we have a dog extremely hard to fault, and some of his admirers say impossible to improve. That he is a dog in a thousand is beyond dispute, and in his possession Mr Lord is to be heartily congratulated. As his breeder, the result of deliberately laid plans, Superior stands as an example of what knowledge and foresight can do. His dam, Seedley Constance, was bought with the avowed intention of breeding her to the best dog Mr Lord then owned, Seedley Squire. As a sire, too, this dog is doing good work. So long as the Collie fancy in the Old Country are able to point to dogs of the calibre of Seedley Superior the future of the breed will never stand in jeopardy, either of extermination or of the loss of the true type......".* Dr Bennett also stated: *"Ch Seedley Superior has not only made his mark on the English show bench by the acquisition of pretty nearly everything worth while, but he established his name as a progenitor of the greatest possible repute when he begot Ch Bayard of Tytton, to mention but one of his sons known to great fame. Superior has also turned out many a good litter for his present owner, and is sought by earnest breeders on account of his superlative quality in head properties."*

Sire Seedley Squire	Champion Squire of Tytton	Ch Balgreggie Baronet	Ch Wishaw Clinker
			Old Hall Duchess
		Helle of Boston	Ch Parbold Piccolo
			Ellwyn Lenore
	Southport Sissie	Ch Anfield Model	Ch Parbold Piccolo
			Bellfield Beauty
		Southport Style	Southport Caledonia
			Well Road Daisy
Dam Seedley Constance	Champion Parbold Peacock	Ch Anfield Model	Ch Parbold Piccolo
			Bellfield Beauty
		Parbold Pepperette	Ch Balgreggie Baronet
			Ch Parbold Pagoda
	Baby (unregistered)	-	-
			-
		-	-
			-

See 'Squire lines' in Appendix I.

Footnote:

1. *On Mr Lord's death in 1923, his Kennel Manager Mr R Rudman took over the Seedley Kennel, and he should not be confused with Mr F Rubmann (later known as Mr F Robson) of Eden fame. (see Eden Examine's footnote on page 53).*

Champion Poplar Perfection

Champion Poplar Perfection was one of Champion Magnet's most prepotent sons and, although Magnet's name is synonymous with the early development of the American Collie, his British stud results were not sufficiently outstanding for him to be highlighted individually. Magnet, bred in 1912 by Mr J R Morley of Bolton, won the Collie Club's Challenge Trophy and gained his English title in 1915. At Crufts the same year judge Mr R Tait (Wishaw) made this comment: "*Ch Magnet is a Collie all over and is hard to fault. His head is ideal in length, shape, eye, and expression, but his ears are not quite what is wanted. In size and shape, he is near perfection and he should leave his mark on the breed.*" At the age of nine years Champion Magnet was exported to Miss Eileen Moretta in New York but, contrary to popular belief, there is no record of him ever having gained his American title despite several sources attributing him with this accolade. Once in the States he sired two Champions and was entitled 'Sire Supreme'. Despite gaining a reputation as the founder of the American Collie, the impact of the 'Magnet line' was through his British bred son Champion Poplar Perfection and grandson Champion Eden Emerald, both of whom followed him to the States.

Before Magnet left England he sired the two Champions, Poplar Perfection and Laund Legislator. Champion Poplar Perfection inherited his sire's good qualities, especially head type, presumably from his tail male line as the tail female side of his pedigree was unimportant, only extending three generations to his great granddam Windsor Judy. Champion Poplar Perfection won his first Challenge Certificate before shows were

1916

Breeder/Owner: Mr A Ray

K.C. Stud Book No. 279X

Sable & White Dog

D.O.B. 1 February 1916

Sire: Champion Magnet

Dam: Pickwick Peeper

3 CHALLENGE CERTIFICATES

banned for the duration of the war, following which he was campaigned to his title. Before leaving England for Clara Lunt's Alstead Kennels at Belle Mead in New Jersey, he sired several noteworthy progeny including Freshfield Freedom (ex Oswald Molly), Champion Thane of Athelney (ex Greta of Athelney, a granddaughter of Denny Lively Bird); and sibling Champions Eden Enrapture, Eden Etiquette, Eden Elegance, Backwoods Fashion, and Eden Emerald (ex Eden Elenora, a daughter of Eden Emily).

Perfection's sable and white son, Champion Thane of Athelney, was bred by Mr L H Hayter in 1922. Although not particularly prominent as a sire Thane was consistent in the show ring winning at every show he attended, between 1924 and 1927, gaining eleven Challenge Certificates from eight different judges in the process. He also won the Collie Club's Challenge Trophy in 1925 and 1926, and by winning the Collie Challenge Trophy at Bath Championship Show for four consecutive years, followed by his daughter winning the same trophy the following year, in 1928, Mr Hayter was presented with the Trophy for posterity.

Champion Poplar Perfection's most important sons were the siblings Champion Eden Emerald[1] (ex Eden Elenora) and Champion Backwoods Fashion (formerly registered as Eden Edward). Emerald inherited his sire's superb head qualities and gained his title comfortably at three consecutive shows during 1923. Before leaving to join his sire at the Alstead Kennels, he left an outstanding contribution to posterity through one son, sable and white Eden Educator (ex Eden Endive). This branch influenced the Chapelburns and Helengowans whilst Emerald's tricolour grandson, Eden Extreme (ex Eden Elvira), played a dominant role in the improvement of the Beulah lines through his blue merle son Champion Glenack Kingfisher and sibling grandchildren Beulah's Nightshadowing and Beulah's Nightshade, born in 1932. Champion Poplar Perfection was great grandsire of Champion Laund Lindrum (see page 48) and, via his son Champion Eden Emerald, was eight generations behind Eden Examine who sired Champion and Irish Champion Lochinvar of Ladypark (see page 58).

Perfection's other important son, Champion Backwoods Fashion (brother of Champion Eden Emerald) sired Backwoods Feature (ex Champion Backwoods Famous). Feature sired Champion Backwoods Fellow (see page 50) who made a huge impact on the Beulah Collies of Mrs Nadine George.

Sire Champion Magnet	Tonge Admiration	Clarksfield Superior	Seedley Superior
			Countess of Clarksfield
		Clarksfield Countess (unregistered)	-
			-
	Southport Seal	Parbold Picador	Master Willie
			Moss Hill Vera
		Leyland Lucy	Ch Ormskirk Foxall
			Leyland Ladybird
Dam Pickwick Peeper	Parbold Privateer	Parbold Proclamation	Billesley Briton
			Billesley Bess
		Parkside Paulette	Parbold Prior
			Cringlebrook Crystal
	Pickwick Poppy	Ch Seedley Stirling	Parkside Pro Patria
			Seedley Sylvia
		Windsor Judy (unregistered)	-
			-

See 'Squire lines' in Appendix I.

Footnote:

1. *A great great grandson of Champion Eden Emerald was American Champion Honeybrook Big Parade from whom most winning American Collies are descended, notably through Big Parade's grandson American Champion Silver Ho Parader, sire of thirty-seven American Champions.*

Champion Laund Lindrum (formerly known as Glenack Glow)

As a boy Mr Stansfield[1], of Rawtenstall, was attracted to the Collies of Mr R H Whittaker, a contemporary of Mr H Ainscough (Parbold), Mr R H Lord (Seedley), and Mr T Stretch (Ormskirk). Mr Stansfield's foundation bitch, Pure Gem (Seedley Squire ex Lady Temple) and his first notable Collie, Master Willie (Champion Anfield Model ex Sweet Mary) were both behind Champion Laund Limit, the first Laund Champion.

The following comments, by Mr W E Mason, are to be found in The Collie Folio of December 1913 (Vol. 9, no.94): *"Mr Stansfield has very pronounced opinions as to which strain are most prone to produce the sort everyone likes. His theory is that a judicious mixture of Anfield Model and Southport Sample blood-lines has satisfied him best of all and he is quietly pursuing that policy. And who shall say his reasonings are not sound? The proof of the pudding is still in the eating thereof, and there is still lots of good pudding around Rawtenstall way!"*

The Laund kennel was to dominate the first half of the twentieth century and by 1948 Mr Stansfield had either bred or campaigned fifty-nine Champions. His most famous Collies were Champions Luminous and Logic (both by Champion Laund Limit), Langton, Legislator, Latto and Lindrum. Logic, born in 1920, was the first post-war Challenge Certificate winner, winning eight in one year and two the following year, all from different judges. He was then sold to the United States of America, along with his brother Luminous, where they both became American Champions and were instrumental in founding the Bellhaven and Alstead kennels. The crossing of these two dogs with the progeny of Champion Magnet proved most successful in the development of the American Collie.

1928

The highlight of Mr Stansfield's show success was at Birmingham in 1924 when he won all four Collie Challenge Certificates, two with Rough Collies, Laund Lukeo and Lucia, and two with Smooth Collies, Laund Latha and Champion Fellman.

Four years later Laund Lindrum appeared on the scene, winning his first Challenge Certificate in 1930, in the ownership of Mr Stansfield, before being sold to Mrs James (Mariemeau) who campaigned him to his title. **Champion Laund Lindrum**'s claim to fame was to be through his most influential son, Mrs James' Champion Knight of Monaster (ex It's A Gift). One Monaster son, Champion The Laird of Killartry, produced Miss May Young's Alphington Land Girl, the granddam of Champion Riffelsee Son O' Lad of Ugony (Champion Lad of Ladypark ex Golden Rod of Wooden). At the West of England Ladies' Kennel Society Show in 1952 Son O'Lad was awarded Reserve Best in Show, the first Rough Collie to achieve such a high honour at a post-war all-breeds Championship Show.

Champion Laund Lindrum headed an early dominant post-war strain through another Monaster son, the unshown Thane of Mariemeau. This included such great sires as Champions Gunner of Mariemeau and Gunner of Glenturret (see page 60) who were to influence many of the Danvis, Jefsfire, Larkena and Sandiacre Collies. This line was to end following the birth of Champion Antoc Vicar of Bray in 1965 (see page 76).

Sire Eden Eldred	Annandale Extra	Ch Eden Extra	Eden Eric
			Alloway Ideal
		Eden Emily	Ch Laund Limit
			Denny Lively Bird
	Oswald Lady	Ch Poplar Perfection	Ch Magnet
			Pickwick Peeper
		Oswald Molly (unregistered)	Ch Laund Luminous
			St Helen's Style
Dam Glenack Juliet	Ch Laund Latto	Laund Lally	Ch Laund Laird
			Laund Lillith
		Spotland Seraph	Ch Magnet
			Ch Seedley Seraph
	Hackbridge Illustrious	Ch Magnet	Tonge Admiration
			Southport Seal
		Landgirl	Ch Laund Luminous
			Suburbia Model Queen

See 'Piccolo and Lindrum lines' in Appendix I.

Breeder: Mr C F Pyle

Owner: Mr W W Stansfield/Mrs James

K.C. Stud Book No. 45LL

Sable & White Dog

D.O.B. 4 June 1928

Sire: Eden Eldred

Dam: Glenack Juliet

4 CHALLENGE CERTIFICATES

Denny Lively Bird, a great granddaughter of Champion Anfield Model and Champion Squire of Tytton, was a paternal great great granddam of Champion Laund Lindrum. She resulted from a grandfather to granddaughter mating and can be traced back through Eva (1878), a daughter of Tricolour, to the bitch Fly in 1860 (see '(Roberts') Old Lassie-family 1', Appendix II). Lively Bird's first litter, to Champion Poplar Perfection, produced Denny Dinah, eight generations behind Beulah's Nightblack and Beautiful. In her second litter, to Seedley Secure, Lively Bird whelped Dennie Darkie who influenced the Edens, Ladyparks, Deloraines, Clanayres and Shearcliffes. Her third litter, to Champion Laund Limit, produced Eden Emily who was the paternal great granddam of Champion Laund Lindrum and the dam of 'Ladypark', Miss Phyllis Grey's first Collie.

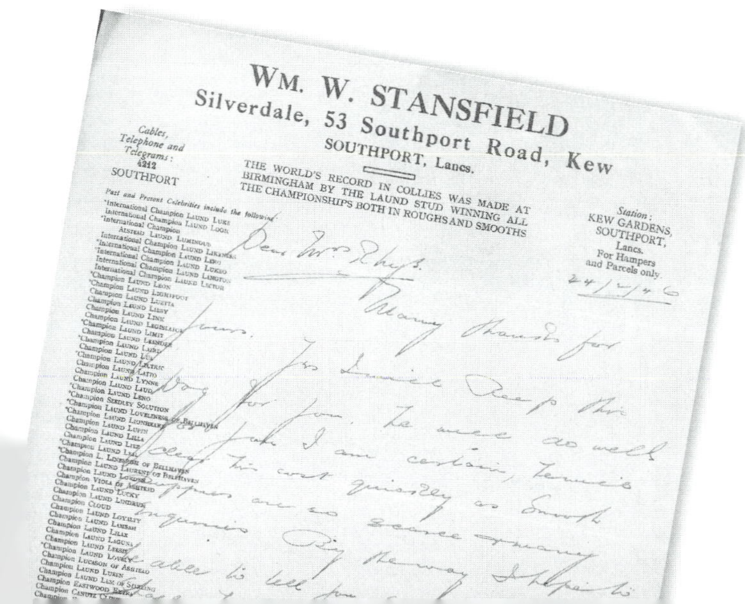

WM. W. STANSFIELD

Silverdale, 53 Southport Road, Kew

SOUTHPORT, Lancs.

Cables, Telephone and Telegrams: 4212 SOUTHPORT

THE WORLD'S RECORD IN COLLIES WAS MADE AT BIRMINGHAM BY THE LAUND STUD WINNING ALL THE CHAMPIONSHIPS BOTH IN ROUGHS AND SMOOTHS

Station: KEW GARDENS, SOUTHPORT, Lancs. For Hampers and Parcels only.

Champion Knight of Monaster, a Lindrum son.

Photo courtesy of Hugh Jones.

Part of Mr W W Stansfield's letterhead – courtesy of Mrs Ada Bishop.

Footnote:

1. *After Mr Stansfield's death his daughter, Mrs Ada Bishop, retained the Laund name and she is still to be seen at the Smooth Collie Club Shows in her position as President.*

Picture courtesy of the Officers and Committee of the Collie Association

Champion Backwoods Fellow

1930

Breeder/Owner: Mr F W Ball

K.C. Stud Book No. 275MM

Sable & White Dog

D.O.B. 3 June 1930

Sire: Backwoods Feature

Dam: Backwoods Fritter

4 CHALLENGE CERTIFICATES

WINNER OF THE COLLIE CLUB'S CHALLENGE TROPHY IN 1935[1]

Champion Backwoods Fellow was closely line-bred to his great grandsire Champion Poplar Perfection (see page 46) and, although not a big dog, inherited his beautiful head, ear carriage and expression from him. Fellow was also white-factored and carried an immense coat with a broad white collar.

Fellow was the inaugural winner of the newly formed Collie Association's Founder's Trophy, which was presented by two Founder Members Nadine George (Beulah) and Clare Molony (Westcarrs). According to Hazel Hunt (Rifflesea): *"Both these ladies considered this dog as near perfection as had yet been seen. He was their ideal and their inspiration".*

Clare Molony (Westcarrs) made an earlier reference to Champion Backwoods Fellow as follows:
"....... probably the best of the many champions from this famous kennel. An outstandingly beautiful dog in his prime, my mental picture of him is of an almost perfect Collie in every respect, and probably the best I ever saw, even though my memory goes back to the great Emerald and Thane. He also left his mark on the breed, principally in the Beulah Kennel".

Champion Backwoods Fellow's greatest influence was clearly in the establishment of the Beulah and Ladypark Collies of Mrs Nadine George and Miss Phyllis Grey respectively. He sired Beulah's Nightmail[2] (ex Champion Eden Electora by Eden Electron) and siblings Champion Backwoods Fanfare and Beulah's Goldenshade (ex Beulah's Nightshade). Nightmail sired only two litters but he provided the breed with the two Champions, Beulah's Golden Feather and Golden Favor[3], whilst Champion Backwoods Fanfare sired Leyland Lima, dam of siblings Beulah's Nightblack and Beautiful, Lyncliffe Lancer and Champion Lyncliffe Blue Lady.

Because of Fellow's white-factoring, Beulah's Goldenshade was unfortunately heavily mis-marked, being predominantly white with sable patches. As a result he was never exhibited, although he proved a noteworthy sire producing Champion Beulah's Golden Future (ex Golden Florida). Future gained his title at the Kensington Canine Society's Show, at Alexandra Palace on 22 July 1939, just three days before the outbreak of war.

Most of these Collies are to be found in the extended pedigree of Champion and Irish Champion Lochinvar of Ladypark, Miss Phyllis Grey's legendary 'King of Collies'(see page 58).

Sire Backwoods Feature	Ch Backwoods Fashion (formerly Eden Edward)	Ch Poplar Perfection	Ch Magnet
			Pickwick Peeper
		Ch Eden Elenora	Ch Eden Extra
			Eden Emily
	Ch Backwoods Famous	Ch Eden Extra	Eden Eric
			Alloway Ideal
		Hallwood Shine	Cragside Chieftain
			Hallwood Secret
Dam Backwoods Fritter	Backwoods Farrier	Ch Fashion's Superior	Ch Backwoods Fashion
			Backwoods Dainty
		Backwoods Futurist	Freshfield Freedom
			St Helen's Sylph
	Backwoods Folio	Freshfield Freedom	Ch Poplar Perfection
			Oswald Molly (unregistered)
		Sandbank Sylvia	Ch Poplar Perfection
			Osborne Ladyship

See 'Squire lines' in Appendix I.

Footnotes:

1. *For several years the Backwoods Collies were very successful with Mr Ball winning the Challenge Trophy with Champions Backwoods Freedom, Future and Fellow in 1927, 1933 and 1935 respectively.*
2. *Beulah's Nightmail, originally owned by Mrs George, was sold to Mr J Lister in 1936 and his name changed to Knottyash Sensation.*
3. *Beulah's Golden Favor, exported to the St Adrian's Kennel of Mr & Mrs James Christie in North Hanover, Massachussetts, gained his American title in 1941.*

Eden Examine with handler. *Photo courtesy Hugh Jones*

Eden Examine (formerly Worsboro' Model)

1944

Breeder: Mr F Hirst

Owner: Mr H Horsfield

K.C. Stud Book No. 985AF

Sable & White Dog

D.O.B. 28 February 1944

Sire: Lyncliffe Lancer

Dam: Seagull

1 CHALLENGE CERTIFICATE

Mr F Rubmann[1], subsequently known as Fred Robson, established the Eden Kennel in Carlisle, some of his Collies being registered as early as 1904. Mr Rubmann/Robson was active for the next sixty years and, being a butcher, managed to maintain a large number of dogs throughout the war years.

In February 1944 Mr F Hirst (Hirspen) bred a litter which included the three brothers Worsboro' Model, Masterpiece of Hawkridge (formerly Bellroy of Bellrenia, and before that Glenwern Crusader), and King Raq of Hirspen, the only one to bear Mr Hirst's affix. Early in 1945 Mr Fred Robson purchased Worsboro' Model for an undisclosed sum and changed his name to **Eden Examine**. Sired by tricolour Lyncliffe Lancer, brother of Beulah's Nightblack and Beautiful, this dark sable and white possessed a good head and expression, adequate bone and overall soundness. His show career was apparently unremarkable, which may explain his frequent change of ownership prior to gaining his Stud Book number at the age of four in the ownership of Mr Horsfield. Records suggest Examine won five stud book qualifying places at three shows over a two year period, the highlight of his show career being firsts in both Limit and Open classes plus the Challenge Certificate at Blackpool under judge Miss Clare Molony (Westcarrs). Many breed historians believed that Eden Examine was unfortunate not to have gained his title but, on joining the Mywicks Kennel, Mr Mycroft retired him from the show ring to stand at stud.

Eden Examine's dominance, as a stud force, changed the direction of the breed as a whole by establishing several sire lines that were to dominate post-war Rough Collies. Used extensively Examine produced several influential progeny including Champion Mywicks Fashioness, Champion Mywicks Model Examiner, Champion Lad of Ladypark (sire of Champion Riffelsee Reward of Glenmist-see page 62), Lad's younger brother Champion and Irish Champion Lochinvar of Ladypark (see page 58), Rimington Kittieholm Pilot, and Abbot of Arranbeck. Whilst Rimington Kittieholme Pilot influenced many of the Jefsfire, Bririch, Duntiblae and Carramar Collies through grandson Champion Mywicks Meadowlancer (see page 64), Irish bred Abbott of Arranbeck drew breeders' attention away from the Lochinvar and Meadowlancer lines, exerting his influence through grandson Champion Defender of Dunsinane to Defender's grandson Dazzler of Dunsinane (see page 72).

Sire Lyncliffe Lancer	Am. Ch Beulah's Silver Don Mario	Beulah's Nightshadowing	Ch Glenack Kingfisher
			Beulah's Nightshadow
		Ch Beulah's Silver Merienda	Ch Backwoods Flutter
			Beulah's Silver Tern
	Leyland Lima	Ch Backwoods Fanfare	Ch Backwoods Fellow
			Beulah's Nightshade
		Merlow Moonbeam	Ch Freshfield Flair
			Knottyash May Queen
Dam Seagull	Masterpiece of Faux	Ch Alphington Achievement	Alphington Diamond King
			Alphington Sunshine
		Alphington Primula	Alphington Golden Melody
			Alphington Dainty
	Laund Larissa	Piper of Mariemeau	Ch Mariemeau Fantail
			Seftonian Sunflower
		Delwood Suzanne	Laund Lorky (formerly Tong Trier)
			Delwood Pamela

See 'Squire and Examine lines' in Appendix I.

Footnote:

1. *The Collie Folio, Volume 10 no.106, of December 1914 includes an advertisement from the Eden Kennels of a Mr F Rubmann, of Fisher Street, Carlisle, which features his latest Champion, Eden Ethel (Parkside Propatria ex Seedley Flossie). According to the Kennel Gazette of February 1915 siblings Eden Elegant and Eden Enchanter (Wishaw Rival ex Eden Ethel, d.o.b. 26.03.14) were registered by breeder/owner Mr F Rubmann. In September of the same year the Kennel Gazette contains the registration of Eden Engineer, litter brother to Elegant and Enchanter, born 26.03.14, bred by a Mr F Robson of Fisher Street, Carlisle! With Britain at war with Germany during this time one can only speculate as to why Mr Rubmann apparently changed his name to Robson!*

Champion Beulah's Golden Flora

Champion Beulah's Golden Flora (R) with her son, Champion and Irish Champion Lochinvar of Ladypark (L)

Photo courtesy of John and Carol Walton

Mrs Nadine George first registered the 'Beulah' affix in 1926 with her first show dog Babette O' Beulah. Six years later Beulah Nightshade (Champion Glenack Kingfisher ex Beulah's Nightshadow, formerly Knatchbull Judith) altered Mrs George's fortunes, heralding her long run of success, with the Beulahs dominating the Collie scene for many years. Mrs George was in the fortunate position of owning sufficient stock for maintaining valuable blood-lines in all three colours, and several of her Collies played significant roles in the breed's post-war improvement. At the outbreak of the second-world war, she evacuated several of her Beulah males to the United States and Canada in the hope of preserving their lines.

Beulah Nightshade's unshown son, Goldenshade (by Champion Backwoods Fellow), a predominantly white Collie with sable patches, secured his place in history by siring Champion Beulah's Golden Future, the last pre-war Champion. He subsequently sired the first post war Champion in Beulah's Golden Futureson, whose main claim to fame was as sire of **Champion Beulah's Golden Flora**.

Miss Phyllis Grey, of the Ladypark Kennels, purchased Beulah's Golden Flora from Nadine George as a puppy.

1945

Breeder: Mrs N K George

Owner: Miss P M Grey

K.C. Stud Book No. 1835AF

Sable and White Bitch

D.O.B. 25 February 1945

Sire: Champion Beulah's Golden Futureson

Dam: Beulah's Golden Kiska

3 CHALLENGE CERTIFICATES

Flora's greatest achievements were the two beautifully line-bred litters she whelped in 1946 and 1947, both sired by Eden Examine (Examine's sire Lyncliffe Lancer being litter brother to Flora's granddam, Nightblack and Beautiful). The first litter of four puppies included Lass of Ladypark and Champion Lad of Ladypark, whilst the repeat mating produced the legendary Champion and Irish Champion Lochinvar of Ladypark (see page 58).

Champion Beulah's Golden Flora's show ring successes came in 1948 when she won her Stud Book number with a third in Limit Bitch at the Caledonian Canine Association's Show followed by her first Challenge Certificate at Altringham Agricultural Society under Mr F Swann. 1949 saw her back in the ring to take her second Challenge Certificate at Leicester and her crown at Southern Counties under Clare Molony. Miss Grey 'did the double' that day as Flora's son, Lochinvar of Ladypark, also won his third Challenge Certificate and title, this dual achievement giving Miss Grey her very first two Champions.

The following extract is taken from an advertisement, placed in the Collie Association's Handbook of 1952, and provides an insight into Mrs Nadine George's successful Beulah Collies: *"This kennel was founded with the intention of producing not only exhibition dogs, but companion and household guards. Thereby assisting to make the Collie once again a popular dog ..... success in the show ring has been gained in many countries – Many devoted and much loved household pets have come and gone, such as Feather, Goldenshade and Futureson – It cannot claim to have bred a 'Lassie-Come-Home'- although the famous Pan, mascot of the American Air Force, was born a Beulah, and is grandfather of Ch Golden Fusonkin. The kennel today is divided into lines, consisting of two sable and white - both descended from Ch Backwood's Fellow. The first through Beulah's Goldenshade and the second through Int. Ch[1] Beulah's Golden Favor. There is too the tricolour merle line. Pure colour bred for 8 generations on the sire's side with no direct introduction of sable and white blood – Hence the beautiful clear blue of all the Beulah Blues."*

Sire Champion Beulah's Golden Futureson	Ch Beulah's Golden Future	Beulah's Goldenshade	Ch Backwoods Fellow
			Beulah Nightshade
		Beulah's Golden Florida	Backwoods Farrier
			Backwoods Florabella
	Ch Beulah's Golden Feather	Knottyash Sensation[2]	Ch Backwoods Fellow
			Ch Eden Electora
		Beulah's Golden Florida	Backwoods Farrier
			Backwoods Florabella
Dam Beulah's Golden Kiska	Beulah's Golden Fanfarist	Ch Backwoods Fanfare	Ch Backwoods Fellow
			Beulah Nightshade
		Kentish Rose	Sterling of Sedgemoor
			Medway Floss
	Beulah's Nightblack and Beautiful	Am Ch Beulah's Silver Don Mario	Beulah's Nightshadowing
			Ch Beulah's Silver Merienda
		Leyland Lima	Ch Backwoods Fanfare
			Merlow Moonbeam

See 'Lima / (Roberts') Old Lassie-family 1' in Appendix II, and 'Squire lines' in Appendix I.

Footnotes:

1. *"Int. Ch" is used in this context to signify that Golden Favor won his title in more than one country, and in this case he was both a British and American Champion.*
2. *Knottyash Sensation was formerly known as Beulah's Nightmail.*

Lilac of Ladypark

Photo: courtesy of Hazel Hunt

1945

Breeder: Miss H L R Edgley (now Hazel Hunt)

Owner: Miss P M Grey & others

Blue Merle Bitch

D.O.B. 3 August 1945

Sire: Maroel Blue Mandarin

Dam: Beulah's Night Flare

Hazel Edgley, later known as Hazel Collins and currently Hazel Hunt, began her Riffelsee[1] Kennel with eight-week old Beulah's Golden Fantasy[2], a great granddaughter of Beulah's Nightshade. As Fantasy was the only bitch in the litter Hazel agreed to return her to Mrs George for a litter and, mated to Beulah's Nightvictorious, an unshown tricolour brother of American Champion Beulah's Silver Don Mario, Golden Fantasy whelped Champion Beulah's Night Fame, Night Flame and Night Flare. As a replacement for Fantasy, Hazel received Night Flare who whelped **Lilac of Ladypark** in her first litter and Riffelsee Royalist (by Champion Lad of Ladypark) in her second. Night Flare's first litter contained only two puppies, but unfortunately she killed the tricolour puppy and so badly savaged the blue merle, Lilac, that she was hand reared by Miss Grey.

Due to her traumatic start to life Lilac of Ladypark was unable to be exhibited although she was to prove of great importance to the post-war breeding of both sables and blue merles, establishing a bitch line that endures to this day. From four litters, each to different dogs, she produced six offspring that gained Stud Book qualifications, including two Champion bitches. It is interesting to note that, although Lilac was a blue merle, her first litter was sired by the sable and white dog Lucky of Ladypark, producing the sable and white Champion Lena of Ladypark. Mated to Champion and Irish Champion Lochinvar of Ladypark, Champion Lena whelped the four Collies, Lena's Golden Son and the three Champions Lilt of Ladypark, Eden Rip of Ladywell, and International Champion Libretto of Ladypark, sire of sibling Champions Liberty and Limpid of Ladypark. Through Libretto, Lilac of Ladypark was to become the great great great granddam of Champion Pattingham Pacemaker (see page 70).

In a subsequent litter Lilac of Ladypark was mated to Westcarrs Black Bisley, producing Lobelia of Ladypark, Sombreseawave from Shiel, and Champion Silvaseabear from Shiel. Silvaseabear stayed with Margaret Osborne proving her worth by becoming the kennel's first Champion and establishing the Shiel name throughout the Collie world. Six of her progeny, from five litters by four different dogs, gained Stud Book recognition, four of these earning a total of five Challenge Certificates.

In 1951 Lilac became the granddam of blue merle siblings Westcarrs Blue Minerva and Champion Westcarrs Blue Minoru. Minoru annexed five Challenge Certificates, winning the Collie Club's prestigious Challenge Trophy twice in 1955. This made him the first blue merle male, and only the second of this colour to win this award, the blue merle bitch Champion Blue Ruin having been the inaugural winner in 1888.

Lilac, via her grandchildren Blue Minoru and Blue Minerva, is behind most post-war British blue merles influencing the clear blue colours of the Shiel, Crosstalk, Bririch, and Carramar Collies.

Sire Maroel Blue Mandarin	Ch Eden Diadem	Ashtead Aristocrat	Ch Ashtead Applause
			Ockham Louise
		Delwick Diana	Ch Netherkeir Starboy
			Surprise of Ashtead
	Blue Baroness	Bruce of Waldemar	Eden Electron
			Pelton Blue Frisetta
		Bleuette of Waldemar	Backwoods Fireman
			Westcarrs Blue Moonlight
Dam Beulah's Night Flare	Beulah's Nightvictorious	Beulah's Nightshadowing	Ch Glenack Kingfisher
			Beulah's Nightshadow
		Ch Beulah's Silver Merienda	Ch Backwoods Flutter
			Beulah's Silver Tern
	Beulah's Golden Fantasy	Ch Beulah's Golden Future	Beulah's Goldenshade
			Beulah's Golden Florida
		Ch Beulah's Golden Feather	Knottyash Sensation
			Beulah's Golden Florida

See '(Salter's) Mountshannon Mona-family 10' in Appendix II, and 'Piccolo lines' in Appendix I.

Footnotes:

1. *Riffelsee was the original spelling of Hazel Hunt's affix, but due to a Kennel Club error some years ago it was changed to Rifflesea.*
2. *After whelping two litters Beulah's Golden Fantasy was exported to Sweden.*

Champion & Irish Champion Lochinvar of Ladypark

Picture courtesy of Dog World

The Ladypark Kennel was established in 1922 with Miss Phyllis Grey's first bitch 'Ladypark', by Champion Eden Extra ex Eden Encore (Doon Rival ex Salford Sensation) and after breeding Collies in a small way for twenty-four years Miss Grey purchased Beulah's Golden Flora as a puppy. The following year Flora was mated to Eden Examine and, from a litter of only four puppies, Miss Grey kept Lass of Ladypark for herself and sold a dog puppy to Dr K G Collins, the future husband of Hazel Edgley (now Hazel Hunt of Rifflesea Collies). This puppy was to become Champion Lad of Ladypark.

A year later Miss Grey repeated the mating of Flora and Examine, resulting in the birth of the great Lochinvar, known as the 'King of Collies'. Champion Lochinvar of Ladypark won his first Challenge Certificate at Bath in May 1948, just eleven days after brother Lad won his first ticket, and during the following year Lochinvar annexed his second Challenge Certificate at the Croydon, Coulsdon and Purley Show and his title at Southern Counties under Clare Molony, where Miss Grey 'did the double' by making up her first two Champions in Lochinvar and his dam Beulah's Golden Flora. Two years later, in 1951, Champion Lochinvar gained his Irish title and had the distinction of winning Best of Breed at Crufts, an achievement he was to repeat in 1957 at the age of ten years.

As well as being a superb show dog he was a prepotent sire, proving dominant for his sable colouring. Siring three Champions in his first litter, his record includes thirteen British Champions, fourteen different Challenge Certificate winners, and numerous overseas Champions. Among his famous offspring were Champion Leonertes of Ladypark, winner of ten Challenge Certificates; Pattingham Kismet, sire of

1947

Champion Pattingham Pacemaker (see page 70); siblings Champion Lilt of Ladypark and International Champion Libretto[1] of Ladypark; sibling Champions Maid of Ladypark and Rose of Ladypark, dam of Frank Mitchell's Champion Riffelsee Reward of Glenmist CD[2] (see page 62); and Champions Westcarrs Whistler, Loyal of Ladypark, Eden Rip of Ladywell and Walbrooke Stormy Petrel.

Champion and Irish Champion Lochinvar of Ladypark was born at a crucial time when breeding stock was sadly depleted after the war but, despite his popularity, his influence did not survive many generations, the longest line extending to Champion Antoc Midnight Cowboy (see page 92) Lochinvar's greatest gift to posterity, without doubt, was shared with Champion Mywicks Meadowlancer as they were both grandsires of Leecroft Leading Lady, the dam of Dazzler of Dunsinane (see page 72).

In Miss Grey's own words: *"Roy, as he is called at Ladypark, traces his ancestry back in a direct line to Trefoil (1873), progenitor of the modern Collie, and descends in a direct line from such Collie greats as Eden Examine, Lyncliffe Lancer, Beulah's Nightvictorious, Eden Emerald, Poplar Perfection and Southport Sample."*

In the Kennel Gazette, 1994 Mrs Aileen Speding (Antoc) made the following comments about Lochinvar: *"In a breed not given to campaigning its Champions, no one dog or bitch stands out by virtue of its show wins alone, and for me, the greatest ever Rough Collie was "The King" himself, Int Ch[3] Lochinvar of Ladypark. Born in 1947, owned and bred by Miss P M Grey, this upstanding, handsome sable and white dog came at a time in Collie history when breeders, who had managed to maintain a nucleus of their kennels throughout the difficult war years, were struggling to regain type and temperament. Carrying the famous blood-lines of the past (Beulah, Laund, Eden, Backwoods, Mariemeau, Delwood) he had impeccable breeding, good looks, and a wonderful temperament. His show record was impressive: he gained his UK and Irish Champion titles, won the CC at Crufts for the first time in 1951 and again in 1957 at ten years of age. I was fortunate enough to see him on both occasions. His head was not as good as that of his older brother, Ch Lad of Ladypark, but his body shape, coat, soundness, and charisma were in a class of their own. Rough Collies were fortunate indeed to have such a dog at this time and, mated to bitches of varying types and breeding, he was able to stamp the Lochinvar Look on to many of his offspring."*

Sire Eden Examine	Lyncliffe Lancer	Am. Ch Beulah's Silver Don Mario	Beulah's Nightshadowing
			Ch Beulah's Silver Merienda
		Leyland Lima	Ch Backwoods Fanfare
			Merlow Moonbeam
	Seagull	Masterpiece of Faux	Ch Alphington Achievement
			Alphington Primula
		Laund Larissa	Piper of Mariemeau
			Delwood Suzanne
Dam Champion Beulah's Golden Flora	Ch Beulah's Golden Futureson	Ch Beulah's Golden Future	Beulah's Goldenshade
			Beulah's Golden Florida
		Ch Beulah's Golden Feather	Knottyash Sensation
			Beulah's Golden Florida
	Beulah's Golden Kiska	Beulah's Golden Fanfarist	Ch Backwoods Fanfare
			Kentish Rose
		Beulah's Nightblack and Beautiful	Am. Ch Beulah's Silver Don Mario
			Leyland Lima

See 'Examine lines' in Appendix I, and 'Lima / (Roberts') Old Lassie-family 1' in Appendix II.

Footnotes:

1. *Libretto of Ladypark was exported to Mrs Garabelli's Cambiano Kennels in Italy where he gained his International title under FCI rules.*
2. *C.D. is a Working Trials award and means 'Companion Dog'.*
3. *In Britain the term 'International Champion' was more often used as a courtesy title for those dogs gaining their titles in more than one country. Lochinvar was an English and Irish Champion but there is no record of him ever having been campaigned elsewhere.*

Breeder/Owner: Miss P M Grey

K.C. Stud Book No. 696AF

Sable & White Dog

D.O.B. 1 February 1947

Sire: Eden Examine

Dam: Champion Beulah's Golden Flora

6 CHALLENGE CERTIFICATES

Champion Gunner of Glenturret

Picture courtsey of the Officers & Committee of the Collie Association/ Sandra Wigglesworth

Champion Gunner of Glenturret was closely line-bred to Champion Laund Lindrum, again resulting from the popular combination of grandsire to granddaughter mating. Gunner's tail female line can be traced back through his great great granddam Radiant Princess, half sister to Silver Emblem, to Mr Claypole's unregistered bitch Curzon Jess, in the 1890's.

Champion Gunner of Glenturret's main claim to fame was through sons Champion Jefsfire Strollaway (ex a great granddaughter of Lochinvar) and Champion Danvis Damascus[1] (a grandson of Lochinvar and Champion Danvis Deborah), paternal and maternal grandsires respectively of the beautifully line-bred and influential foundation bitch of the Rokeby kennels–Champion Witchcraft of Rokeby (see page 74). Witchcraft was the granddam of Champion Sandiacre String of Pearls (see page 82) who carried no fewer than sixteen lines, in five generations, to Gunner.

He also had a great part to play in the early Antoc and Corydon kennels, among others, through his great great grandson Champion Larkena Vanara Golden Victor (ex Champion Starlet of Glenmist, daughter of Champion Riffelsee Reward of Glenmist, page 62) who sired Champion Antoc Vicar of Bray for Aileen Speding (see page 76). Victor was also the double grandsire of Corydon Quo Vadis, sire of John and Barbara Blake's Champion bitch Corydon Qui Vive (see page 86).

The following article, entitled 'The Glenturret Collies', is taken from a Kennel Gazette of the mid 1950's: *"Mr Macpherson has for several years been a prominent figure in the Collie world, and last year made a*

1952

Champion Jefsfire Strollaway, a son of Gunner.
Photo courtesy of Kathy Green

successful debut as a championship show judge. Many years ago he was a successful Scottish Terrier exhibitor. David really came into prominence when he made Gunner of Mariemeau a champion. Today he is really in the limelight with his sensational Gunner of Glenturret, who was rested after being reserve CC at Manchester. However, he made a real come-back at Bearsden Members show, where in a record Scottish entry he won best in show under Mr Alex Murray. Since then he has won a CC at Edinburgh, CC and best of breed at Richmond, and other wins include best in show at the Scottish Collie Club open show. His CC show report read:'Gunner of Glenturret, outstanding winner, has all the essentials a good Collie requires, type, eye, and expression, flowing coat of right texture'. His stud fee is £6.6s.0d.,plus return carriage. A point for breeders to note is that his dam was of championship class."

Kath and Alan Jeffries (Jefsfire) commented in the 'Rough Collie Forum', Dog World 24 July 1998: *"Ch. Gunner of Glenturret', a sable dog of substance whose construction enabled him to cover the ground with effortless ease. Classic head with correct ears and eyes to create that expression that keenly awaits the next command. A tailor-made coat of correct weather proof texture enhanced the picture that lingers still".*

Breeder/Owner: Mr D McPherson

K.C.Stud Book No. 65AM

Sable & White Dog

D.O.B. 8 July 1952

Sire: Champion Gunner of Mariemeau

Dam: Vanity of Glenturret

3 CHALLENGE CERTIFICATES

Sire Champion Gunner of Mariemeau	Thane of Mariemeau	Ch Knight of Monaster	Ch Laund Lindrum
			It's a Gift
		The Ladye of Mariemeau	Mariemeau Brilliantine
			Mariemeau Genesta
	Patricia of Mariemeau	Mariemeau Blue Rannoch	Ch Laund Lindrum
			Mariemeau Idylle
		Princess of Mariemeau	Ch Mariemeau Fantail
			Sapho of Mariemeau
Dam Vanity of Glenturret	Cragienure Chancellor	Ch Gunner of Mariemeau	Thane of Mariemeau
			Patricia of Mariemeau
		Cragienure Crystal	Sensation of Bellrenia
			Cragienure Camellia
	Eden Golden Queen of Riglea	Townhouse Diamond King	Laund Cragienure Camouflage
			Valerie of Killartry
		Beauty of Riglea	Eden Esquire
			Radiant Princess

See 'Lindrum lines' in Appendix I, and '(Claypole's) Curzon Jess-family 2' in Appendix II.

Footnotes:

1. *Champion Danvis Damascus went Best in Show at the South Wales Kennel Association's Championship Show in Cardiff, in 1961, and was the first post-war Rough Collie to win this award at an 'all breeds' Championship Show.*

Champion Riffelsee Reward of Glenmist C.D

Photos courtesy of Hazel Hunt

Champion Lad of Ladypark, sire of **Champion Riffelsee Reward of Glenmist**, was from Miss Grey's Beulah's Golden Flora and he was transferred as a puppy to Dr and Mrs K G Collins of the Riffelsee Collies. Lad was a highly intelligent, versatile and active dog, well known in the West Country for his stage appearances doing two seasons in Prince Littler's 'Sleeping Beauty' at the Bristol Hippodrome and the Bristol Old Vic. He played the part of the shepherd dog no less than a hundred and forty-four times.

Champion Lad of Ladypark and Champion Rose of Ladypark, older brother and daughter of Lochinvar respectively, were campaigned to their titles by Hazel Collins. Lad's first Challenge Certificate, at the West of England Ladies' Kennel Society Championship Show in 1948, was also the first for both breeder and owner. Rose and Lad were mated together on three occasions producing a Champion in each litter–Champion Riffelsee Resplendence, Champion and Irish Champion Riffelsee Regality of Dunsinane, the first of Audrey Chatfield's many Champions, and Champion Riffelsee Reward of Glenmist. Lad also sired Ugonys Son o' Lad of Riffelsee for Miss May Young; Riffelsee Royalist (ex Beulah's Night Flare, a half brother of Lilac of Ladypark), who in turn sired the outstanding blue merle siblings Champion Westcarrs Blue Minoru and Westcarrs Blue Minerva for Miss Clare Molony; and Frank Mitchell's Champions, Lovely Lady of Glenmist and Pattingham Gay Lady of Glenmist (dam of Champion Pattingham Pacemaker-see page 70). Rose's fourth litter, to Riffelsee Royalist, produced Riffelsee Rosemary who went to the Jefsfire Kennels. Rosemary's tail female line led to granddaughter Sandiacre Jefsfire Gay Tweed, the granddam of Champion Sandiacre String of Pearls (see page 82).

1953

Left: Reward's dam, Champion Rose of Ladypark, as a nine month old puppy. **Right:** Champion Lad of Ladypark aged three years, an older brother of Lochinvar and sire of Reward.

Frank Mitchell purchased Riffelsee Reward as his foundation bitch. She was a true 'all round' Collie combining both intelligence and beauty and, apart from gaining her Obedience CD and show title, she also produced some very important progeny. Mated three times to Champion Liberty of Ladypark she produced seven Collies to achieve Stud Book entry, including the four Champion daughters Sapphire, Sceptre, Spellbinder and Starlet. Sapphire continued the family tradition by whelping four Champions–the two sons Glenmist Golden Legacy[1] and Pattingham Gay Legend of Glenmist, and daughters Lovely Lady of Glenmist and Pattingham Gay Lady of Glenmist (by Riffelsee Royalist). Gay Lady proved to be a most useful bitch producing siblings Pattingham Pretty Jetta and Precious Lady, who were behind the Geoffdon, Erjon and Claredawn Collies respectively, and Champion Pattingham Pacemaker. Starlet whelped Champion Debonair of Glenmist and Champion Larkena Vanara Golden Victor, sire of Champion Antoc Vicar of Bray (see page 76). Victor was also behind Corydon Coalblack Maid (ex Ralvera's Donna's Maid) and Corydon Don Vicisti (ex Corydon Bella Donna) and when these two were eventually mated together they produced Corydon Quo Vadis, sire of Qui Vive (see page 86).

At the West of England Collie Society's first Championship Show in 1956, Frank exhibited Reward, Sceptre and Sapphire under Mr S A Martin, each winning their respective classes. In the challenge Frank piloted Sceptre to the Challenge Certificate whilst Hazel handled Reward to the Reserve ticket. Four years later, at Windsor Championship Show, Frank exhibited three generations of Rough Collies in both beauty and obedience classes. Champion Riffelsee Reward of Glenmist worked obedience Test C; her daughter Champion Sapphire (granddam of Champion Pattingham Pacemaker) worked Test A; and Reward's granddaughter Champion Lovely Lady performed in the Novice Test. Champion Riffelsee Reward at Glenmist qualified twice at Working Trials, holding the record for being the only Champion Rough Collie with a CD certificate. It is primarily for this reason that she deserves inclusion here.

Breeder: Dr KG & Mrs H Collins (now Hazel Hunt)

Owner: Mr F Mitchell

K.C.Stud Book No. 1516AP

Sable & White Bitch

D.O.B. 29 May 1953

Sire: Champion Lad of Ladypark

Dam: Champion Rose of Ladypark

3 CHALLENGE CERTIFICATES

WINNER OF TWO WORKING TRIALS QUALIFIERS

Sire Champion Lad of Ladypark	Eden Examine	Lyncliffe Lancer	Am. Ch Beulah's Silver Don Mario
			Leyland Lima
		Seagull	Masterpiece of Faux
			Laund Larissa
	Ch Beulah's Golden Flora	Ch Beulah's Golden Futureson	Ch Beulah's Golden Future
			Ch Beulah's Golden Feather
		Beulah's Golden Kiska	Beulah's Golden Fanfarist
			Beulah's Nightblack and Beautiful
Dam Champion Rose of Ladypark	Ch & Irish Ch Lochinvar of Ladypark	Eden Examine	Lyncliffe Lancer
			Seagull
		Ch Beulah's Golden Flora	Ch Beulah's Golden Futureson
			Beulah's Golden Kiska
	Laird's Rose	Air Commander	Ch The Laird of Killartry
			Sedgemoor Symphony
		Mystic Maid	Roundrobin
			Silver Emblem

See '(Claypole's) Curzon Jess–family 2' in Appendix II, and 'Examine lines' in Appendix I.

Footnote:

1. *In 1966 Champion Glenmist Golden Legacy went Best in Show at Southern Counties, under F Warner-Hill, having first taken the Group under Fred Curnow. He was one of only two Rough Collies to go Best in Show at an 'all breeds' Championship Show.*

Champion Mywicks Meadowlancer

Photo courtesy of Dareen Bridge

Champion Mywicks Meadowlancer's tail male line descended from Trefoil, through grandsire Eden Examine, continuing through the Duntiblaes and Bririchs of the 1960's and 1970's, whereas his tail female line began in the early twentieth century, fading away at his dam Shoinemaw Sheena[1]. Jimmy Tait (Aberthorne) attributes much of Meadowlancer's success as follows: "*Most of the type and influence produced by this dog was, without doubt, due to his lovely dam who was a beautiful bitch in her own right, and a size smaller than most of her contemporaries.*"

Meadowlancer was a Rough Collie of distinction on two counts, proving to be a tremendous ambassador for the breed in the show ring as well as a sire of note. Gaining his second Challenge Certificate with Best of Breed at Crufts in 1956 and his title six days before his first birthday, 'Kim' gained a total of fifteen Challenge Certificates from eight different judges, including Crufts and the British Collie Club's Championship Show on four occasions. He was also the holder of the British Collie Club's Challenge trophy for Best in Show in 1957, 1959 and 1961.[2]

Meadowlancer played a major role in diverting breeders' attentions away from the influence of the Lochinvar line. His head and expression were a revelation at that time and breeders wishing to improve these points in their own stock flocked to use him. He sired thirteen Champions, eight bitches and five dogs including Ralvera's Meadowmaid; siblings Danvis Sheba of Simbastar, Mywicks Satine of Simbastar and Deborah of Dunsinane; Shearcliffe Vampire; siblings Jefsfire Happy Byname and Jefsfire Lucky Byname; Rhodelands Boy, and Duntiblae Dog Watch, the last three of these being instrumental in perpetuating the male lines for several further generations. Alan and Kath Jeffries' Champion Jefsfire Lucky Byname sired Champion Thistleblue Blueland Boy, who was three generations behind Vera Hickson's Bririch Champions, Black Keino, Blue Rock and Blue Unit; Mr Ball's tricolour, Champion Rhodelands Boy, sired Mrs Joyce Sargeant's beautifully coloured blue merle Champion Carramar Boy Blue, winner of ten Challenge

1955

Breeder/Owner: Mr J E Mycroft

K.C.Stud Book No. 2216AN

Sable & White Dog

D.O.B. 16 March 1955

Sire: Mywicks Monitor

Dam: Shoinemaw Sheena

15 CHALLENGE CERTIFICATES

WINNER OF THE COLLIE CLUB'S CHALLENGE TROPHY IN 1957, 1959, & 1961

Certificates including Best of Breed at Crufts 1966 in an entry of 405 Rough Collies. Rhodelands Boy was the grandsire of Lyn Westby's Champion Lowerpark Black Buccaneer, winner of the Collie Club's Challenge Trophy in 1962 and the dog behind many of the Bririch Collies; and Diane Cochrane's Champion Duntiblae Dog Watch was the sire and grandsire respectively of Champions Duntiblae Dogstar and Duntiblae Dingo.

As a producer Champion Mywicks Meadowlancer exerted the greatest influence over his female progeny, particularly Champion Mywicks Satine of Simbastar, the all-time bitch record holder with fifteen Challenge Certificates (see page 66). His greatest gift to posterity, however, was through his granddaughter Leecroft Leading Lady, the dam of Dazzler of Dunsinane (see page 72).

The following two critiques, from the Kennel Gazette 1994, summed up Champion Mywicks Meadowlancer: *"A shaded sable male born in 1955, and homebred by Joe Mycroft. I think it is safe to say 'Kim' was a 'head' dog. Being outstanding in this department, breeders had not seen the like of his expression before and even though he lacked a little in construction, flocked to use him. Fortunately he was not dominant sable, and sired some good tricolour Champions among his many Champion progeny".* (Derek Smith, Clickam).

".... it is for his beautiful daughters he must be remembered, those wonderful headed bitches with such melting expressions and all the feminine attributes which combined to make the Rough Collie bitch the most beautiful of any breed. In one litter Lancer sired three such bitches, with the tricolour Ch Mywicks Satine of Simbastar destined to become the bitch CC record holder. My own personal choice from his lovely daughters is between Ch Mywicks Merlow Moonbeam and Ch and Int Ch Deborah of Dunsinane". (Jimmy Tait, Aberthorne).

Sire Mywicks Monitor	Rimington Kittieholme Pilot	Eden Examine	Lyncliffe Lancer
			Seagull
		Homeward Treasure	Thane of Mariemeau
			Alphington Lass
	Rimington Panda	Lyncliffe Lancer	Am. Ch Beulah's Silver Don Mario
			Leyland Lima
		Walshaw Duchess	Lyncliffe Lancer
			Laund Larkspur
Dam Shoinemaw Sheena	Lyncliffe Thyland Lad	Lyncliffe Landseer	Beulah's Nightvictorious
			Ch Lyncliffe Blue Lady
		Spaton Lass	Rimington Kittieholme Pilot
			Tatton Lass
	Eden Engraving of Shoinemaw	Eden Extra Model	Sensation of Bellrenia
			Eden Elma
		Eden Edwina	Killartry Rex
			Biddy of Daddystown

See 'Examine lines' in Appendix I, and '(Baillie's)Yieldshields Beaute-family 4' in Appendix II.

Footnotes:

1. *Other members of Shoinemaw Sheena's family are still active through Eden Edwina's full sister Eden Epaulet.*
2. *It is thought Meadowlancer also won the Challenge Trophy in 1956, but in the absence of an engraved plaque or record of Best of Breed in the Stud Books, it cannot be proved.*

Champion Mywicks Satine of Simbastar

Photo courtesy of the Officers & Committee of the Collie Association

Champion Mywicks Satine of Simbastar was out of Leecroft Ladyfair, litter sister to Dazzler of Dunsinane's dam Leecroft Leading Lady, being from a litter of five bitches and two dogs (Sabine and Shane). Of the bitches Sheba, Satine, Sherry, Shirlee and Deborah, three became champions, namely Champion Mywicks Satine of Simbastar, Champion Danvis Sheba of Simbastar, and Champion and International Champion Deborah of Dunsinane. Satine, or 'Blackie' as she was known at home, was sold to Mr Mycroft who added the Mywicks prefix. In 1966 Mr Rippon became a partner in the Mywicks Kennel and, upon the death of Mr Mycroft the following year, Satine became the property of Mr Rippon.

Satine remains the bitch record holder with fifteen Challenge Certificates[1], equalling the number awarded to her sire Meadowlancer. Her tickets were won under fourteen different judges, adding Best of Breed on eleven occasions.

Satine also proved herself in the whelping box by producing six litters. Her first, by Mywicks Model Examiner, produced Skipper of Simbastar, the grandsire of Leecroft Lover Boy of Dunsinane. Inbred to her sire Meadowlancer for her second litter, Satine whelped two dogs and four bitches, from which tricolour daughter Colrenes Mywicks Merlow Moonbeam subsequently gained her title. But it was Moonbeam's sable sister, the strangely named Mywicks Silver Lining, who was to make the greatest impact on the breed's future.

1960

Mywicks Silver Lining was, indubitably, Satine's most noteworthy offspring, influencing the breed through her daughter Mywicks Solette of Brettonpark (by half brother Inglebrook Golden Dandy), the foundation bitch of the Brettonpark Kennels. From Solette two main branches of tail female influence were to develop through sisters Brettonpark Sweet Melody, born in 1968, and Brettonpark Gaiety Girl from a repeat mating the following year (both by Leecroft Lover Boy of Dunsinane). Sweet Melody's influence extends through many of the Hillandale, Emryks, Triburle and Geosan Collies, whilst Gaiety Girl is behind all the Brettonparks in direct tail female line, her main influence being behind one litter, sired by Dazzler of Dunsinane, which produced siblings Champion Brettonpark Vanity Fair (see page 84) and Brettonpark Bobbee Dazzler, double great granddam and grandsire respectively of Champion Arranbrook Mr Chips of Aberhill (see page 98). Gaiety Girl's great granddaughter, Brettonpark Burnished Gold, became a pivotal bitch for the Arranbrook Kennel of Mr and Mrs Basing and her name can be found behind many of the Erjon, Sandiacre, Lynway, Lynaire and Camanna Collies.

Although Champion Mywicks Satine of Simbastar only whelped four Collies to gain Stud Book recognition, there is no disputing her influence on present day Rough Collies.

Miss Margaret Osborne (Shiel) commented many years ago: "*...of Satine I consider that there was no better bitch. She was not specially outstanding to look at, being rather short of white markings, but she was constructed perfectly and moved as a result superbly (these are the first two items I look for when judging),and all the rest of her fitted in. She is one of the very few collies who when I think of her are absolutely crystal clear in my memory, she was absolutely correct for size (which puts many of today's bitches to shame) and was virtually a perfect mover. I know when I gave her a CC in '62 I wrote endlessly about her in my report! She was gorgeous*".

In the Kennel Gazette 1994, Aileen Speding (Antoc) wrote: *"I consider myself extremely fortunate that, awarding CCs for the first time at Windsor 1962, she was shown under me, to gain her third CC. Three and a half years later, at Birmingham City, she won her ninth CC from me. A deep jet black, with well-defined tan markings, she was extremely well constructed, a very sound, effortless mover, with a beautifully balanced head, melting expression, and neat, well-placed ears which she used to great advantage. Her final CCs were won in 1970 when over 10 years old, and having had several litters; a tribute to her lasting qualities"*.

Breeder: Mrs D Illingworth

Owners: Messrs J E Mycroft & D Rippon

K.C.Stud Book No. 1349AU

Tricolour Bitch

D.O.B. 25 July 1960

Sire: Champion Mywicks Meadowlancer

Dam: Leecroft Ladyfair

15 CHALLENGE CERTIFICATES – The all-time Bitch Record Holder

WINNER OF THE COLLIE CLUB'S CHALLENGE TROPHY IN 1964

Sire Champion Mywicks Meadowlancer	Mywicks Monitor	Rimington Kittieholme Pilot	Eden Examine
			Homeward Treasure
		Rimington Panda	Lyncliffe Lancer
			Walshaw Duchess
	Shoinemaw Sheena	Lyncliffe Thyland Lad	Lyncliffe Landseer
			Spaton Lass
		Eden Engraving of Shoinemaw	Eden Extra Model
			Eden Edwina
Dam Leecroft Ladyfair	Look-at-Me -of Ladypark	Ch & Irish Ch Lochinvar of Ladypark	Eden Examine
			Ch Beulah's Golden Flora
		Ch Limpid of Ladypark	Int. Ch Libretto of Ladypark
			Lindy Lou of Ladypark
	Leecroft Black Magic	Ch Mywicks Meadowlancer	Mywicks Monitor
			Shoinemaw Sheena
		Pride of May	Lookout of Ladypark
			Golden Sky of Whitetip

See '(Lord's) Seedley Lassie-family 16' in Appendix II, and 'Examine lines' in Appendix I.

Footnote:

1. *Despite some breeders maintaining that Satine was awarded sixteen Challenge Certificates, only fifteen are recorded in the Stud Book. It is interesting to note Mr Rippon's advertisment in the 1970 Yorkshire Collie Club Handbook: "STOP PRESS!! 'Satine' won her 16th CC and was Best in Show at the Collie Association Championship Show."*

Champion Bririch Silver Dream

Champion Bririch Silver Dream won her first Challenge Certificate at the Collie Association's Championship Show, under Ada Bishop, at the tender age of nine months. She became Vera's first Champion, gaining her title in 1963. A consistent winner, the photograph shows her winning Best Veteran (all breeds) at Blackpool Championship Show in 1971.

Champion Bririch Silver Dream's sire, Crosstalk Silverstar, descends from a prepotent tail female line extending seventeen generations from Mr Baillie's unregistered Yieldshields Beaute, in the early twentieth century, via Mrs Caygill's outstanding tricolour brood bitch, Black Ricky. The combination of Crosstalk Silverstar and Bririch Merry Mischief proved most successful producing two important bitch lines through Champion Bririch Silver Dream and younger sister Bririch Silver Lace. Champion Bririch Silver Dream was more influential, her lines being found behind every Bririch Collie and, together with Silver Lace, she influenced numerous Rough Collie kennels. Bririch Silver Lace proved of particular importance to Mr Broderick's Shearcliffe blue merle line, and from them to the Ingledene Kennel of Val and John Geddes. Their foundation bitch, Leawyn Annabelle, great granddaughter of Silver Lace, whelped Ingledene Black Rose (by Irish Champion Cregagh Pattingham Paymaster) and Ingledene Black Sequin (by Pattingham Premonition), the latter bitch being the great granddam of Champion Ingledene First Love (see page 118), second of four generations of home-bred Ingledene Champion bitches.

Champion Bririch Silver Dream exerted her principal influence in two kennels, whelping Clickam Bririch Night Glamour (by Champion Carramar Boy Blue), dam of Derek Smith's Champion Clickam Night Superior and, from a subsequent litter, Bririch Blue Lilac. Lilac influenced the Bririch Kennel by whelping siblings Bririch Blue Adona and Bririch Black Andrena (by Champion Lowerpark Black Buccaneer). Bririch Black Andrena was responsible for continuing the sable line through daughter Bririch Golden Belita (by Dazzler), who whelped sable Champions, Bririch Goldemblem and Bririch Gold Edition, and tricolour sister Champion Bririch Night Enchantment (by Champion Royal Ace of Rokeby). Blue Adona was the granddam of

1961

Champion Bririch Blue Chiffon who was behind such lovely dogs as Champions Blue Rock of Bririch and Bririch Blue Yvette through tricolour son Champion Bririch Black Keino, and great grandson Champion Bririch Blue Unit. Champion Bririch Blue Yvette, born early in 1977, was a most beautiful bitch excelling in colour, conformation and flowing movement. She won nine Challenge Certificates making her top winning Rough Collie for 1978. Blue Yvette was one of the last of the Bririch Collies to be seriously campaigned along with her son Champion Bririch Blue Ripple, and one of his daughters Serenity Blue of Bririch, Vera's final Challenge Certificate winner.

Breeder: Mr T McKenna

Owner: Mrs V Streeter (now Vera Hickson)

K.C. Stud Book No. 2624AU

Blue Merle Bitch

D.O.B. 3 February 1961

Sire: Crosstalk Silverstar

Dam: Bririch Merry Mischief

3 CHALLENGE CERTIFICATES

Left: Champion and International Champion Bririch Blue Chiffon, great great granddaughter of Champion Bririch Silver Dream
Right: Champion Bririch Blue Yvette, granddaughter of Blue Chiffon
Photos courtesy of RJ Kenward/V Hickson

Sire Crosstalk Silverstar	Ch Westcarrs Blue Minoru	Riffelsee Royalist	Ch Lad of Ladypark
			Beulah's Night Flare
		Lobelia of Ladypark	Westcarrs Black Bisley
			Lilac of Ladypark
	Black Ricky	Alstonians Normington	Ch Cezar of Corbieux
			Lamour of Ladypark
		Glendoran Golden Miranda	Eden Excellent
			Eden Epaulet
Dam Bririch Merry Mischief	Bririch Carnedd Countryman	Ch Liberty of Ladypark	Int. Ch Libretto of Ladypark
			Lindy Lou of Ladypark
		Carnedd Gypsy	Laund Limitless
			Delwood Marietta
	Cloverfield Charleston	Cloverfield Westcarrs Black Barn Dance	Ch Wetscarrs Blue Minoru
			Westcarrs Black Ballet
		Cloverfield Cobweb	Lupin of Ladypark
			Danethorpe Silverdream

See '(Milroy's) Florrie-family 3' in Appendix II, and 'Examine lines' in Appendix I.

Champion Pattingham Pacemaker

Danethorpe Laugh of Ladypark, a Lochinvar daughter and great granddam of Pacemaker, earned her Stud Book number by winning a second place in the Limit Class at the Scottish Kennel Club's Show in 1952. Margaret Franklin purchased Laugh, on breeding terms, from Harry Underwood as the Pattingham foundation bitch, and it was agreed that he would have a dog puppy from her first litter, to be sired by International Champion Libretto of Ladypark. Despite whelping several subsequent litters, each sired by a different Ladypark Champion, Laugh's first one was to prove her most important. The only dog puppy in the litter was duly returned to Harry Underwood whilst Pattingham Polka was sold to Floss Chapman's Deloraine Kennel as a brood bitch. From three litters Polka produced four Champions in Deloraine Decorative, Distinctive, Dinah-mite, and Don Juan. Pattingham Prelude and Pattingham Lullaby, also from Laugh's first litter, stayed with Margaret Franklin, Lullaby eventually becoming the first Pattingham Champion. When mated back to her double grandsire Lochinvar she whelped Pattingham Kismet, sire of Champion Pattingham Pacemaker.

Champion Pattingham Pacemaker, or 'Bracken' as he was known at home, was a beautifully line-bred dog with the prepotent blood of many of the famous Beulahs and Ladyparks behind him. Bracken won five Challenge Certificates claiming his title as a Collie of Distinction, not only by winning Reserve Best in Show (All breeds) at Richmond in 1963, but by winning the Non-Sporting Group at Crufts[1] in 1964, the only Rough Collie to do so since the last war. Although Pacemaker did not feature particularly strongly as a sire he influenced the Antoc Kennel through son Glamour Boy of Glenmist, the sire of Champion Antoc the Boyfriend and grandsire of Champion Antoc Haymaker respectively.

Recent reminiscences by Margaret Franklin will best serve to illustrate Pacemaker: *"As far as my own personal experience of life with my own beloved Collies is concerned, I owe a debt of gratitude to Miss Phil*

1961

Grey's Ch Lochinvar of Ladypark. I remember Lochinvar with deep affection. He was one of those rare stud dogs who had the ability to bestow on his progeny his type, quality and sweetness of temperament. He and his fellow Ladyparks were responsible for my successful Pattingham line of the fifties, sixties and early seventies. I have written on previous occasions about my 'once in a lifetime dog' Ch Pattingham Pacemaker. He gave me such joy and companionship for over thirteen years. He was born in 1961 and by the age of 6 weeks, he had developed the happy extrovert character that remained with him all his long life. His show career brought me much pleasure, as he always did his best in the ring, and rose to all occasions with great charm and enjoyment. At home he was the perfect companion to all the family, and liked nothing better than to join in my teenage sons' games. Often my heart would leap into my mouth when I saw him catching hard cricket balls in his mouth! Such was Bracken – Peace to his bright memory."

In the Kennel Gazette, 1994, Rene Cozens (Bhyllsacre) commented: *"In my opinion the greatest ever Rough Collie was Ch Pattingham Pacemaker. Although I never had the privilege of 'going over him', being very new to dogdom when his star was at its zenith, I remember him so well on my first visit to Crufts, when 'Bracken' won the Non-Sporting Group. Having just acquired a young son of his, naturally my excitement at this victory was tremendous, but his very appearance held me spellbound. He had a most beautifully balanced head, with perfect ear carriage. His super conformation was enhanced by his immaculate shaded sable coat. His movement was so sound, but what set him apart from his peers, for me, was his wonderful personality. He had an extra helping of charisma when he was born – and it showed!"*

Sire Pattingham Kismet	Ch & Irish Ch Lochinvar of Ladypark	Eden Examine	Lyncliffe Lancer
			Seagull
		Ch Beulah's Golden Flora	Ch Beulah's Golden Futureson
			Beulah's Golden Kiska
	Ch Pattingham Lullaby	Int. Ch Libretto of Ladypark	Ch & Ir. Ch Lochinvar of Ladypark
			Ch Lena of Ladypark
		Danethorpe Laugh of Ladypark	Ch & Ir. Ch Lochinvar of Ladypark
			Proud Lassie
Dam Champion Pattingham Gay Lady of Glenmist	Riffelsee Royalist	Ch Lad of Ladypark	Eden Examine
			Ch Beulah's Golden Flora
		Beulah's Night Flare	Beulah's Nightvictorious
			Beulah's Golden Fantasy
	Ch Sapphire of Glenmist	Ch Liberty of Ladypark	Int. Ch Libretto of Ladypark
			Lindy Lou of Ladypark
		Ch Riffelsee Reward of Glenmist	Ch Lad of Ladypark
			Ch Rose of Ladypark

See 'Examine lines' in Appendix I, and '(Claypole's) Curzon Jess-family [2]' in Appendix II.

Owner/Breeder: Mrs M. Franklin

K.C.Stud Book No. 279AV

Sable & White Dog

D.O.B. 15 July 1961

Sire: Pattingham Kismet

Dam: Champion Pattingham Gay Lady of Glenmist

5 CHALLENGE CERTIFICATES

RESERVE BEST IN SHOW (ALL BREEDS) – RICHMOND 1963

WINNER OF THE NON-SPORTING GROUP - CRUFTS 1964

Footnote:

1. *Champion Pattingham Pacemaker was actually the third Rough Collie to win the Non-Sporting Group at Crufts. Previous winners were Champion Wishaw Leader in 1906 (see page 38), Laund Luminous in 1916 and Laund Lauder in 1922. At this stage the Non-Sporting Group included the Working and Utility breeds and it was not until 1967 that these were divided into separate Groups. In 1999 the Working Group was split into Working and Pastoral groups.*

Dazzler of Dunsinane

Photos by courtesy of Audrey Chatfield

Dazzler of Dunsinane went back to Eden Examine on both sides of his pedigree . In tail male he traced back through his grandsire, Mrs Audrey Chatfield's Champion Defender of Dunsinane (ex Rinth Recluse, strongly line-bred to both the Lyncliffes and the Beulahs) and on his dam's side through Lochinvar and Meadowlancer. Interestingly Dazzler's dam, Leecroft Leading Lady, was full sister (later litter) to Leecroft Ladyfair, dam of Champion Mywicks Satine of Simbastar (see page 66).

Dazzler was a rather small and unremarkable dog, but as Audrey comments: "*he did, however, possess an excellent eye, head and expression....*". He was exhibited as a puppy but Audrey found difficulty in getting sufficient body on him and he never regenerated a full coat once his puppy moult was over. As he did not particularly enjoy or excel in the show ring, he was retired to stud, a function he also did not particularly relish refusing to mate bitches indoors. Despite all of this Dazzler's impact was significant. His arrival changed breeders' perception of Collie head and expression and, whereas Meadowlancer in the late fifties had diverted attention from Lochinvar, Dazzler was now to draw breeders' attentions away from Meadowlancer. Once again it can be seen that attentions were now concentrated on the male line of just one Collie and his influence was to dominate the breed for ever, with the majority of British Rough Collies extending through Dazzler right back to Trefoil and Shamrock.

Dazzler was obviously a prepotent sire but, despite his progeny tending to look similar, they did not resemble him. He sired nine UK Champions including siblings Ramsey of Rokeby and Dunsinane Rosalinda of Rokeby, Sandiacre Secondhand Rose, Deloraine Doll Face, Dunsinane Robin Hood of Rokeby and Brettonpark Vanity Fair but without doubt his most important litter was the first one he sired to Champion Witchcraft of Rokeby. This contained sibling Champions Royal Ace of Rokeby, Romney of Rokeby and Deburgh Rose Marie. Royal Flush of Rokeby and Champion Dunsinane Robin Hood of Rokeby, resulting from a repeat

1962

Breeder/Owner: Mrs A.F. Chatfield

Sable & White Dog

D.O.B. 14 June 1962

Sire: Champion Dorgano Demander of Dunsinane

Dam: Leecroft Leading Lady

WINNER OF THE COLLIE ASSOCIATION'S CHAMPION LOCHINVAR OF LADYPARK STUD DOG TROPHY IN 1969 & 1970

mating five years later, influenced the Corydon and Myberns Kennels whereas Royal Ace (see page 78) and Romney influenced the breed on a far wider scale.

Other offspring who featured prominently in forwarding Dazzler's influence to the present day were Royal Ace's half brother, Champion Ramsey of Rokeby (see page 80), Sandiacre Softly Softly (ex Champion Sandiacre String of Pearls – see page 82), and litter brother and sister Brettonpark Highlander of Dunsinane and Champion Brettonpark Vanity Fair (see page 84).

Through Brettonpark Highlander, Dazzler was the grandsire of Pelido Black Prince who influenced many of the Pelido blue merles and tricolours through one particular blue merle son, Champion Cathanbrae Polar Moon at Pelido. Champion Brettonpark Vanity Fair, Dazzler daughter and sister to Highlander, was mated to her half brother Champion Ramsey to produce Champion Brettonpark Whatziname (see page 90).

Alan Clarke (Lynway) made the following observations on Dazzler: "*The name Dazzler of Dunsinane is synonymous with the production of quality Collies of both sexes. We went to use him even before Betty Eglin, but unfortunately we did not manage to get a mating on that occasion. He had a lovely head and good construction and the ability not only to produce good children but children that threw on in future generations. I still believe that his blood has a beneficial effect on the breed today.*"

Left: Champion Dorgano Demander of Dunsinane, Dazzler's sire

Right: Champion Defender of Dunsinane, Demander's sire and Dazzler's grandsire

Sire Champion Dorgano Demander of Dunsinane	Ch Defender of Dunsinane	Irish Ch Dunsinane Alaric of Arranbeck	Abbot of Arranbeck
			Astrakhan of Arranbeck
		Rinth Recluse	Lyncliffe Loadstar
			Rinth Remembrance
	Foxshot Charmer	Whitelea Winley	Ch Amber Lad of Glenacre
			Ch Girley of Whitelea
		Foxshot Surprise	Rowlyn Lad
			Danethorpe Darkly
Dam Leecroft Leading Lady	Look-at-Me of Ladypark	Ch. & Ir. Ch Lochinvar of Ladypark	Eden Examine
			Ch Beulah's Golden Flora
		Ch Limpid of Ladypark	Int. Ch Libretto of Ladypark
			Lindy Lou of Ladypark
	Leecroft Black Magic	Ch Mywicks Meadowlancer	Mywicks Monitor
			Shoinemaw Sheena
		Pride of May	Lookout of Ladypark
			Golden Sky of Whitetip

See 'Examine and Dazzler lines' in Appendix I, and '(Lord's) Seedley Lassie-family 16' in Appendix II.

Champion Witchcraft of Rokeby

Photo courtesy of Hugh Jones

Champion Witchcraft of Rokeby, or 'Amber' as she was affectionately known, was Betty Eglin's foundation bitch, beautifully line-bred along Danvis and Jefsfire lines with four lines going back to Champion Gunner of Glenturret.

Amber whelped nine offspring to gain Stud Book qualifications in Britain, five of these becoming British Champions. She also produced six European Champions to grandson Champion Ramsey of Rokeby and four European Champions to Dazzler of Dunsinane. Of the three Champions Witchcraft produced from her union with Dazzler, Romney of Rokeby and Royal Ace of Rokeby remained in the home kennel, whilst Deburgh Rose Marie of Rokeby was owned and campaigned to her title by Miss V N Morris. From a repeat mating of Witchcraft and Dazzler, five years later, came Royal Flush of Rokeby and Champion Dunsinane Robin Hood of Rokeby. Royal Flush influenced the Corydon Kennel through Corydon King Hector, grandsire of Champion and Australian Champion Little Caesar at Corydon, whilst Robin Hood influenced the Myberns Kennel, being great grandsire of Champion Myberns Minstrel (see page 102).

From Witchcraft's union with grandson Champion Ramsey of Rokeby, she produced Champion Rauno of Rokeby, best remembered as the sire of Champion Sandiacre Sweet Lorraine (ex Champion Sandiacre String of Pearls), and the tricolours Nite Shade of Rokeby and Knight Marksman of Rokeby. Nite Shade was the dam of Champion Fernmoss Nite Lark of Rokeby and International Champion Knight Avenger of Rokeby, whilst Knight Marksman sired Crossfell's Cathanbrae Dresden Blue and Champion Cathanbrae Willow

1963

Breeder/Owner: Mr & Mrs J Eglin

K.C.Stud Book No. 2746AX

Tricolour Bitch

D.O.B. 31 October 1963

Sire: Prospecthill Rustler of Rokeby

Dam: Retta of Rokeby

3 CHALLENGE CERTIFICATES

Pattern, grandsire of Champion Cathanbrae Polar Moon at Pelido. Before leaving for France, Knight Avenger of Rokeby sired a litter to Champion Asoka Gay Mist (Champion Asoka Clayswood Blue Venture ex Champion Kingsville Corviross Gay Silver) producing Acorus Blue Grass and Acorus Blue Erica of Rokeby. Blue Grass became the only blue merle Rokeby Champion, whilst Erica went out to the Spanish Kennel of artist Senor Pardo de Santayana. Not only was she the first blue merle Collie in Spain but she also annexed her International title.

In the 1987 International Collie Handbook Mrs Betty Eglin commented:*"..... a year later we purchased our first sable bitch. We called her Miss Chief and she was the beginning of the Rokeby line ..... I would keep my own stud dogs and breed all my own stock. I outcrossed Dazzler three times, twice with Champion Witchcraft and once with Ch Romney. I bought the first litter sired by Ch Royal Ace because the dam was line bred to Ch Mywicks Meadowlancer and from that litter I kept Ch Rosalie. One further outcross to Ch Asoka Clayswood Blue Venture to bring in the blue line. The development of the line on this basis allowed me to breed the type of Collie that was both distinctive, elegant and intelligent. They had their faults of which I was aware but, taking them as a whole, they fitted the Standard. Working along these lines, faults were more easily eliminated and I worked with the devil I knew rather than the devil I didn't!"*

In the same publication Mrs Eglin made comments on some of her favourite Rokeby Collies:*"For his true Collie character, a perfect gentleman at all times, it has to be Royal Ace and in bitches, Ch Witchcraft for her wonderful intelligence, ring presence and of course her ability to breed so many wonderful Champions. In all she bred fifteen Chs in five litters and Ch Royal Ace sired twenty seven Chs*[1] *in the eight years he was at public stud."*

Sire Prospecthill Rustler of Rokeby	Ch Jefsfire Strollaway	Ch Gunner of Glenturret	Ch Gunner of Mariemeau
			Vanity of Glenturret
		Jefsfire Satin Sensation	Ch Larkena Rexley of Larkfield
			Whitelea Watastra
	Jefsfire Rosalie	Jefsfire Copper Laddie	Ch Gunner of Glenturret
			Glamour of Hanoi
		Jefsfire Dusky Dawn	Ch Gunner of Glenturret
			Jefsfire Satin Sensation
Dam Retta of Rokeby	Ch Danvis Damascus	Ch Gunner of Glenturret	Ch Gunner of Mariemeau
			Vanity of Glenturret
		Danvis Delsia	Ch & Irish Ch Lochinvar of Ladypark
			Ch Danvis Deborah
	Miss Chief of Rokeby	Netherkeir Torch-fire	Torchfire
			Coronation Girl
		Alloa's Masterpiece	Ferry of Narragansette
			Happy of Narragansette

See '(Claypole's) Curzon Jess-family 2' in Appendix II, and 'Lindrum lines' in Appendix I.

Footnote:

1. The total number of Champions, produced by both Witchcraft and her son Royal Ace, was for Champions produced worldwide and not just the UK.

Photo courtesy of
Aileen Speding

Champion Antoc Vicar of Bray

1965

Breeder/Owner: Mrs A Speding

K.C. Stud Book No. 2969AY

Sable & White Dog

D.O.B. 5 March 1965

Sire: Champion Larkena Vanara Golden Victor

Dam: Antoc Rose Marie

9 CHALLENGE CERTIFICATES

WINNER OF THE COLLIE CLUB'S CHALLENGE TROPHY, 1971

WORKING GROUP FINALIST, CRUFTS 1972

Investigation into **Champion Antoc Vicar of Bray**'s tail female line shows his dam, Antoc Rose Marie, extending back to Mr Bell's unregistered bitch Stanhope Village Belle around the turn of the nineteenth century.

Vicar's maternal granddam, Antoc Tawny Lyric, produced two important daughters in Champion Antoc Daydream and Antoc Rose Marie. Mated to Glamour Boy of Glenmist (by Champion Pattingham Pacemaker–see page 70), Daydream continued the female line down through granddaughter Antoc Dearly Beloved. This line fades eight generations later in 1990, with Rhodabern Brown Sugar in one branch and, in a second, in 1993, with Amalie Black Penny at Lewarne. Champion Antoc Daydream's granddaughter, Champion Antoc April Love (by Champion Antoc Midnight Cowboy), deserves mention by winning Reserve in the Working Group at Crufts, 1974, at the tender age of ten and a half months (see page 93). Daydream's half sister, Antoc Rose Marie (by Pattingham Kismet, the sire of Champion Pattingham Pacemaker) influenced the male lines through her son Champion Antoc Vicar of Bray.

Vicar was most successful as a stud force, particularly his 'K' litter to 'aunt', Champion Antoc Daydream (Champion Debonair of Glenmist ex Antoc Tawny Lyric). He sired four dogs and three bitches, among them Antoc King's Rhapsody, Australian Champion Antoc Knight Templar, and Antoc Kittiewake. Rhapsody was behind Sangreat Sasha, tail male grandsire and great grandsire of Sangreat Sorrocco of Arranbrook and Champion Arranbrook Mr Chips of Aberhill respectively (see page 98); Knight Templar influenced many of the early Pelido Collies through grandson Champion Pelido Copper Beech; and Kittiwake was granddam of sibling Champions Ravensbeck Moonlight of Antoc and Antoc Midnight Cowboy (see page 92).

Champion Antoc Vicar of Bray and his tricolour grandson Champion Antoc Midnight Cowboy are noteworthy for promoting the Rough Collie breed, by virtue of their successes in the Veteran Stakes classes at 'All Breeds' Championship Shows.

In an article entitled 'Some Thoughts about Antoc' (International Collie Handbook 1986), Aileen Speding reminisces about Vicar: *"He was an impressive dog with a coat the colour of deep burnished copper, with the whitest of natural white markings I have ever seen. His showmanship was faultless, his manners perfect, and he never let me down in the ring in his long and glorious career. He won his first CC aged 9 months, and his ninth at 7 years at Crufts 1972, where he was also a finalist in the Working Group. He won BIS at the British Collie Club the year before, and made his final show appearance at the British the year after to win the Reserve CC. He sired many winners including Champions at home and abroad, and mated to Ch Daydream produced the K litter that is still influencing Collie breeding today.........to have bred and owned such an outstanding dog is a privilege given to so few of us, and Vicar will always be that extra special dog for me."*

Sire Champion Larkena Vanara Golden Victor	Ch Larkena Rabelias	Larkena Royalist	Ralvera's Craiglyn Commando
			Larkena Rhonda
		Lavish of Ladypark	Ch Liberty of Ladypark
			Lancer Leonie
	Ch Starlet of Glenmist	Ch Liberty of Ladypark	Int Ch Libretto of Ladypark
			Lindy Lou of Ladypark
		Ch Riffelsee Reward of Glenmist	Ch Lad of Ladypark
			Ch Rose of Ladypark
Dam Antoc Rose Marie	Pattingham Kismet	Ch. & Ir. Ch Lochinvar of Ladypark	Eden Examine
			Ch Beulah's Golden Flora
		Ch Pattingham Lullaby	Int Ch Libretto of Ladypark
			Danethorpe Laugh of Ladypark
	Antoc Tawny Lyric	Ch Liberty of Ladypark	Int Ch Libretto of Ladypark
			Lindy Lou of Ladypark
		Antoc Tawny Token	Ch Ugony's Son o' Lad of Riffelsee
			Sherry of Shencolne

See 'Lindrum lines' in Appendix I, and 'Jeannie / (Bell's) Stanhope Village Belle-family 13' in Appendix II.

Champion Royal Ace of Rokeby

Photo courtesy of Maurice Haslam/Hugh Jones

Born in Champion Witchcraft of Rokeby's first litter to Dazzler of Dunsinane, **Champion Royal Ace of Rokeby** was one of three Champions, the others being bitches Romney and Deburgh Rose Marie of Rokeby. Royal Ace was half brother of Champion Ramsey of Rokeby, also by Dazzler.

As well as being successful in the show ring, by gaining seven Challenge Certificates, Royal Ace's main claim to fame was through his stud work. He sired thirty-eight Rough Collies gaining Stud Book recognition, including twelve British and thirteen overseas Champions. His British Champions included Rosalie of Rokeby; Westlynns Witchcraft; Sandiacre String of Pearls (see page 82); siblings Bririch Gold Edition and Bririch Night Enchantment, both with four Challenge Certificates; Nellwyns Black Beauty; and Baronstar Black Diamond, winner of six Challenge Certificates.

Royal Ace, together with half brother Ramsey, now head the current principal sire lines with Royal Ace the more influential of the two, through son Champion Bririch Gold Edition (ex half sister Bririch Golden Belita, great granddaughter of Champion Bririch Silver Dream-see page 68). Gold Edition remained at the home kennel where, apart from winning four Challenge Certificates, he sired five Champions including Corydon Polymeros of Bririch, Fernmoss Editorial of Bririch and Kidlaine Konrad. Champion Kidlaine Konrad extends his sire's influence through son Champion Aberthorne Arrester (see page 100). The union of Champion Bririch Gold Edition and Champion Corydon Hippolyta, a most successful combination, also deserves

1965

Breeder/Owner: Mr & Mrs J Eglin (later Mrs B Eglin)

K.C.Stud Book No. 289AZ

Sable & White Dog

D.O.B. 20 May 1965

Sire: Dazzler of Dunsinane

Dam: Champion Witchcraft of Rokeby

7 CHALLENGE CERTIFICATES

mention. Through Hippolyta's daughter, Corydon Polyhanna, came a line of prepotent sable Corydon male Champions including Handsome Hero, Handsome Hotspur, Gold Star and Il Supremo.

Of Royal Ace, Audrey Chatfield (Dunsinane) commented in the Kennel Gazette, 1994: *"Sired by the famous Dazzler of Dunsinane x Ch Witchcraft of Rokeby, he was not only a great show dog but was also dominant sire, passing on his qualities to a variety of blood lines. Winner of seven CCs (including Crufts) and six Reserve CCs, he was a force to be reckoned with. A big, strong dog, a real Collie gentleman possessed of a gentle dignified temperament which he unfailingly passed to his offspring – these included nearly thirty Champions at home and abroad as well as many other CC winners."*

Royal Ace son, Champion Bririch Gold Edition at eleven years of age

Photo courtesy of Vera Hickson

Sire: Dazzler of Dunsinane	Ch Dorgano Demander of Dunsinane	Ch Defender of Dunsinane	Ir. Ch Dunsinane Alaric of Arranbeck
			Rinth Recluse
		Foxshot Charmer	Whitelea Winley
			Foxshot Surprise
	Leecroft Leading Lady	Look-at-Me of Ladypark	Ch. & Ir. Ch Lochinvar of Ladypark
			Ch Limpid of Ladypark
		Leecroft Black Magic	Ch Mywicks Meadowlancer
			Pride of May
Dam: Champion Witchcraft of Rokeby	Prospecthill Rustler of Rokeby	Ch Jefsfire Strollaway	Ch Gunner of Glenturret
			Jefsfire Satin Sensation
		Jefsfire Rosalie	Jefsfire Copper Laddie
			Jefsfire Dusky Dawn
	Retta of Rokeby	Ch Danvis Damascus	Ch Gunner of Glenturret
			Danvis Delsia
		Miss Chief of Rokeby	Netherkeir Torch-fire
			Alloa's Masterpiece

See 'Dazzler and Royal Ace' lines in Appendix I, and '(Claypole's) Curzon Jess-family 2' in Appendix II.

Footnote:

1. *Champion Bririch Goldemblem, full brother to Champion Bririch Gold Edition, was exported to Mrs Bates' Heathfield Kennel in the United States, and was one of the last Rough Collies to cross the Atlantic to assist in the improvement of American blood-lines.*

Champion Ramsey of Rokeby

Photo courtesy of Hugh Jones

Champion Ramsey of Rokeby's dam, Champion Romney of Rokeby, deserves a mention, being one of Witchcraft's important progeny. Winner of five Challenge Certificates she was also a spectacular brood bitch. In one litter to her sire Dazzler, she produced the two Champions Ramsey and Rosalinda of Rokeby, and from her union with full brother Royal Ace whelped Corydon Regality of Rokeby, the dam of John and Barbara Blake's first Challenge Certificate winner Champion Corydon Qui Vive (see page 86). In 'The Judges' Choice', Kennel Gazette 1994, Albert Wight (Sharval) referred to Champion Romney as follows: *"....One of the earliest of a long line of Champions produced by the late Mrs Eglin. Wonderfully successful as a puppy and quickly gaining her title, she took the show ring by storm, by virtue of her sheer look of quality, shapeliness and soundness in action. Always presented to perfection and responsive to her handler, she also proved her worth as a brood bitch. One of her sons was the superbly headed Ch Ramsey of Rokeby who also had a great influence on the breed."*

Champion Ramsey of Rokeby was not a particularly big dog and, being so closely line-bred he was rather shy. However he excelled in head and expression, qualities which many of his progeny were fortunate to inherit. Ramsey sired ten British and fifteen European Champions including Bririch Idcam Amanda, Rauno of Rokeby, siblings Geoffdon Westlynns Wayside Boy and Westlynns Star, Brettonpark Whatzizname, Corydon Quinault, Claredawn Clansman and Cliona Sapphire.

Champion Ramsey and his half brother, Royal Ace, head the current principal sire lines and although Royal

1966

Breeder/Owner: Mrs B Eglin

K.C.Stud Book No. 1677BC

Sable & White Dog

D.O.B. 4 June 1966

Sire: Dazzler of Dunsinane

Dam: Champion Romney of Rokeby

4 CHALLENGE CERTIFICATES

Ace proved the more influential of the two it is interesting to note that several of Ramsey's Challenge Certificate-winning progeny were out of Royal Ace daughters. Two of Ramsey's sons were to prove of real significance, these being Champion Corydon Quinault and Champion Brettonpark Whatzizname. Prior to Quinault's export to Australia his influence was predominantly focused on the home kennel as his most important son, Champion and Australian Champion Little Caesar at Corydon, established a prepotent sire line extending to the present day via son Handsome Hotspur.

Ramsey's most notable son proved to be Champion Brettonpark Whatzizname (see page 90) who made his influence felt far and wide especially through Sangreat Sorrocco of Arranbrook, sire of Champion Arranbrook Mr Chips of Aberhill (see page 98).

Champion Romney of Rokeby, dam of Champion Ramsey

Photo: courtesy of Kathy Green

Barry Makepeace (Lynaire) commented in 'The Judges' Choice', Kennel Gazette 1994:

"In my opinion the greatest ever Rough Collie was Ch Ramsey of Rokeby, a small dark sable who had the most wonderful head, eye and expression. The result of a father/daughter mating, here was a dog which went on, like his sire Dazzler of Dunsinane, to change the breed. He had the ability to pass on his own qualities to bitches of many different lines. One of the many Champions he sired was Ch Brettonpark Whatzizname, a prepotent sire behind so many of today's winners."

In the same article Aileen Speding (Antoc) said of him: *"Ch Ramsey was a smallish dog for those days, but he was so elegant and had a beautiful clean, quality head, and of course, proved to be a great sire, although he was a very reluctant show dog and rarely made the most of himself."*

Sire Dazzler of Dunsinane	Ch Dorgano Demander of Dunsinane	Ch Dorgano Demander of Dunsinane	Ir. Ch Dunsinane Alaric of Arranbeck
			Rinth Recluse
		Foxshot Charmer	Whitelea Winley
			Foxshot Surprise
	Leecroft Leading Lady	Look-at-Me of Ladypark	Ch. & Ir. Ch Lochinvar of Ladypark
			Ch Limpid of Ladypark
		Leecroft Black Magic	Ch Mywicks Meadowlancer
			Pride of May
Dam Champion Romney of Rokeby	Dazzler of Dunsinane	Ch Dorgano Demander of Dunsinane	Ch Defender of Dunsinane
			Foxshot Charmer
		Leecroft Leading Lady	Look-at-Me of Ladypark
			Leecroft Black Magic
	Ch Witchcraft of Rokeby	Prospecthill Rustler of Rokeby	Ch Jefsfire Strollaway
			Jefsire Rosalie
		Retta of Rokeby	Ch Danvis Damascus
			Miss Chief of Rokeby

See 'Dazzler lines' in Appendix I, and '(Claypole's) Curzon Jess-family 2' in Appendix II.

Champion Sandiacre String of Pearls

Champion Sandiacre String of Pearls was a great great granddaughter of Riffelsee Rosemary (Riffelsee Royalist ex Champion Rose of Ladypark), the Sandiacre foundation bitch. 'Pearlie' was tightly line bred to Champion Gunner of Glenturret, via half brothers Champion Jefsfire Strollaway and Champion Danvis Damascus. Enjoying a spectacular puppy career she had gained her title by the age of eighteen months.

As well as distinguishing herself in the show ring she proved to be an excellent brood bitch being behind a superb line of world-wide Sandiacre Champions. Whelping five quality litters to different dogs, six of her offspring gained Stud Book recognition. When mated back to her grandsire Dazzler in 1970, the fabulous dominant sable Sandiacre Softly Softly was the result. 'Copper' won a first prize at Crufts under Mrs Pru Green, a Reserve Challenge Certificate at the London Collie Club under Mrs Vera Hickson, and the Champion Lochinvar of Ladypark Stud Dog Trophy in 1972. A consistent winner as a puppy he finally lost interest in the show ring and was retired to stud, a job he enjoyed far more! Softly Softly distinguished himself by siring eight Champions including Sandicare Sweet Georgia Brown and Romadale Rothschild, and excelled at producing beautiful bitches with dreamy expressions.

From 'Pearlie's' second litter, by Champion Rauno of Rokeby, Sandra and Jack retained Champion Sandiacre Sweet Lorraine who was to continue the influence by producing three Champions to three different dogs: Champion Sandiacre Sweet Valentine (by half brother Irish Champion Cregagh Sandiacre Strolling), the dam of English and Irish Champion Sandiacre Sonny Jim of Lassina; Champion Sandiacre Stripper (by Glenorka Governor General); and Champion Sandiacre Silence is Golden (by Sangreat Sorrocco of Arranbrook) who, having won Best of Breed at Crufts 1981, went on to become a Working Group finalist. Silence is Golden was subsequently the sire of Champion Sandiacre Silence Please. Pearlie's third litter, by

1967

Breeder: Mr C R Chambers

Owner: Mrs S Wigglesworth

K.C.Stud Book No. 2225 BC

Sable & White Bitch

D.O.B. 9 September 1967

Sire: Champion Royal Ace of Rokeby

Dam: Colrenes Seawitch of Sandiacre

3 CHALLENGE CERTIFICATES

Brettonpark Highlander of Dunsinane, produced Champion Sandiacre Seed Pearl, the dam of Champion Sandiacre Sweet Georgia Brown (by Softly Softly).

Sandiacre Collies are synonymous with the production of elegant dogs and bitches with sweet expressions and the kennel continues to make its presence felt through such Collies as Slap 'n'Tickle, Stop 'n' Think, Set 'n' Match, Social Climber, and their latest sable male Champion, Sandiacre Sacre Bleu.

Left: Sandiacre Softly Softly (Pearlie's son by Dazzler of Dunsinane) **Centre:** Champion Sandiacre Sweet Lorraine (Pearlie's daughter by Champion Rauno of Rokeby) **Right:** Champion Sandiacre Sweet Valentine (Pearlie's granddaughter by Irish Champion Cregagh Sandiacre Strolling ex Champion Sandiacre Sweet Lorraine)
Photos courtesy of McFarlane/Sandra Wigglesworth

Sandra Wigglesworth reminisces as follows:
"String of Pearls was sired by Ch Royal Ace of Rokeby ex Colrenes Seawitch of Sandiacre. When this mating took place the intention was to combine relative bloodlines where the common denominator was the sable male Ch Gunner of Glenturret. In five generations 'Pearlie' carried sixteen lines to this famous dog, (a dog which we had only read about and saw one picture only). All the afore mentioned are ancestors of our present day Collies, and I personally feel that Dazzler of Dunsinane, through his children, changed the breed significantly by stamping a beautiful head, eye and expression on his progeny. This combined well with the Rokeby blood lines, which also descended from Ch Gunner of Glenturret. We condensed acombination of these lines to produce the type of Sandiacre Collie which I feel has the attributes of the Glenturret influence for conformation and movement, combined with the good heads and sweetness of expression inherited from Dazzler."

Sire Champion Royal Ace of Rokeby	Dazzler of Dunsinane	Ch Dorgano Demander of Dunsinane	Ch Defender of Dunsinane
			Foxshot Charmer
		Leecroft Leading Lady	Look-at-Me of Ladypark
			Leecroft Black Magic
	Ch Witchcraft of Rokeby	Prospecthill Rustler of Rokeby	Ch Jefsfire Strollaway
			Jefsfire Rosalie
		Retta of Rokeby	Ch Danvis Damascus
			Miss Chief of Rokeby
Dam Colrenes Seawitch of Sandiacre	Jefsfire Fury	Jefsfire Chateauroux Fellow	Ch Jefsfire Strollaway
			Chateauroux Lady Corzet
		Alanward Jefsfire Joystar	Ch Jefsfire Strollaway
			Jefsfire Sallubrious
	Sandiacre Jefsfire Gaytweed	Franwyns Jefsfire Starmaker	Ch Jefsfire Strollaway
			Starlight of Southwardedge
		Jefsfire Gaytime	Ch Statesman of Southwardedge
			Riffelsee Rosemary

See '(Claypole's) Curzon Jess-family 2' in Appendix II, and 'Dazzler and Royal Ace lines' in Appendix I.

Champion Brettonpark Vanity Fair

Photo courtesy of Joyce Skilbeck

When Thelma and Gordon Duncan were first married they purchased two sable and white puppies one of which was Mywicks Solette of Brettonpark. Very tightly line-bred to Meadowlancer, Solette was a daughter of the strangely named sable and white bitch Mywicks Silver Lining who resulted from a father to daughter mating. When Silver Lining was mated to her half brother (by Meadowlancer) she produced Mywicks Solette who was destined to become Thelma and Gordon's foundation bitch.

Mated to Leecroft Lover Boy of Dunsinane, pictured opposite, Solette produced a promising litter from which Thelma kept the sable and white bitch Brettonpark Sweet Melody, a Reserve Challenge Certificate winner, and the unshown Brettonpark Gaiety Girl, from a repeat mating the following year. Gaiety proved her weight in gold for, when mated to Dazzler, she whelped a superb litter from which came Brettonpark Highlander of Dunsinane, Brettonpark Bobbee Dazzler, Brettonpark Fan Fair and Champion Brettonpark Vanity Fair.

Champion Brettonpark Vanity Fair, a precocious youngster, gained her title by the time she was eleven months of age in addition to winning numerous Best in Show, Reserve Best in Show, Best Puppy in Show and Best of Breed awards, gaining her Junior Warrant in the process. Besides enjoying a superb, if short, show career Vanity was extremely useful as a brood bitch establishing two branches to her family. Mated to Champion Ramsey of Rokeby she whelped Champion Brettonpark Whatziziname (see page 90) and, from a repeat mating the following year, Duntiblae Brettonpark Even Chance. Brettonpark Joyfulness, Vanity's daughter by Champion Royal Ace of Rokeby, mated to uncle Bobbee Dazzler, produced Brettonpark Burnished Gold of Arranbrook who subsequently whelped a fantastic litter containing the three Champions, Arranbrook Polly Peachum, Arranbrook Summer Wind of Camanna and Champion Arranbrook Mr Chips of Aberhill (see page 98).

1969

Breeder/Owner: Mr D G & Mrs T Duncan

K.C.Stud Book No. 400BE

Sable & White Bitch

D.O.B. 4 May 1969

Sire: Dazzler of Dunsinane

Dam: Brettonpark Gaiety Girl

3 CHALLENGE CERTIFICATES

In a litter sired by her son Whatzizname, Champion Brettonpark Vanity Fair whelped Brettonpark Vienna Charm (dam of Brettonpark Country Tweed, by Champion Aberthorne Arrester) who influenced the Erjon, Angelfield and Emryks Kennels among others. Duntiblae Brettonpark Even Chance, Vanity's son and Whatzizname's younger brother, influenced the Lowerpark, Amalie and Lassina Kennels. Besides siring Lyn Westby's Champion Lowerpark Izafella, sire of Anne Hollywood's Ambassador of Amalie, Even Chance was the grandsire of Lassina Lovely Boy who influenced the early Lassinas through son Champion and Irish Champion Sandiacre Sonny Jim of Lassina (ex Champion Sandiacre Sweet Valentine). Vanity's dominance eventually stretched so wide that few kennels escaped her influence, particularly through great granddaughter Arranbrook Razzledazzle. When mated to Sangreat Sorrocco of Arranbrook, Razzledazzle whelped Arranbrook Spring Rain at Lynaire, Arranbrook Swingtime of Sandiacre, and the two Champions Arranbrook Song of Gold at Brilyn and Arranbrook Sugar 'n' Spice of Rixown.

Leecroft Lover Boy of Dunsinane, maternal grandsire of Champion Brettonpark Vanity Fair

Photo courtesy of Audrey Chatfield

Sire Dazzler of Dunsinane	Ch Dorgano Demander of Dunsinane	Ch Defender of Dunsinane	Ir. Ch Dunsinane Alaric of Arranbeck
			Rinth Recluse
		Foxshot Charmer	Whitelea Winley
			Foxshot Surprise
	Leecroft Leading Lady	Look-at-Me of Ladypark	Ch & Ir. Ch Lochinvar of Ladypark
			Ch Limpid of Ladypark
		Leecroft Black Magic	Ch Mywicks Meadowlancer
			Pride of May
Dam Brettonpark Gaiety Girl	Leecroft Lover Boy of Dunsinane	Ch Dorgano Demander of Dunsinane	Ch Defender of Dunsinane
			Foxshot Charmer
		Leecroft Loobi-Loo	Skipper of Simbastar
			Leecroft Black Magic
	Mywicks Solette of Brettonpark	Inglebrook Golden Dandy	Ch Mywicks Meadowlancer
			Brooklea Wendy
		Mywicks Silver Lining	Ch Mywicks Meadowlancer
			Ch Mywicks Satine of Simbastar

See '(Lord's) Seedley Lassie-family 16' in Appendix II, and 'Examine lines' in Appendix I.

Champion Corydon Qui Vive

The following quotation is extracted from John and Barbara Blake's advertisement in the International Collie Handbook of 1998, which was their fortieth year in Rough Collies: *"When Barbara and her sister, Christine, were granted the affix CORYDON in 1958, little did they dream how significant it would become. The first CORYDON litter, sired by Ch Liberty of Ladypark, was born that year. In 1960 the affix was transferred to John and Barbara and when a great granddaughter of Ch Liberty produced her first litter in 1962 (sired by Ch Jefsfire Strollaway) Corydon Bella Donna was retained and she gave us Corydon Don Vicisti. He sired Corydon Quo Vadis who sired Ch Corydon Qui Vive."*

Corydon Regality of Rokeby, **Champion Corydon Qui Vive**'s dam, resulted from the brother to sister mating of Champions Royal Ace and Romney of Rokeby, which means that Qui Vive was strongly line-bred to Champion Jefsfire Strollaway through Champion Witchcraft of Rokeby and Corydon Bella Donna.

As well as her show ring successes, Champion Corydon Qui Vive whelped two influential offspring in tricolour Champion Corydon Quinault (by Champion Ramsey of Rokeby) and sable Champion Corydon Hippolyta (by Corydon King Hector). During his stud career Quinault sired several great Collies but by far the most significant were siblings Champion and Australian Champion Little Caesar at Corydon and Champion Dameral Aristedes (ex Champion Everlovin' Emily at Corydon-see page 96). Although Hippolyta became the first Corydon Champion, beating her dam Qui Vive to the title by just a few weeks, Quinault was actually the Kennel's first Challenge Certificate-winner and first male Champion.

1970

Breeder/Owner: Mr & Mrs J J Blake

K.C.Stud Book No. 3186BG

Tricolour Bitch

D.O.B. 19 August 1970

Sire: Corydon Quo Vadis

Dam: Corydon Regality of Rokeby

3 CHALLENGE CERTIFICATES

Champion Corydon Quinault, a Qui Vive son

Champion Corydon Hippolyta's first litter, to Champion Baririch Gold Edition, produced Corydon Polyhanna, Vera Hickson's Champion Corydon Polymeros of Bririch being whelped in a subsequent litter. Polyhanna continued the line, producing a total of seven offspring to gain Stud Book recognition, from four litters to three different dogs. Although Polyhanna whelped three daughters, each of which produced Champions and Challenge Certificate-winning progeny, she is best remembered for sons Champion and Australian Champion Corydon Handsome Hero (by Qui Vive's son, Champion Corydon Quinault) and Champion Corydon Handsome Hotspur (by Champion and Australian Champion Little Caesar at Corydon), as well as granddaughter Champion Corydon Glory Hallelujah, who was two generations behind Corydon Silver Moon, the dam of Champion Phreelancer Phrosty Moon Over Corydon (see page 124). Handsome Hero had far greater successe in the show ring than as a stud force, gaining his Junior Warrant and twelve Challenge Certificates, nine with Best of Breed awards. He was shortlisted for the Working Group several times, and in 1979 won the Working Group at the East of England Show and the Champions' Stakes class, on the second day at Birmingham, before leaving for Australia. Champion Corydon Handsome Hotspur remained in the home kennel siring twenty-four Rough Collies gaining Stud Book entry, including the three Champions, Corydon Gold Spur, Sandiacre Slap 'n' Tickle and Sassari Deadeyed Dick. Gold Spur continued his sire's influence by producing several Stud Book qualifying progeny, including singleton Challenge Certificate winner Corydon Whisper Willow, Champion Alssala Canny Bairn at Corydon and Champion Corydon La Stupenda. Canny Bairn (ex granddaughter of Champion Sandiacre Sweet Lorraine and Champion and Irish Champion Sandiacre Sonny Jim of Lassina) sired three Challenge Certificate-winning progeny, whilst La Stupenda whelped John and Barbara's recent Champion, Corydon Il Supremo (by multi-titled Sogno del Narciso with Pelido). Two of Supremo's early litters produced Corydon Primadonna for the home kennel, and siblings Brooklynson Headliner and Champion Brooklynson Golden Fashion for the Steve and Angela Barratt/Derek Smith partnership. Golden Fashion won her first two Challenge Certificates as a puppy, gaining her title shortly afterwards to become top Rough Collie puppy of the Millennium year. Prima Donna qualified for the finals of the Dog World/Beta 'Pup of the Year'competition, and Headliner qualified for the finals of both 'Pup of the Year' and the Pet Plan 'Junior of the Year', becoming the first dog to qualify for both finals in the same year.

Sire Corydon Quo Vadis	Corydon Don Vicisti	Ch Larkena Vanara Golden Victor	Ch Larkena Rabelias
			Ch Starlet of Glenmist
		Corydon Bella Donna	Ch Jefsfire Strollaway
			Chuckaluck's That's My Girl
	Corydon Coalblackmaid	Ch Larkena Vanara Golden Victor	Ch Larkena Rabelias
			Ch Starlet of Glenmist
		Ralvera's Donnasmaid	Ch Ralvera's Meadowmarquis
			Ralvera's Delightful Donna
Dam Corydon Regality of Rokeby	Ch Royal Ace of Rokeby	Dazzler of Dunsinane	Ch Dorgano Demander of Dunsinane
			Leecroft Leading Lady
		Ch Witchcraft of Rokeby	Prospecthill Rustler of Rokeby
			Retta of Rokeby
	Ch Romney of Rokeby	Dazzler of Dunsinane	Ch Dorgano Demander of Dunsinane
			Leecroft Leading Lady
		Ch Witchcraft of Rokeby	Prospecthill Rustler of Rokeby
			Retta of Rokeby

See '(Claypole's) Curzon Jess-family 2' in Appendix II, and 'Lindrum lines' in Appendix I.

Pelido Black Prince

'Blackie' was sired by Brettonpark Highlander of Dunsinane, litter brother to Champion Brettonpark Vanity Fair, the dam of Champion Brettonpark Whatzizname (see pages 84 and 90).

Despite **Pelido Black Prince** not featuring particularly prominently in the show ring, annexing only one Reserve Challenge Certificate at Birmingham City in 1973 under Audrey Chatfield, he proved most useful as a sire. He produced Champions in all three colours, these being blue merle, Cathanbrae Polar Moon at Pelido (ex Cathanbrae Southern Belle), sable and white dog Pelido Sparticus (ex Brettonpark Golden Dream of Pelido, the maternal granddam of Champion Pelido Double Fantasy – see page110), and tricolour bitch Pelido Black Belle (ex Pelido Waltz in Springtime). All have had their fair share of publicity, with Polar Moon featuring on the cover of the Kennel Gazette in January 1995, Sparticus on the cover of Dog World's 1993 Annual, and Black Belle also featuring on the front cover of an earlier edition of the Kennel Gazette.

Pelido Black Prince's greatest claim to fame is through son Champion Cathanbrae Polar Moon at Pelido, born in June 1976. Polar Moon, winner of seven Challenge Certificates, sired several Rough and Smooth Champions including the Rough dog Champion Upperton Blue Brand, sire of former post-war Challenge Certificate record holder Champion Tameila Gordon Bennet (see page 116), and Smooth bitch[1] Champion Astrellita Blue Movie of Glenmist who, not content with winning twenty nine Challenge Certificates, was also capable of working cattle.

At Birmingham National, in 1978, judge Barbara Blake commented on Polar Moon as follows: *"Superbly constructed blue who has more than fulfilled his early promise. He is maturing into a grand dog with excellent bone and substance without coarseness. His head is balanced and moulded with just the right amount of stop and beautifully shaped and placed eyes which give him an almost laughing expression in such wonderful bloom that he commands any ring he enters. CC and BOB and he upheld the honour of the breed by being selected in the group. Well done."*

1971

Breeder/Owner: Mr & Mrs P W Burtenshaw

K.C.Stud Book No. 3039BH

Tricolour Dog

D.O.B. 28 February 1971

Sire: Brettonpark Highlander of Dunsinane

Dam: Pelido Doretta of Dunsinane

In a limited stud career Pelido Black Prince's grandson, Pelido Hot Chocolate, proved useful in the home kennel influencing the Pelido blues and tricolours through sons Champion Alenzone's Blue Stratos at Pelido, grandson Champion Pelido Guilty and great grandson Champion Pelido Blue Bolero. Blackie's influence is also to be found behind many of the Rickwood blue merles, via sibling grandchildren Rickwood Black Symphony and Rickwood Sapphire (by Champion Cathanbrae Polar Moon at Pelido) who, when mated together produced sibling Champions, Rickwood Fine 'n' Dandy and Rickwood Musetta.

Of Pelido Black Prince, Lisa Burtenshaw comments: " *Blackie was the most gentle and sweet natured dog, with wonderful bone and substance, beautifully sound and a very BLACK coat. Like many of our oldies, he was a much loved house pet.*"

L to R: Champion Jeffield Esquire (Ch & Aus. Ch Little Caesar at Corydon ex Shanbe Strollawhile at Jeffield); Pelido Black Prince's offspring, Champion Pelido Black Belle, Champion Cathanbrae Polar Moon at Pelido and Champion Pelido Sparticus; Champion Pelido Angel Fingers (Ch Pelido Copper Beech ex Black Prince daughter, Pelido Polka); Champion Pelido Silver Lady (Ch Cathanbrae Polar Moon at Pelido ex Pelido Minuetto Allegretto); and Champion Jaden Mr Blue at Pelido (Pelido Midnight Love Affair ex Pelido Cleopatra in Blue of Jaden).

Sire Brettonpark Highlander of Dunsinane	Dazzler of Dunsinane	Ch Dorgano Demander of Dunsinane	Ch Defender of Dunsinane
			Foxshot Charmer
		Leecroft Leading Lady	Look-at-Me of Ladypark
			Leecroft Black Magic
	Brettonpark Gaiety Girl	Leecroft Lover Boy of Dunsinane	Ch Dorgano Demander of Dunsinane
			Leecroft Loobi-Loo
		Mywicks Solette of Brettonaprk	Inglebrook Golden Dandy
			Mywicks Silver Lining
Dam Pelido Doretta of Dunsinane	Don Panza of Dunsinane	Leecroft Lover Boy of Dunsinane	Ch Dorgano Demander of Dunsinane
			Leecroft Loobi-Loo
		Leecroft Larrissa	Skipper of Simbastar
			Leecroft Black Magic
	Dulcimer of Dunsinane	Leecroft Lover Boy of Dunsinane	Ch Dorgano Demander of Dunsinane
			Leecroft Loobi-Loo
		Admiration of Christholme	Ch Dorgano Demander of Dunsinane
			Damask of Dunsinane [2]

See 'Dazzler lines' in Appendix I, and '(Claypole's) Curzon Jess-family 2 in Appendix II.

Footnotes:

1. *On 1 January 1994 the Kennel Club ceased to register the offspring of Rough/Smooth Collie matings, including recessive Rough puppies produced from Smooth to Smooth matings.*
2. *Black Prince's tail female great great granddam, Damask of Dunsinane, traces back five generations to Champion Rose of Ladypark.*

Photo courtesy of Mary Farnes

Champion Brettonpark Whatzizname

Champion Brettonpark Whatzizname, or 'Woolly' as he was affectionately known, was a dominant sable double grandson of Dazzler of Dunsinane, being out of Thelma and Gordon Duncan's famous Champion Brettonpark Vanity Fair (see page 84), a sister of Brettonpark Highlander of Dunsinane.

Whilst 'Woolly' was still a youngster Thelma arranged with Audrey Chatfield for him to be sent abroad but, at the last minute, decided she could not bear to part with him. Little did she know then what an incredible impact this dog was destined to have on the future of the Rough Collie, through such notable males as Champion Arranbrook Mr Chips of Aberhill, Champion Brilyn Supertramp, Champion Karava Kornishman, Champion Pelido Double Fantasy, Champion Lynway Sandknocker, and Champion Brilyn Rum'n Black.

Champion Brettonpark Whatzizname and his younger brother, Duntiblae Brettonpark Even Chance, sired many winning Collies including several Champions of both sexes, but Whatzizname proved to be the most influential of the two. He sired twenty-five Rough Collies gaining Stud Book entry, including four Champions, Regan of Romadale, Pied Piper of Aberhill at Rixown, Arcot Abelle Helene and Sylcroft Sweet Success. Whatzizname's initial claim to fame was through son Sangreat Sorrocco of Arranbrook who, apart from siring Sandra Wigglesworth's Champion Sandiacre Silence is Golden, produced that famous litter of 1976 which included three sable Champions–the bitch Arranbrook Polly Peachum, and dogs Arranbrook Summer Wind of Camanna and Arranbrook Mr Chips of Aberhill (see page 98). From a repeat mating, four years later, Sorrocco sired Arranbrook Cleopatra at Lynway, dam of Champion Lynway Sandknocker (see page112).

'Woolly' is best summed up by Thelma Duncan's comments in the 1984 Yorkshire Collie Handbook: *"When mated to Ch Ramsey of Rokeby, Ch Vanity Fair produced our Ch Whatzizname who we are proud to say is behind so many winners of today. Woolly has been a wonderful dog to own, very intelligent, a thinking dog, king of the castle here at Brettonpark. Never shown extensively as he wasn't always the best of show dogs – it would depend very much how he felt on the day. A super stud dog to deal with."*

Alan Mather (Rubec) commented in 'The Judges' Choice', Kennel Gazette 1994:*"A beautifully headed dog, with all the attributes to give that elusive expression, plus outline and movement to match, he was admired by many. He proved a fine ambassador for the breed and Mr and Mrs Duncan."*

Sire Champion Ramsey of Rokeby	Dazzler of Dunsinane	Ch Dorgano Demander of Dunsinane	Ch Defender of Dunsinane
			Foxshot Charmer
		Leecroft Leading Lady	Look-at-Me of Ladypark
			Leecroft Black Magic
	Ch Romney of Rokeby	Dazzler of Dunsinane	Ch Dorgano Demander of Dunsinane
			Leecroft Leading Lady
		Ch Witchcraft of Rokeby	Prospecthill Rustler of Rokeby
			Retta of Rokeby
Dam Champion Brettonpark Vanity Fair	Dazzler of Dunsinane	Ch Dorgano Demander of Dunsinane	Ch Defender of Dunsinane
			Foxshot Charmer
		Leecroft Leading Lady	Look-at-Me of Ladypark
			Leecroft Black Magic
	Brettonpark Gaiety Girl	Leecroft Lover Boy of Dunsinane	Ch Dorgano Demander of Dunsinane
			Leecroft Loobi-Loo
		Mywicks Solette of Brettonpark	Inglebrook Golden Dandy
			Mywicks Silver Lining

See 'Dazzler lines' in Appendix I, and '(Lord's) Seedley Lassie-family 16' in Appendix II.

1971

Breeder/Owner: Mr & Mrs D G Duncan

K.C.Stud Book No. 115BG

Sable & White Dog

D.O.B. 19 March 1971

Sire: Champion Ramsey of Rokeby

Dam: Champion Brettonpark Vanity Fair

3 CHALLENGE CERTIFICATES

Champion Antoc Midnight Cowboy

Photo courtesy of F Garwood/Dog World/Aileen Speding

Champion Antoc Midnight Cowboy and tricolour sister, Champion Ravensbeck Moonlight of Antoc, were bred by Peggy House of the Ravensbeck Collies. Sired by Antoc Griffin, they were fifth generation home-bred Antocs, being grandchildren of Champion Antoc Vicar of Bray (see page 76).

Besides winning multiple Challenge Certificates Merlin also followed in Vicar's footprints, being particularly successful as a veteran. A finalist in the Pedigree Chum Veteran Stakes, in three successive years, Merlin holds a record which so far remains unbroken.

Merlin sired four Champions in all colours - one blue merle, two sable and one tricolour - appearing to exert a greater influence over bitches. For the home kennel he produced Champion Ravensbeck Sea Jade at Antoc, granddaughter of Antoc the Boyfriend and great granddaughter of Australian Champion Antoc Knight Templar (son of Vicar); and Champion Antoc April Love (ex Antoc High Society), daughter of Champion Antoc Daydream. April Love enjoyed a successful puppy career winning Best of Breed and Reserve in the Working Group at Crufts in 1974, adding third overall in the finals of the 'Pup of the Year' contest. Merlin also sired tricolour Champion Volterra Future Vision (dam of Champion Sonza Star Wars), and Champion Cathanbrae Smokey Joe, out of Champion Cathanbrae Ladypark Lavender Blue[1], one of the last Champions to carry the Ladypark prefix.

Champion Antoc April Love at 10 months old (daughter of Champion Antoc Midnight Cowboy) winning Reserve in the Working Group at Crufts, 1974.
Photo courtesy of Diane Pearce/Aileen Speding

Champion Antoc Midnight Cowboy's blue merle great great granddaughter, Champion Antoc Crystal Rainbow, awarded Working Group 2[2] at the South Wales Kennel Association's Show in 1997, followed this accolade with Best of Breed at Crufts in 1999.

In the Kennel Gazette 1994, Miss D M Young (Ugony) paid tribute to Champion Antoc Midnight Cowboy: *".... A tricolour dog once again; a very sound dog, lovely mover with good front and feet, very balanced. Again, a great showman – and what a laster! Winning the Pedigree Chum Veteran Stakes in '80, '81 and '82 at Richmond, WKC, WELKS, under Joe Cartledge, Harry Jordan, Beefy Sutton.[3] He sired champions in all three colours."*

Breeder: Mrs P House

Owner: Mrs A Speding

K.C.Stud Book No. 683BG

Tricolour Dog

D.O.B. 30 April 1971

Sire: Antoc Griffin

Dam: Ravensbeck Cherry Ripe

8 CHALLENGE CERTIFICATES

PEDIGREE CHUM VETERAN STAKES' FINALIST - 1980, 1981 & 1982.

Sire Antoc Griffin	Rainpark Dandy Lion	Landlubber of Ladypark	Ch Liberty of Ladypark
			Hyacinth of Holmlands
		Rainpark Walnut Whirl	Ch Debs Happy Marquis
			Westcarrs Work of Art
	Antoc Kittiwake	Ch Antoc Vicar of Bray	Ch Larkena Vanara Golden Victor
			Antoc Rose Marie
		Ch Antoc Daydream	Ch Debonair of Glenmist
			Antoc Tawny Lyric
Dam Ravensbeck Cherry Ripe	Ch Antoc Vicar of Bray	Ch Larkena Vanara Golden Victor	Ch Larkena Rabelias
			Ch Starlet of Glenmist
		Antoc Rose Marie	Pattingham Kismet
			Antoc Tawny Lyric
	Ravensbeck Lucy Locket	Duntiblae Dundrum	Ch Pattingham Pacemaker
			Ch Duntiblae Doorknocker
		Ravensbeck Regency Charm	Ch Pattingham Pacemaker
			Dilys of Dunsinane [4]

See 'Examine lines' in Appendix I, and '(Lord's) Seedley Lassie-family 16' in Appendix II.

Footnote:

1. *Champion Cathanbrae Ladypark Lavender Blue, bred by Mr Tams, was litter sister to Champion Asoka Clayswood Blue Venture (by Lacemaker of Ladypark ex Clayswood Blue Slipper).*
2. *On 1 January 1995 the Kennel Club amended the rules governing Best in Show and Group winners. Four dogs are short-listed for each of the Groups, commonly referred to as Group winners 1-4, and two dogs are short-listed for Best in Show, referred to as Best in Show and Reserve Best in Show.*
3. *Group Captain A G Sutton was fondly referred to as 'Beefy'!*
4. *Midnight Cowboy's tail female great great granddam, Dilys of Dunsinane, was full sister, later litter, to Dazzler of Dunsinane.*

Champion & Australian Champion Danvis Ladyvale Blue Mist

Photo courtesy of Diane Pearce/Derek Smith

The joint show record of blue merle litter brothers, Champion & Australian Champion Danvis Ladyvale Blue Mist and Champion & Australian Champion Danvis Ladyvale Blue Macade, make these dogs worthy 'Collies of Distinction'.

Champion and Australian Champion Danvis Ladyvale Blue Mist was the first of the brothers to win high honours. In 1977 he was top Rough Collie gaining his title in three weeks at consecutive shows, starting with Crufts and culminating at the British Collie Club's Show where he went Best in Show. A year later he won his ninth Challenge Certificate at the British Collie Club's show, again with Best in Show. Following his twelfth Challenge Certificate he was exported to Mr Marcovich's Dornbrae Kennels in Australia, where he quickly gained his Australian title.

Although not particularly influential as a sire Blue Mist produced the blue merle dog, Champion Rubec Mist 'n' Blue of Aberhill, and was the maternal grandsire of the blue merle bitch, Champion Lynaire Chiquitita.

In the Kennel Gazette of 1994 Geoff Mildon (Geoffdon) commented: *"Born in 1975, Blue Mist made a sensational impact by winning his first CC at Crufts in 1977 from Miss D M Young, followed by his second and third at consecutive shows; gaining his title and BIS at the British Collie Club and taking home the fabulous Challenge Trophy, a triumph he repeated a year later when winning his ninth CC from Mrs Betty Eglin. With 12CCs to his credit he left these shores to make a name for himself in Australia, but not before making his mark as a sire with Ch Rubec Mist 'n' Blue of Aberhill in the UK, and his grand-daughter Int Ch Grimhaven Blue Opal, the dam of the Italian bred blue Ch Incredibly Blu di Cambiano."*

Champion & Australian Champion Danvis Ladyvale Blue Macade

1975

Photo courtesy of Garwood/Dog World

Champion and Australian Champion Danvis Ladyvale Blue Macade failed to make a similar impact on the breed, but his short show record was nonetheless remarkable. In 1979, not only did he win Best of Breed and his title at Crufts, but annexed Best in Show at the British Collie Club's Show, giving his owner a 'hat trick' of Challenge Trophy wins, and won Reserve Best in Show (all breeds) at Manchester Championship Show. At Crufts the following year, Macade won his ninth Challenge Certificate with Best of Breed, and Reserve in the Working Group. Shortly afterwards Tom Purvis died and Macade was sent to join Blue Mist 'down under' where he emulated his brother by rapidly gaining his Australian title.

Kath Jeffries, of the Jefsfire kennels, judged the Rough Collies at Crufts in 1980 and Blue Macade's critique read as follows: *"Purvis' Ch Danvis Ladyvale Blue Macade, put down to perfection and handled well allowing the dog to give of his best at all times. Good head, well filled muzzle, good underjaw, good ears which he made the most of, level back, lovely arched neck, good body, legs and feet. He presented a lovely profile, his calmness but awareness gave him that extra something that carried him through to BOB and then Reserve in the Group."*

Sire Danvis Jefsfire Johny Walker	Lynway Some Loving	Sandiacre Softly Softly	Dazzler of Dunsinane
			Ch Sandiacre String of Pearls
		Lynway Sugar Sugar	Ch Royal Ace of Rokeby
			Samantha of Sandiacre
	Ch Jefsfire Lucky Lea	Ch Jefsfire Lucky Byname	Ch Mywicks Meadowlancer
			Jefsfire Fashion
		Beaudeer Cherry-Bee	NZ Ch Jefsfire High Return
			Beaudeer Annaback
Dam Sea Dreamer	Clickam Silver Snowstar	Ch Carramar Blue Tweed	Ch Carramar Boy Blue
			Carramar Black Opal
		Clickam Night Flair	Bririch Bedazzle
			Clickam Bririch Night Glamour
	Clickam Night Affection	Ch Carramar Boy Blue	Ch & Int. Ch Rhodelands Boy
			Westcarrs Blue Myrobella
		Clickam Night Attraction	Ch Carramar Blue Tweed
			Clickam Night Flair

See 'Dazzler lines' in Appendix I, and '(Milroy's) Florrie-family 3 in Appendix II.

Breeder: Mr P Davidson

Owner: Mr T Purvis

K.C. Stud Book No. 4567BK

Blue Merle Dog

D.O.B. 26 June 1975

Sire: Danvis Jefsfire Johnny Walker

Dam: Sea Dreamer

12 CHALLENGE CERTIFICATES

WINNER OF THE BRITISH COLLIE CLUB'S CHALLENGE TROPHY - 1977 & 1978

K.C. Stud Book No.1409BM

Blue Merle Dog

9 CHALLENGE CERTIFICATES

WINNER OF THE BRITISH COLLIE CLUB'S CHALLENGE TROPHY - 1979

RESERVE BEST IN SHOW, MANCHESTER 1979

TOP ROUGH COLLIE 1979

RESERVE IN WORKING GROUP, CRUFTS 1980

Champion Everlovin' Emily at Corydon

Photograph taken at the Collie Association's Open Show in 1978, at Weedon, Northamptonshire. Champion Everlovin' Emily at Corydon with her four sons aged ten months. **L to R:** Derek Field with Dameral Aristedes and Emily, Val Plimmer with Emperor Nero at Corydon and Firestone, Darryl Field with Dameral Tawny Tobias and John Blake with Little Caesar at Corydon.
Photo courtesy of John & Barbara Blake

Champion Everlovin' Emily at Corydon was in-bred to Dazzler of Dunsinane and Champion Witchcraft of Rokeby, through siblings Royal Flush of Rokeby, Champions Royal Ace and Romney of Rokeby. Emily's sire and dam were half brother and sister, both out of Regality who was the result of a brother to sister mating. Regality was mated to uncle Royal Flush and produced Emily's sire Corydon King Hector. Emily's dam, Clear Majority of Corydon, was loaned to Mrs Webb on a 'breeding terms' arrangement and Everlovin' Emily was returned to the Corydon Kennel before going to Darryl and Derek Field (Dameral) as a six month old puppy on 'breeding terms'. She was a rather unprepossessing youngster, being slow to mature, but Derek's presentational skills helped to pilot her to five Challenge Certificates. Not just a pretty face, Emily earned the Collie Association's Brood Bitch Trophy on four occasions in addition to being runner-up in five successive years, adding the London & Provincial Collie Club's Brood Bitch Trophy in 1978, and a Best in Show award as a veteran.

Emily excelled as a brood bitch having several litters, and it was the one to Champion Corydon Quinault that confirmed her place as a brood bitch of consequence. This litter contained four very successful dogs, sables Dameral Tawny Tobias and Champion and Australian Champion Little Caesar at Corydon; and tricolours Champion Dameral Aristedes and Emperor Nero at Corydon and Firestone. Aristedes and Little Caesar proved the most successful, both in and out of the show ring, with Aristedes, or 'Smudge' as he was known at home, winning five Challenge Certificates, East Anglian Collie Associations' Collie of the Year for 1978, and top-winning tricolour for five successive years. His most famous offspring were Champion Saheltra Sally Sunshine of Clickam (ex Misty Blue Girl) and Champion Lowerpark Star Spangled (ex Lowerpark Forget-me-Not, a granddaughter of Champion Cathanbrae Polar Moon at Pelido). Sally Sunshine took the ring by storm in 1983, winning five Challenge Certificates from eight shows, plus the Bitch ticket at Crufts in 1984 before being exported to Italy. Star Spangled's grandson, Champion Lowerpark.

Moonlighter at Corydon, was a Junior Warrant winner annexing ten Challenge Certificates, a third place in the Working Group at Paignton and a Group finalist at both Richmond and Bath in 1989. Moonlighter is

1975

Breeder: Mrs E J Webb

Owners: Mr & Mrs D Field

K.C. Stud Book No. 4054BL

Sable & White Bitch

D.O.B. 6 September 1975

Sire: Corydon King Hector

Dam: Clear Majority of Corydon

5 CHALLENGE CERTIFICATES

WINNER OF THE COLLIE ASSOCIATION'S BROOD BITCH TROPHY – 1977 & 1978

LONDON & PROVINCIAL COLLIE CLUB'S BITCH OF THE YEAR – 1978

best remembered as the sire of Champion Corydon Blackcat and great grandsire of the breed's current Challenge Certificate record holder, Champion Phreelancer Phrosty Moon over Corydon (see page 124).

Emily's most notable son was Champion and Australian Champion Little Caesar at Corydon[1]. He gained his British title before being exported to Australia at the age of three and a half and, prior to leaving, sired four Champions – Champion Corydon Handsome Hotspur, Champion and International Champion Chrisarion Capricious, Champion Sindalyn Sherralynda and Champion Jeffield Esquire, as well as Irish Champion Corydon C'est Magnifique. Despite siring in excess of twenty Champions world wide, his most important were British bred Champions Corydon Handsome Hotspur and Jeffield Esquire. Hotspur's greatest sons were Champion Corydon Qui Vive, page 86) and it also extended to the 1997 top winning Rough Collie Champion Ingledene Penny Lover, through her sire Sandiacre Stop 'n' Think, a Hotspur grandson. Champion Jeffield Esquire is behind many of the Pelido, Samhaven and Willowgarth Collies, and the Pelido Kennel has also been strongly influenced by Little Caesar's grandson, Champion Pelido Double Fantasy (see page 110).

After judging Emily at the West of England Ladies' Kennel Society Championship Show in 1978, Alan Jeffries (Jefsfire) wrote the following critique: *"Last time I judged this bitch she was five weeks in whelp and as normal teeming in condition, perhaps a little overweight. She had not quite the coat and looked rather too petite for this competition – beautifully balanced throughout as are her beautiful dog puppies, lovely topline, good head profile, good ears and expression, moved well."*

Sire Corydon King Hector	Royal Flush of Rokeby	Dazzler of Dunsinane	Ch Dorgano Demander of Dunsinane
			Leecroft Leading Lady
		Ch Witchcraft of Rokeby	Prospecthill Rustler of Rokeby
			Retta of Rokeby
	Corydon Regality of Rokeby	Ch Royal Ace of Rokeby	Dazzler of Dunsinane
			Ch Witchcraft of Rokeby
		Ch Romney of Rokeby	Dazzler of Dunsinane
			Ch Witchcraft of Rokeby
Dam Clear Majority of Corydon	Ch Drummajor[2] of Dunsinane	Brettonpark Highlander of Dunsinane	Dazzler of Dunsinane
			Brettonpark Gaiety Girl
		Leecroft Louise	Leecroft Lover Boy of Dunsinane
			Inglebrook Star Lady
	Corydon Regality of Rokeby	Ch Royal Ace of Rokeby	Dazzler of Dunsinane
			Ch Witchcraft of Rokeby
		Ch Romney of Rokeby	Dazzler of Dunsinane
			Ch Witchcraft of Rokeby

See '(Claypole's) Curzon Jess-family 2' in Appendix II, and 'Dazzler lines' in Appendix I.

Footnotes:

1. *Champion Little Caesar at Corydon was exported to Mr & Mrs C West's Westlands Kennels, in Victoria, Australia where he gained his Australian title.*
2. *Audrey Chatfield always refers to Champion Drummajor of Dunsinane as 'Drum Major', whereas the Kennel Club records it as one word - 'Drummajor'. Surprisingly, however, it is recorded as two words on Emily's entry.*

Champion Arranbrook Mr Chips of Aberhill

Photo courtesy of James Keith

Sangreat Sorrocco of Arranbrook, sire of **Champion Arranbrook Mr Chips of Aberhill**, was bred on Meadowlancer lines via Mywicks Solette of Brettonpark, Mywicks Silver Lining and Mywicks Satine of Simbastar (see page 66) and, although only sparingly exhibited, Sorrocco's claim to fame was as a producer siring Champions Arranbrook Sugar 'n' Spice of Rixown, Arranbrook Song of Gold at Brilyn and Sandiacre Silence is Golden. Sorrocco's reputation was secured when he and Brettonpark Burnished Gold of Arranbrook produced that famous litter containing the three Champions, Arranbrook Mr Chips of Aberhill for Shirley Toothill, Arranbrook Summer Wind of Camanna for Anne Hassock, and Arranbrook Polly Peachum for Duna

1976

Sangreat Sorrocco of Arranbrook, sire of Mr Chips
Photo courtesy of James Keith/Lyn Basing

Jones and the Erjons. Although never campaigned to her title Arranbrook Cleopatra of Lynway, born four years later from a repeat mating, earned herself a place in the history books as the dam of Champion Lynway Sandknocker (see page 112). Of this famous litter it was 'Mr Chips' who was to dominate the breed for the next few years, both as a show winner and a major stud force. Winning ten Challenge Certificates, his first one as a puppy, he became possibly the most sought after stud dog siring thirteen champions. Being prepotent he transmitted many dominant qualities to his progeny, especially his classic head properties and good temperament. Champion progeny include Geoffdon Lawmaker, Angelfield Petite Etoile, Jasand Master Ziggy, Pelido Double Fantasy (see page110), Mr Wot of Aberhill and Miss Chips of Aberhill.

Of all his sons Champion Geoffdon Law Maker and Champion Pelido Double Fantasy were destined to provide the greatest influence on present day Rough Collies. The most dominant male line was undoubtedly through Lawmaker and Champion Karava Kornishman (see page) to such distinctive Collies as Champion Ingledene First Love, Champion Jasand Young Winston, Champion Brilyn Rum'n Black, Chrisarion Collier and Champion Phreelancer Phrosty Moon Over Corydon. Apart from the Kornishman influence, Law Maker sired Champion Corydon Gold Star, maternal grandsire of Champion Corydon Gold Spur; and continued to influence many of Ian Brazier's Kybrance Collies and the Geoffdon Collies of Pat and Geoff Mildon, through son and grandson Champion Kybrance Cherokee and Kybrance Cavalier respectively.

In the 'The Judges' Choice', Kennel Gazette 1994, Lisa Burtenshaw (Pelido) wrote *"Ch Arranbrook Mr Chips of Aberhill, a bright golden sable dog born 7 February 1976. His head and expression were the nearest to perfection I have seen; he had the reach of neck, the length in back – all the style and presence one dreams of when showing a Collie. A dog with personality plus,which always catches the eye. The first time I judged at Championship Show level, I gave him his second CC. He went on to win a total of ten CCs, and was the sire of 13 UK Champions and a number of overseas Champions. His type and quality has bred on through his progeny, who in turn have become leading sires in the breed"*.

Sire Sangreat Sorrocco of Arranbrook	Ch Brettonpark Whatzizname	Ch Ramsey of Rokeby	Dazzler of Dunsinane
			Ch Romney of Rokeby
		Ch Brettonpark Vanity Fair	Dazzler of Dunsinane
			Brettonpark Gaiety Girl
	Sangreat Samantha	Sangreat Sasha	Antoc King's Rhapsody
			Supedra Black Orchid
		Ch Burwydne Brendenbury	Burwydne Brave Ruler
			Burwydne Gay Gal
Dam Brettonpark Burnished Gold of Arranbrook	Brettonpark Bobbee Dazzler	Dazzler of Dunsinane	Ch Dorgano Demander of Dunsinane
			Leecroft Leading Lady
		Brettonpark Gaiety Girl	Leecroft Lover Boy of Dunsinane
			Mywicks Solette of Brettonpark
	Brettonpark Joyfulness	Ch Royal Ace of Rokeby	Dazzler of Dunsinane
			Ch Witchcraft of Rokeby
		Ch Brettonpark Vanity Fair	Dazzler of Dunsinane
			Brettonpark Gaiety Girl

See 'Dazzler lines' in Appendix I, and '(Lord's) Seedley Lassie-family 16' in Appendix II.

Footnote:
1. *The Dazzler of Dunsinane Memorial Trophy is run as a competition with progeny earning points at all Yorkshire Collie Club Shows. The trophy is awarded annually to the Top Stud Dog.*

Breeder: Mr & Mrs J Basing

Owner: Mrs S L Toothill

K.C.Stud Book No. 4461BK

Sable & White Dog

D.O.B. 7 February 1976

Sire: Sangreat Sorrocco of Arranbrook

Dam: Brettonpark Burnished Gold of Arranbrook

10 CHALLENGE CERTIFICATES

TOP ROUGH COLLIE STUD DOG – 1980, 1981, 1982 & 1983

WINNER OF THE DAZZLER OF DUNSINANE MEMORIAL TROPHY[1] - 1980

Photo: courtesy of Martin den Otter/Jimmy Tait

Champion Aberthorne Arrester

1976

Breeders/Owners: Mr J Tait & Miss J Skilbeck

K.C.Stud Book No. 368BL

Sable & White Dog

D.O.B. 19 April 1976

Sire: Champion Kidlaine Konrad

Dam: Champion Kreba Contemplation

6 CHALLENGE CERTIFICATES

WINNER OF THE DAZZLER OF DUNSINANE MEMORIAL TROPHY - 1979

Albergo of Aberthorne and his daughter Champion Kreba Contemplation, Arrester's maternal grandsire and dam respectively, were owned by Joyce Skilbeck who in February 1972 became a partner in Jimmy Tait's Aberthorne Kennel. Four years later "Tweedie" was born.

The following extract from Jimmy Tait's article "A Tribute to **Champion Aberthorne Arrester**" (British Collie Handbook 1999) serves as a useful introduction to this Collie of distinction: "*.... The Konrad/Contemplation litter at first looked rather a mixed bag as would be expected with a relative outcross. Though Contemplation was rising five she had a reasonably easy whelping, especially for a first litter but when the puppies were 4 weeks old she contracted Eclampsia which was immediately corrected by the Vet. By now the litter of five dogs and two bitches, a melee of golden and shaded sable and tricolour, had started to sort themselves out and the quality had become apparent. The tricolour bitch, Aphrodisia, became a Champion. Aphrodite, the golden sable bitch, was unbeaten in her classes and exported to France at 16 months - and then, of course, there was Arrester ....*"

Arrester tended to produce sweet expressions, dark eyes and thick coats, features that are still distinctive today. He sired nine British Champions from different bitches, his progeny winning a total of forty-eight Stud Book entry-winning offspring, and amassing a total of forty-six Challenge Certificates. Tweedie's unshown son, Brettonpark Country Tweed, deserves mention here by virtue of the quality of his progeny, especially his daughters. He sired thirty-one Rough Collies gaining Stud Book recognition, including four Champions, and influenced the Mallicot, Pelido, Heysompark, Cramar, Erjon, Angelfield, Westoak, Newloc and Wardette Collies, among others. Champion Aberthorne Arrester's Champion progeny include Myberns Minstrel, Brettonpark Country Fair, Tameila Casey Jones, Dunsinane Detective, Chrisarion Corndolly and Tashadon Tommy Tucker. Arrester established two prepotent branches to the Royal Ace tail male line, through his sable grandsons Champion Myberns Mandane and younger half brother Champion Brilyn Supertramp (both by Champion Myberns Minstrel–see page 102).

In 'The Judges' Choice', Kennel Gazette 1994, Alan Mather (Rubec) commented: *"In my opinion the greatest ever Rough Collie was Ch Aberthorne Arrester. He made a tremendous start to his show career, winning nine classes at a Breed Club Open Show when still a puppy. He developed into an adult who captured the imagination of virtually all who saw him. He quickly gained his title, his virtues being his balanced head pattern and correctly placed eye of the right size which gave that elusive expression we all seek. His ideal conformation and movement, and wealth of coat all came together to make the ideal Collie for a lot of Collie lovers. His greatness was enhanced when he was placed at stud and proved he could pass on his qualities to his children."*

Sire Champion Kidlaine Konrad	Ch Bririch Gold Edition	Ch Royal Ace of Rokeby	Dazzler of Dunsinane
			Ch Witchcraft of Rokeby
		Bririch Golden Belita	Dazzler of Dunsinane
			Bririch Black Andrena
	Kidlaine Kyano	Ch Leverpark Laughan Larilan	Rushmead Dandini of Dunsinane
			Remlaw Royalist of Laughan
		Laund Luciano	Ch Royal Ace of Rokeby
			Ch Laund Livia
Dam Champion Kreba Contemplation	Albergo of Aberthorne	Ch Mywicks Meadowlancer	Mywicks Monitor
			Shoinemaw Sheena
		Display of Dunsinane	Ch Dorgano Demander of Dunsinane
			Ch & Int. Ch Deborah of Dunsinane
	Luna Lace of Ladypark	Ch Royal Ace of Rokeby	Dazzler of Dunsinane
			Ch Witchcraft of Rokeby
		Liza of Grennyne	Clayswood Future Kin
			Deb of Dunsinane

See 'Royal Ace lines' in Appendix I, and '(Salter's) Mountshannon Mona-family 10' in Appendix II.

Champion Myberns Minstrel

Photo courtesy of Ian Entwhistle/Dave Crapper

Mike and Bernice Harris founded their Myberns Kennel on the two bitches Melzar's Moonshadow (Champion Myberns Minstrel's tail female granddam) and Melzar's Miss Wanda (tail female granddam of Minstrel's son Champion Myberns Mandane). Moonshadow's daughter, Myberns Mistibelle, in the first litter registered with the Myberns affix, was the dam of Minstrel. 'Danny', as Minstrel was known at home, was transferred to Dave Crapper's ownership whilst still a puppy. An upstanding, dominant sable dog he matured quickly, gaining his title before the age of fourteen months.

Champion Myberns Minstrel is pictured here at Blackpool in 1978, after winning his first Challenge Certificate from the Puppy Dog class. Judge Albert North wrote in his critique: *"1 and CC. Crapper's Myberns Minstrel. 11 months s/w that commanded attention as he entered the ring, lovely clean head, well balanced, correct stop, good eye placement giving the desired expression, neat ears which today he used to advantage, good conformation, in excellent coat and condition, moved well. I was pleased to give him and his owner their first ticket, congratulations."*

The prepotency of Minstrel's sire, Champion Aberthorne Arrester, was to continue through his two most

1977

Champion Myberns Mandane, son of Minstrel
Photo courtesy of Ian Entwhistle

influential sons Champion Myberns Mandane (ex Myberns Morning Mist) and Champion Brilyn Supertramp (see page 106). Mandane won four Challenge Certificates and in 1985 was awarded the Working Group runner-up to the 'Our Dogs Top Sire' competition, being fourth in all breeds. Mandane produced seven male and four female Champions providing the breed with a more dominant sire line through such Champions as Lynway Sandknocker (see page 112), Lasheen Stolen Property from Jefsfire, and Jankeith Gideon of Myberns. He is also remembered for the union with Abbestone Ruby Red Dress which produced three Champions in Abbestone Ruby Tuesday, Red Adair and Ruby's Love at Myberns. Champion Lasheen Stolen Property from Jefsfire was the maternal grandsire of Champion Jefsfire Francheska, who won her first ticket at Crufts in 1996, under Terry Taylor. Gideon's influence continues through two sons in particular: Pelido Forgotten Dreams, behind the recent Sandiacre Champions, Social Climber and Sacre Bleu; and Champion Myberns Merideon, behind the Jamesfair, Steelhurst, Rhodabern, Troydon and Kourika Collies.

Champion Myberns Minstrel's other important son, Champion Brilyn Supertramp, tended to be more dominant over bitch lines, siring many quality daughters including Champion Ingledene Summer Love.

A double great great grandson of Champion Myberns Minstrel was Champion Percheron Benjamin's Black at Amalie whose influence is felt behind most of Anne Hollywood's recent Amalie Collies such as Blossom's Black at Amalie, Champion Back in Love at Mallicot, Amalie Yorkshire Bitter and Amalie Mild Affair.

In 'The Judges' Choice', Kennel Gazette 1994 Jimmy Tait (Aberthorne) commented: "*....the superb Minstrel must always be a close contender in the list of all time greats, not only for his bloodlines (from which the tail male line consisted of an uninterrupted string of Champions for seven generations) but also for his own breathtaking combination of quality and glamour. He won his first CC at eleven months and was a Champion at 13 months. His most famous sons, Ch Brilyn Supertramp and Ch Myberns Mandane, are at the head of most of the present day kennels and they in turn have done the breed a gigantic service by passing on their many qualities. The Minstrel was a powerful dominant sable dog, but as gentle as a lamb, and was in fact used in schools for many years to illustrate carnivorous dentition.*"

Sire: Champion Aberthorne Arrester	Ch Kidlaine Konrad	Ch Bririch Gold Edition	Ch Royal Ace of Rokeby
			Bririch Golden Belita
		Kidlaine Kyano	Ch Leverpark Laughan Larilan
			Laund Luciano
	Ch Kreba Contemplation	Albergo of Aberthorne	Ch Mywicks Meadowlancer
			Display of Dunsinane
		Luna Lace of Ladypark	Ch Royal Ace of Rokeby
			Liza of Grennyne
Dam: Myberns Mistibelle	Ch Melzar's Marvin of Dunsinane	Ch Drummajor of Dunsinane	Brettonpark Highlander of Dunsinane
			Leecroft Louise
		Cavatina Charm of Melzar	Silstar of Simbastar
			Cavatina Metana of Wittonpark
	Melzar's Moonshadow	Ch Dunsinane Robin Hood of Rokeby	Dazzler of Dunsinane
			Ch Witchcraft of Rokeby
		Rimarlyn's Rhapsody	Ch Leepark Glenbarry
			Salroyd's Sherimar

See 'Royal Ace lines' in Appendix I, and '(Milroy's) Florrie-family 3' in Appendix II.

Breeders: Mr R M & Mrs B Harris

Owner: Mr D B Crapper

K.C.Stud Book No. 2051BM

Sable & White Dog

D.O.B. 23 July 1977

Sire: Champion Aberthorne Arrester

Dam: Myberns Mistibelle

4 CHALLENGE CERTIFICATES

Champion Bhyllsacre Querida Mia

The following testimonials, beginning with Mia's breeder and owner Rene Cozens, suffice to portray this bitch of distinction:

*"**CHAMPION BHYLLSACRE QUERIDA MIA** (1979–1992)*

'Mia' was born on May 1st 1979 whilst a fierce blizzard was raging outside and of course, giving me a hint of the awkwardness which became so much a part of her personality, she arrived right in the middle of the night. It was obvious from the start that she was a pretty puppy, indeed they all were. She was not flashily marked but attractive from all angles. Her name, Querida Mia, came from a song title. People of my generation will surely remember a hit of Dean Martin's entitled '(Day after Day) I'll always love you'. Coming from the Continent the record label had the title in brackets, with the sub-title in its original language of 'Querida Mia'. Years later I remembered this when I was naming my 'Q' litter. Her impressive show career started quietly enough, not gaining a Crufts' qualification until in Junior classes. However, because of maternal duties, she could not attend the great show the following year. After recovering from the litter she returned to the ring in 1981 to win her first CC under judge Lisa Burtenshaw at Paignton, and Reserve in the Working Group. Before the end of that year she had gained her title. Her next show was Crufts in 1982 and here she won the coveted 'Lassie' Trophy for Best of Breed. A few more outings brought two

more CCs, then semi-retirement for further maternal duties. It was in 1987, when 'Mia' was eight years old, that I decided to compete in the Veteran classes. She won CCs from the Veteran class, followed by Best in Show, both at the Midland Collie Club and West of England Collie Society's Championship Shows. In between she attended the West of England Collie Society's Open Show and gained yet another Best in Show from the veteran class – a truly remarkable feat. Three Best in Show wins at the West of England Collie Society Shows is surely a record and, interestingly, she was never beaten by a male as all her CC wins were followed by Best of Breed. Her attempts at motherhood were few and far between, being glamorous was obviously her main priority! Her second litter, to Bhyllsacre All in Gold, was her most successful containing the two Champion daughters, Bhyllsacre Mia'ly Golden and Bhyllsacre Mia'ly a Dream. She never managed to produce a good enough male, but her daughters eclipsed her in that department with Bhyllsacre Make Mine Macho and Bhyllsacre Shades of Gold respectively. 'Mia' was a good, contented Mum but, as soon as weaning time came around, she would 'wash her paws' of the 'motherhood thing' and more or less tell me to 'get on with it'. After suffering a mild stroke at twelve years of age she deteriorated quite noticeably and, eventually, her kidneys gave out. She now lies peacefully under some rose bushes that I planted as a celebration of her glorious life. There will never be another 'Mia'."

In 'The Judges' Choice', Kennel Gazette 1994 Lyn Westby (Lowerpark) made the following comments on Mia: *"She had the correct overall shape, with the right length of body, height, arch of neck, slope to quarters, and bend of stifle required of a working breed – coupled with that balanced, clean head we used to see, and melting expression so difficult to explain, yet always remembered once seen. She was so truly feminine and sound."*

In the same article Ken Bullock (Konelga) wrote:*"........I was delighted to award her second CC at Richmond 1981 and see her progress so well. Her final tally was eight CCs including BOB Crufts 1982 and the last two CCs from Veteran. It is interesting to note that she was never beaten by the Dog CC winner; all her wins culminated in BOB. My critique at that time reads 'I really fell for this delightful bitch. She has a beautiful head, perfectly proportioned, soft expression, from front to rear handled well, moved with drive and purpose, a dense well-textured sable and white coat.' The impression she made on me then has been a lasting one."*

Sire Champion Rokeby the Radical	Rokeby the Renegade	Knight Porter of Rokeby	Ch Royal Ace of Rokeby
			Rokeby Lady Rhonda of Scotforth
		Regalia of Rokeby	Ch Royal Ace of Rokeby
			Romarin of Rokeby
	Pattingham Passing Breeze	Ch Pattingham Prosper	Ch Geoffdon Westlynn's Wayside Boy
			Pattingham Petal
		Pattingham Westlynns Wishful	Ch Ramsey of Rokeby
			Ch Westlynns Witchcraft
Dam Bhyllsacre Limelight	Ch Romadale Rothschild	Sandiacre Softly Softly	Dazzler of Dunsinane
			Ch Sandiacre String of Pearls
		Sandiacre Strawberry Rose of Romadale	Ch Ramsey of Rokeby
			Ch Sandiacre Secondhand Rose
	Jayhaven Morning Star of Bhyllsacre	Bracken of Bhyllsacre	Antoc Griffin
			Manorfields Dream Willow
		Pattingham Paisley	Lynway Some Loving
			Pattingham Sandiacre Sincerity

See '(Lucas') Miss Perfection-family 6' in Appendix II, and 'Royal Ace lines' in Appendix I.

1979

Breeder/Owner: Mrs I Cozens

K.C.Stud Book No. 1149BP

Sable & White bitch

D.O.B. 1 May 1979

Sire: Champion Rokeby the Radical

Dam: Bhyllsacre Limelight

8 CHALLENGE CERTIFICATES

RESERVE IN THE WORKING GROUP AT PAIGNTON - 1981

Champion Brilyn Supertramp

Photo by courtesy of Lene Halvorsen/Brian Hawkins

Champion Brilyn Supertramp was an impressive golden sable dog who enjoyed a most successful show career winning his Junior Warrant, four Challenge Certificates and three Reserve Challenge Certificates in addition to gaining the Top Stud Dog accolade in two successive years.

Champion Brilyn Supertramp and Champion Myberns Mandane were Champion Myberns Minstrel's most influential sons, with Supertramp's Stud Book progeny coming very close to equalling those sired by Champion and Irish Champion Lochinvar of Ladypark. It is also interesting to note that whilst 'Trampus' predominantly influenced the distaff or female side, Mandane tended to exert greater influence on male lines.

Among Supertramp's many Champion sons were Jayverly Super Ted, Rifflesea Romantasy and Tiganlea Touche, but it was the untitled Lanteague Golden Harvest and Bhyllsacre All in Gold who were mostly responsible for the continuation of Supertramp's lines to the present day. Trampus was the paternal grandsire of Champion sisters Bhyllsacre Mia'ly Golden and Mia'ly a Dream (by Bhyllsacre All in Gold ex Champion Bhyllsacre Querida Mia), and greatgrandsire of siblings Champion and International Champion Ingledene Power of Love and Ingledene Ria'ly a Love, dam of Champion Ria'ly Famous at Bhyllsacre.

1979

Supertramp's influence on male lines has also been strongly felt through yet another grandson, Champion Lanteague Harvest Moon of Silvermoor (by Lanteague Golden Harvest), who sired Champion Lanteague Black Magic at Brilyn, dam of Champion Brilyn Rum'n Black (see page 120).

Champion Brilyn Supertramp stamped his quality on bitch lines siring numerous beautiful and useful bitches including Champion Ingledene Summer Love (the first of four generations of Ingledene bitch Champions), Lanteague Heart of Gold at Pelido, Champion Brilyn Dawn Delight and Champion Kaywell Babooshka at Geoffdon. The combination of Supertramp and Double Fantasy lines proved most successful for Brian and Sue Hawkins, producing a very strong line of Brilyn bitches such as Champions Brilyn Satin Dream and Brilyn Satin'n Silk of Carostar. These Supertramp/Double Fantasy lines were also combined to produce Champion Silvermoor's Hollyberry at Amalie (by Supertramp's grandson Champion Lanteague Harvest Moon at Silvermoor), winner of ten Challenge Certificates, the eight gained in 1991 being sufficient to make her the UK's top winning Rough Collie that year.

At Leeds Championship Show in 1980, judge Norma Lister (Abbestone) placed Trampus first in a Puppy Dog class of twenty-two and her critique read as follows: *"Super young dog of obvious quality presented to the minute in full bloom, well balanced head on a good neck, good body shape and level topline which he kept on the move. Moved soundly on good legs and feet. In a line-up of lovely dogs I was pleased to award him the Res CC which he well deserved, a future champion without doubt."*

The following year Jean Lawson judged at Southern Counties and commented: *"Hawkins' Brilyn Supertramp, most glamorous golden sable, has the most lovely expression combined with a good masculine head, elegant neck, good spring and depth of rib, well let down hocks, coarse stand away coat to finish the picture. Standing he looks like a Collie should, a dog of beauty. Moved well when he wanted to. CC and BOB, and was pleased to see him finish in the last four of the group."*

Sire Champion Myberns Minstrel	Ch Aberthorne Arrester	Ch Kidlaine Konrad	Ch Bririch Gold Edition
			Kidlaine Kyano
		Ch Kreba Contemplation	Albergo of Aberthorne
			Luna Lace of Ladypark
	Myberns Mistibelle	Ch Melzar's Marvin of Dunsinane	Ch Drummajor of Dunsinane
			Cavatina Charm of Melzar
		Melzar's Moonshadow	Ch Dunsinane Robin Hood of Rokeby
			Rimarlyn's Rhapsody
Dam Brilyn Duchesse Lace	Sangreat Sorrocco of Arranbrook	Ch Brettonpark Whatzizname	Ch Ramsey of Rokeby
			Ch Brettonpark Vanity Fair
		Sangreat Samantha	Sangreat Sasha
			Ch Burwydne Brendenbury
	Brilyn Golden Girl	Ch Brettonpark Whatzizname	Ch Ramsey of Rokeby
			Ch Brettonpark Vanity Fair
		Beechmere Cream Cracker	Sandiacre Softly Softly
			Beechmere Super Sue[2]

See 'Royal Ace lines' in Appendix I, and '(Rae's) Yellow Primrose-family 15' in Appendix II.

Breeder/Owner: Mr B Hawkins

K.C.Stud Book No. 911BP

Sable & White Dog

D.O.B. 2 July 1979

Sire: Champion Myberns Minstrel

Dam: Brilyn Duchesse Lace

4 CHALLENGE CERTIFICATES

TOP STUD DOG[1] 1987 & 1988

Ch Brilyn Supertramp's tail female extension into family 15

Beechmere Super Sue
1973
|
Chateauroux Sunbeam
1968
|
Moneystone Lassie
1965
|
Sable Thunder Flash
1963
|
Cilla's Lady
1960
|
Lillian's Lady
1956
|
Royden Thunderflash
1952
|
Bakewell Belle
1948
|
Bakewell Ideal
1947
|
Dawn of Harcongyll
1944

continued on (Rae's) Yellow Primrose-family 15

Footnote:

1. *'Dog World's' top stud dog competition is run on a points system. When a collie gains a first challenge certificate its sire is awarded 5 points. An additional point is awarded for each subsequent challenge certificate won by that dog during the same year.*
2. *Supertramp's tail female family extends through twelve generations before a significant bitch appears. See extension in the right hand panel and '(Rae's) Yellow Primrose-family 15.*

Photo courtesy of McFarlane/R Anderton

Champion Karava Kornishman

1980

In the 1994 Kennel Gazette article, 'The Judges' Choice', Geoff Mildon (Geoffdon) commented on Karava Kornishman as follows: *"Born in September 1980, he won his first CC from Mrs Ada Bishop (Laund) at the tender age of eleven months and gained his title at two years old. Perhaps a little on the small size for some judges, he is nevertheless a beautifully balanced, soundly constructed Collie, with good neck and shoulders, excellent legs and feet, and a clean refined head, and he had a lovely expression. His re-appearance in the ring, in Veteran classes, has shown that all these qualities had been retained and he had a dignified yet friendly temperament. At stud he has proved to be one of our 'greats'."*

Champion Karava Kornishman, or 'Ross' as he was affectionately known, won his first Challenge Certificate, whilst still a puppy, at Leicester Championship Show. The highlight of his career came just after his second birthday when, at Lancashire and Cheshire Collie Club's Championship Show under Margaret Franklin, he gained the Open Dog class, the Challenge Certificate, Best of Breed and Best in Show to give the Karava Kennel its first Champion.

Kornishman rapidly established himself as a stud force becoming the UK's top producing tricolour in the half century since the last war. He sired thirty-four Rough Collies who gained entry to the Kennel Club Stud Books, including nine Champions in all three colours. His male Champion progeny included Penpriory Playboy of Karava; Jasand Young Winston; Keegan of Karava, Wardette Duncan Disorderly and Black Phantom of Beechwyre, each with four Challenge Certificates; and Sunnhyhurst Siegfried of Karava with five Challenge Certificates. Amongst 'Ross' Champion daughters were Karava Blue Kreation; Kidlaine Kwaeda of Karava with four Challenge Certificates; and Ingledene First Love with six Challenge Certificates (see page 118). Kornishman's qualities were inherited by two of First Love's influential offspring, Ingledene Love is the Drug and Ingledene Ria'ly a Love, dam of Champion Ria'ly Famous at Bhyllsacre. The Lynaire Kennel was influenced through Kornishman son Lynaire Man in Black, grandsire of Champion Midnight Flyer of Lynaire at Aberhill, and Man in Black's younger brother Lynaire Midnight Blue (ex Champion Lynaire Chiquitita), sire of Champions Aberhill Bluwatch and Rothpen Silver Orchid.

Champion Karava Kornishman's dominance over the sire lines has been consolidated by two of his grandsons, Champion Brilyn Rum'n Black (see page 120) and Chrisarion Collier (see page 122), both sired by Champion Jasand Young Winston but out of different bitches.

Sire Champion Geoffdon Law Maker	Ch Arranbrook Mr Chips of Aberhill	Sangreat Sorrocco of Arranbrook	Ch Brettonpark Whatzizname
			Sangreat Samantha
		Brettonpark Burnished Gold of Arranbrook	Brettonpark Bobbee Dazzler
			Brettonpark Joyfulness
	Geoffdon Isabella	Ch Duntiblae Dodgem of Geoffdon	Ch Geoffdon Westlynns Wayside Boy
			Duntiblae Geoffdon Vanity Fair
		Franwyns Fascination of Geoffdon	Pattingham Portrayal
			Foxearth Flame of Franwyns
Dam Karava Kastille	Laughan Larinka	Leecroft Lover Boy of Dunsinane	Ch Dorgano Demander of Dunsinane
			Leecroft Loobi-Loo
		Remlaw Royalist of Laughan	Ch Royal Ace of Rokeby
			Remlaw Pat's Choice
	Kidlaine Kamille	Ch Aberthorne Arrester	Ch Kidlaine Konrad
			Ch Kreba Contemplation
		Anlyn Alicia	Ch Kidlaine Konrad
			Tiree Lass[1]

See 'Dazzler lines' in Appendix I, and 'Lima-family 1' in Appendix II.

Footnote:

1. *Kornishman's tail female family extends through eleven generations before any significant bitch appears. See extension in the right hand panel and Lima-family 1 (extension to '(Roberts') Old Lassie').*

Breeder/Owner: Mr & Mrs R Anderton

K.C. Stud Book No. 3122BQ

Tricolour Dog

D.O.B. 17 September 1980

Sire: Champion Geoffdon Law Maker

Dam: Karava Kastille

3 CHALLENGE CERTIFICATES

Ch Karava Kornishman's tail female extension into family 1

Tiree Lass
1972
|
Miss Moodies
1970
|
Sharons Fair Lady
1965
|
Shona of Landover
1959
|
Lovely Romance of Landover
1958
|
Jocelyn Cherry
1956
|
Spring Morn from Shiel
S & W-1953
|
Shiel's Beulah's Night Flower
Tri-1945
|
Beulah's Golden Kiska
S & W-1943

continued on Lima-family 1

Champion Pelido Double Fantasy

The following quotation, taken from 'The Story of **Champion Pelido Double Fantasy**', written by Lisa Burtenshaw for the Autumn 2000 edition of 'Collie Seasons', serves to introduce 'Champion Mummy's Pet':

" Fantasy's grandmother, the sable Brettonpark Golden Dream (later: at Pelido) was purchased from Mr & Mrs Duncan, as a puppy, by Mr & Mrs A J Green, and from there she went to Mr & Mrs Warner (Silvermear). Golden Dream came to us en route to a pet home. On her arrival she was just off a litter with her previous owner. I felt I should get her into better condition before she went to her new home. Because of this the would-be new owners changed their minds. Golden Dream was a feminine bitch, not big, very well made, lovely neck, clean head and super eye and expression. She was by Ch Brettonpark Whatzizname ex Brettonpark Fan Fair, a sister of Ch Brettonpark Vanity Fair (Whatzizname's mother). Golden Dream was mated to the sable Ch Little Caesar at Corydon to produce the sable lady Pelido French Knickers……For her first litter Knickers was mated to Ch Arranbrook Mr Chips of Aberhill because I thought he was a wonderful specimen of the breed. On 14 March 1981 she gave birth to four bitches and one dog."

1981

Breeder/Owner: Mr & Mrs P W Burtenshaw

K.C.Stud Book No. 1957BS

Sable & White Dog

D.O.B. 14 March 1981

Sire: Champion Arranbrook Mr Chips of Aberhill

Dam: Pelido French Knickers

3 CHALLENGE CERTIFICATES

Pelido Double Fantasy was the only dog in this litter, and he was named after a John Lennon/Yoko Ono album of the same name. Double Fantasy, a dominant sable excelling in head and expression, was a precocious youngster enjoying a successful show career. He gained his Junior Warrant by the age of ten months, followed by the three Challenge Certificates required for his title in 1984. His first ticket came at the Midland Collie Club under Ray Mitchell (Damirayan); his second at the Scottish Kennel Club's Show under Anne Hassock (Camanna); and at the London Collie Club's Show he won his crown with Best in Show, under judge Anne Lister (Abbestone). Her critique of Fantasy read: *"What a dog, sheer class, have always admired him and, after going over him, everything I thought was confirmed; lovely rib cage and bodyshape, most lovely rich colour which was presented first class, moved as if he owned the ring, so sound. But his head, which I just couldn't get past, is absolutely right, flat skull so clean, beautiful well placed stop and rounded muzzle, and to make my day complete his eyes are just heart stopping, almond shaped, dark and set just right. This sort of eye and expression is our beautiful breed, they describe it in one fell swoop-the nature and heart of gold that is our beautiful Collie. CC, his third, so richly deserved. One of his daughters won minor puppy bitch, obviously he is passing on his good looks. He will be a great asset to the breed, BIS unanimously."*

Despite being one of Mr Chips' most prolific offspring, Double Fantasy did not produce as dominant a sire line as that of Champions Geoffdon Law Maker and Karava Kornishman. He did, however, sire thirty seven Rough Collies gaining Stud Book entry including the seven Champions, Lanteague Heart of Gold at Pelido, Pelido Precocious at Angelfield, Pelido Delta Dawn of Daviston, Pelido French Maid, Pelido Careless Love, Lynaire Honeychile and Starbrook Touch of Gold at Lynaire. The last of these dogs was his most successful son winning ten Challenge Certificates, eight Reserve Challenge Certificates and a Group 3 placing at Border Union in 1995. Double Fantasy's influence was also felt in numerous other kennels including the Amalie, Aspera, Samhaven, Gerian, Trenley, Deanjan, Lyswood and Shasam Collies, although his greatest impact has been on the home kennel.

Of Fantasy's offspring, Lisa comments: *"If you ask me who I consider to be Fantasy's most influential (grand)son/(grand)daughter, I would probably say Ch Pelido Careless Love. He is the sire of three Champions, including Int. It. Lux. UK. Ch Sogno del Narciso with Pelido, who himself is the sire of three UK Champions, namely Ch Pelido Italian Affair, Ch Markenfield Asti Spumante, and Ch Corydon Il Supremo, who in turn is the sire of Ch Brooklynson Golden Fashion. This lady was BIS at the BCC Show and took the bitch CC at Crufts, at the tender age of ten months!"*

Sire Champion Arranbrook Mr Chips of Aberhill	Sangreat Sorrocco of Arranbrook	Ch Brettonpark Whatzizname	Ch Ramsey of Rokeby
			Ch Brettonpark Vanity Fair
		Sangreat Samantha	Sangreat Sasha
			Ch Burwydne Brendenbury
	Brettonpark Burnished Gold of Arranbrook	Brettonpark Bobbee Dazzler	Dazzler of Dunsinane
			Brettonpark Gaiety Girl
		Brettonpark Joyfulness	Ch Royal Ace of Rokeby
			Ch Brettonpark Vanity Fair
Dam Pelido French Knickers	Ch & Aus. Ch Little Caesar at Corydon	Ch Corydon Quinault	Ch Ramsey of Rokeby
			Ch Corydon Qui Vive
		Ch Everlovin' Emily at Corydon	Corydon King Hector
			Clear Majority at Corydon
	Brettonpark Golden Dream at Pelido	Ch Brettonpark Whatzizname	Ch Ramsey of Rokeby
			Ch Brettonpark Vanity Fair
		Brettonpark Fan Fair	Dazzler of Dunsinane
			Brettonpark Gaiety Girl

See 'Dazzler lines' in Appendix I, and '(Lord's) Seedley Lassie-family 16' in Appendix II.

Photo courtesy of Fr Nicaise/Alan Clarke

Champion Lynway Sandknocker

1982

Breeders/Owners: Mesdames A M & D L Clarke

K.C.Stud Book No. 1175BT

Sable & White Dog

D.O.B. 30 November 1982

Sire: Champion Myberns Mandane

Dam: Arranbrook Cleopatra of Lynway

3 CHALLENGE CERTIFICATES

Champion Lynway Sandknocker's dam, Arranbrook Cleopatra at Lynway, was from a repeat mating, four years on, of the now famous litter comprising Champions Arranbrook Mr Chips of Aberhill, Arranbrook Polly Peachum and Arranbrook Summerwind of Camanna.

Sandknocker, or 'Ted' as he was known to his friends, was a precocious youngster who gained his Junior Warrant in style, adding three Challenge Certificates before retirement to the life of a stud dog where he earned his place in Collie history. Ted influenced many kennels, siring twenty-eight Rough Collies gaining Stud Book entry. Of these, four gained their titles, the sibling Champions Emryks 'Owd Peculiar and Emryks April Affair at Lynway, Champion Matai Don Quixote, and Champion Lasheen Simply Red at Lynway, the last three each gaining five Challenge certificates. Champion Emrks 'Owd Peculiar heads the principal sire line through son Champion Emryks Runnaway, winner of seven Challenge Certificates and top male Rough Collie in 1991, the Challenge Certificate with Best of Breed at Crufts in 1992 and the Reserve Challenge Certificate the following year. Runnaway was also a successful sire producing three Champions, Emryks Running Bear at Brilyn, Brilyn Satin Symphony, and Hillandale Miss Elation at Peptide. Champion Matai Don Quixote heads Sandknocker's second sire line, which extends through Champions Abbeywater Faberge at Evad and Elsamos Starmaker at Mallicot. Faberge has sired thirteen Rough Collies with Stud Book entries, including the two Champions, Elsamos Starmaker at Mallicot and the bitch Trenley Teasle with four Challenge Certificates. He is also currently influencing the Geosan, Robroz, Deanjan, and Rickwood Collies.

Two other sons, Erjon Eyecatcher and home-bred International Champion Lynway Seldom Sober[1], were to perpetuate Sandknocker's influence, with the tricolour Eyecatcher exerting the greatest influence by producing winners in all three colours. He sired eleven Rough Collies gaining Stud Book recognition, including the two Champions, Camanna Chicken George and Pelido Estee Lauder and, having incorporated both Eyecatcher and Seldom Sober's influence into her present Show Collies, Anne Hollywood's Amalie Kennel produced Amalie Mild Affair, currently on two Challenge Certificates. Finally, Champion Lynway Sandknocker influenced the breed in Ireland through son and grandson Champion and Irish Champion Lasheen Simply Red at Lynway and Irish Champion Lowerpark Limited Edition respectively.

At Bath in 1985, judge Vic Salt (Woodlyn) commented: *"My dog CC and BOB was Clarke's Lynway Sandknocker. It was the first time I had seen this dog, his head handles well, good mould of foreface, flat skull, neat pair of ears, good eye and expression. His reach of neck and body shape, together with his rich colour, made the overall picture complete; should not be long before he gets his title."*

Sire Champion Myberns Mandane	Ch Myberns Minstrel	Ch Aberthorne Arrester	Ch Kidlaine Konrad
			Ch Kreba Contemplation
		Myberns Mistibelle	Ch Melzar's Marvin of Dunsinane
			Melzar's Moonshadow
	Myberns Morning Mist	Ch Drummajor of Dunsinane	Brettonpark Highlander of Dunsinane
			Leecroft Louise
		Melzar's Miss Wanda	Ch Brettonpark Whatzizname
			Melzar's Marchioness
Dam Arranbrook Cleopatra at Lynway	Sangreat Sorrocco of Arranbrook	Ch Brettonpark Whatzizname	Ch Ramsey of Rokeby
			Ch Brettonpark Vanity Fair
		Sangreat Samantha	Sangreat Sasha
			Ch Burwydne Brendenbury
	Brettonpark Burnished Gold of Arranbrook	Brettonpark Bobbee Dazzler	Dazzler of Dunsinane
			Brettonpark Gaiety Girl
		Brettonpark Joyfulness	Ch Royal Ace of Rokeby
			Ch Brettonpark Vanity Fair

See 'Royal Ace lines' in Appendix I, and '(Lord's) Seedley Lassie-family 16' in Appendix II.

Footnote:

1. Seldom Sober gained a single Challenge Certificate in 1989, prior to leaving Britain for the Rosegarden Kennels of Birgit and Claus-Peter Fricke in Germany.

Champion Jasand Young Winston

1983

Breeder/Owner: Mrs J Round

K.C.Stud Book No. 2986BU

Sable & White Dog

D.O.B. 12 March 1983

Sire: Champion Karava Kornishman

Dam: Jasand Tuppence Coloured

3 CHALLENGE CERTIFICATES

DOG WORLD'S TOP STUD DOG IN 1992 & 1995

Although **Champion Jasand Young Winston** was lightly used at stud he sired several top quality Collies including Champion Jasand Jack Daniels for the home kennel, winner of eight Challenge Certificates and Reserve in the Working Group at the West of England Ladies' Kennel Society Championship Show; litter brothers Chrisarion Collier (see page 122) and Champion Chrisarion Carbon Copy for Jasand; Champion Myskveil Made to Measure for Seriema with four Challenge Certificates; and siblings Champion Brilyn Rum'n Black, Champion Brilyn Painted Lady and International Champion Brilyn Dark Delight (ex Champion Lanteague Black Magic at Brilyn). Winston has also sired a number of dual and single Challenge Certificate-winning offspring to his credit, one of these being daughter Strolester Mis'Understood at Jasand. When mated to Champion Jasand Master Ziggy she whelped Champion Jasand Gigolo, winner of three Challenge Certificates, two with Best in Show the British Collie Club's Championship Show in 1990.

Champion Jasand Young Winston is currently influencing the breed, primarily through two tricolour sons Champion Brilyn Rum'n Black (see page 120) and Chrisarion Collier, with the blending of these bloodlines being especially successful in the home kennel, producing Winston's granddaughter Champion Jasand True Blue (by Champion Brilyn Rum'n Black) and great grandson Champion Jasand Going Places (by Chrisarion Collier). A Young Winston grandson, Champion Phreelancer Phrosty Moon Over Corydon (by Rum'n Black), is the current Challenge Certificate record holder (see page 124).

Winston's granddaughter, Champion Jasand True Blue (Truly), won her first Reserve Challenge Certificate and Reserve Best Puppy in Show at the National Working Breeds Show at seven and a half months of age. At Bournemouth, one month later, Truly annexed Best Puppy in the Working Group, repeating this success at the Darlington Championship Show before going on to win Best Puppy in Show. She won the Ladypark Trophy with an outstanding one hundred and forty points (the runner-up had just forty-six points) and gained her title at the age of fifteen months. Her final tally was five Challenge Certificates, three with best of Breed, adding Best in Show on two occasions, and five Reserve Challenge Certificates including Crufts in 1998. Unfortunately Truly died tragically one month after her fourth birthday, but had previously whelped a most successful litter, sired by Winston's son Chrisarion Collier. Winston featured very heavily in the pedigree being grandsire, great grandsire and double great great grandsire of the puppies. From this litter the tricolour bitch, Jasand Panama Hatty, and blue merle dog, Champion Jasand Going Places, winner of a Junior Warrant[1] and eleven Challenge Certificates, were retained for the home kennel.

Sire Champion Karava Kornishman	Ch Geoffdon Law Maker	Ch Arranbrook Mr Chips of Aberhill	Sangreat Sorrocco of Arranbrook
			Brettonpark Burnished Gold of Arranbrook
		Geoffdon Isabella	Ch Duntiblae Dodgem of Geoffdon
			Franwyns Fascination of Geoffdon
	Karava Kastille	Laughan Larinka	Leecroft Lover Boy of Dunsinane
			Remlaw Royalist of Laughan
		Kidlaine Kamille	Ch Aberthorne Arrester
			Anlyn Alicia
Dam Jasand Tuppence Coloured	Ch Arranbrook Mr Chips of Aberhill	Sangreat Sorrocco of Arranbrook	Ch Brettonpark Whatzizname
			Sangreat Samantha
		Brettonpark Burnished Gold of Arranbrook	Brettonpark Bobbee Dazzler
			Brettonpark Joyfulness
	Aberhill Prima Donna of Jasand	Ch Pied Piper of Aberhill at Rixown	Ch Brettonpark Whatzizname
			Friendly Lass of Lingwell
		Aberhill Carousel	Seafire Sentinel
			Winrix Sweet Serenade

See 'Dazzler lines' in Appendix I, and 'Jeannie/ (Bell's) Stanhope Village Belle-family 13' in Appendix II.

Footnote:

1. For additional information on the Junior Warrant (JW) see Appendix IV.

Champion Tameila Gordon Bennet

Photo by Paul Hodgson

Champion Tameila Gordon Bennet's reputation is due to his marvellous show record, rather than as a producer of note, being distinctive as the holder of the breed's post-war record with sixteen Challenge Certificates, eleven with Best of Breed awarded by fifteen judges, plus thirteen Reserve Challenge Certificates from twelve judges. He held this position until superseded by Champion Phreelancer Phrosty Moon Over Corydon in the final year of the twentieth century (see page 124).

Gordon Bennet, or Tramp as he was better known, had a phenomenal start to his show career. Campaigned from the age of eleven months he won all his classes at his first three shows, gaining his Junior Warrant with ease, and adding a Reserve Challenge Certificate[1] at his first Championship Show under judge Aileen Speding[1] at the Midland Collie Club's Show in 1987. His inaugural Challenge Certificate was awarded at Crufts, and by the time he was two years old he had annexed seven Challenge Certificates, six Reserve Challenge Certificates and 'Dog World's' Top Dog of the Year.

Despite blue merles having limited opportunities for the continuation of blood-lines Gordon Bennet sired six Rough Collies gaining Stud Book recognition. These included daughters Seriema Matchmaker; Gemastra Snowdrop; Tameila Dark Gem, winner of a Junior Warrant and a Reserve Challenge Certificate; and blue

1986

Breeder/Owner: Mrs A Hodgson

K.C. Stud Book No. 116BW

Blue Merle Dog

D.O.B. 18 January 1986

Sire: Champion Upperton Blue Brand

Dam: Tameila Blue Charm

16 CHALLENGE CERTIFICATES

DOG WORLD'S TOP ROUGH [2] COLLIE IN 1988 & 1993

merle Lassina Let it be Love, Challenge Certificate and Best of Breed winner at the Crufts Centenary Show in 1990, under Iris Combe. Let it be Love's tricolour sister, Lassina Love in the Night of Ladyfayre, was the dam of Champion Ladyfayre Blue Lagoon of Karava, the great grandsire of Champion Jasand Going Places. Tramp's sons included Lassina Lovely Boy Blue, sire of Lynmead Magic Moondrops and Newarp Winter Mischief; and Wendardebs Bloo Wizard, sire of Champion Wendardebs Bloo Swiz of Abbestone.

Following her judging appointment at the 1988 Crufts Show, Sandra Wigglesworth (Sandiacre) had this to say about Tramp: *"When I first saw this beautiful merle in the ring I had a penchant towards him, as he is completely balanced throughout. Standing he presents a superb profile, lovely neck let into correct shoulders and perfect topline; excellent hindquarters which, together with his ebullient temperament, moved confidently and freely round the ring. I found his head clean with the correct parallel planes, good foreface, correct stop and all this, together with his most gorgeous eye and expression and well placed ears, presented a Collie which befits the Standard in nearly all aspects. His coat was at its best which was perfectly groomed and of the most glorious colour and, to my mind, perfect merling – the very quintessence of the blue merle. At 2 years old I feel his best days are still to come as he could be a fraction bigger. Despite this I could honestly say I found him to be the dog which typified outstanding merit and quality. It gave me great pleasure to award him his first CC."*

Champion Tameila Gordon Bennet, one of a minority of consistent show-winning dogs to continue his successes into old age, was awarded his final Challenge Certificate by Brian House (Lassina) following his Veteran class win at the London and Provincial Collie Club's Championship Show in 1994. Brian's critique read: *"Hodgson's Ch Tameila Gordon Bennet, b/m and needs no introduction. In my mind certainly one of the best heads and expressions on a b/m, beautiful eye and good body shape, in terrific condition, moved well. CC, his sixteenth and still more to come on this form. Wish he was mine."*

Sire Champion Upperton Blue Brand	Ch Cathanbrae Polar Moon at Pelido	Pelido Black Prince	Brettonpark Highlander of Dunsinane
			Pelido Doretta of Dunsinane
		Cathanbrae Southern Belle	Ch Cathanbrae Willow Pattern
			Cotsbelle Heavenly Blue from Cathanbrae
	Upperton My Blue Heaven	Upperton Chief Scout	Upperton Cherokee Chief
			Upperton Jewel Song
		Upperton Lavender Princess	Ch Cathanbrae Willow Pattern
			Upperton La Belle Helene
Dam Tameila Blue Charm	Int. Ch Incredibly Blu di Cambiano	Int. Ch Lupupick Blu di Cambiano	Silver Dag vom Holderfeld
			New Moon Nera di Cambiano
		Int. Ch Grimhaven Blue Opal	Glenalan's Night Fury of Clickam
			Grimhaven Grey Mist
	Tameila Tar Baby	Ch Tameila Casey Jones	Ch Aberthorne Arrester
			Ch Dark Delight of Tameila
		Cinlock's Tavena's Spanish Lace	Cinlock's Candyman
			Sandiacre Spanish Eyes

See 'Dazzler lines' in Appendix I, and '(Lucas') Miss Perfection-family 6' in Appendix II.

Footnotes:

1. *In the nine years between Gordon Bennet earning his Stud Book number with the Reserve Challenge Certificate from Aileen Speding in 1987, and his last appearance when he collected 3rd in the Open Dog class from Arthur Lumb at Leeds in 1986, he earned a place in every Stud Book except Volume 123 which covered 1995.*
2. *Dog World's Top Dog competition is sponsored by Pedigree Petfoods and Championship Show Winners are allotted points for Challenge Certificate wins, additional points being given for best of breed, group wins and best in show or reserve best in show awards.*

Champion Ingledene First Love

The Ingledene kennel of Val and John Geddes was established in the 1970's with foundation bitch Leawyn Annabelle (by Bririch Black Cavalier), a granddaughter of Shearcliffe Blue Star (ex Bririch Silver Lace, sister to Champion Bririch Silver Dream). It was not until the late 1980's, however, that John and Val Geddes' first bitch of significance, the multi-Challenge Certificate-winning **Champion Ingledene First Love**, was produced. 'Cherry', as she was affectionately known, was second in a line of four consecutive home-bred tail female 'Love' champions, a current record for bitch lines in Britain. Champion Ingledene Summer Love (by Champion Brilyn Supertramp ex Ingledene Spring Song) was the first, followed by Champion Ingledene First Love (by Champion Karava Kornishman). Next came Champion Ingledene Cherish the Love (by Champion Easy Come at Drenoss, a grandson of Champion Aberthorne Arrester) and finally Champion Ingledene Penny Lover (by Sandiacre Stop 'n' Think).

1987

Breeder/Owner: Mr & Mrs J N Geddes

K.C. Stud Book No. 1275BY

Sable & White Bitch.

D.O.B. 31 May 1987

Sire: Champion Karava Kornishman

Dam: Champion Ingledene Summer Love

6 CHALLENGE CERTIFICATES

GROUP WINNER OF THE PUPPY LINCOLN STAKES, MANCHESTER 1988

UK's TOP WINNING ROUGH COLLIE 1990

WINNER OF THE PEDIGREE PETFOODS (ALL BREEDS) CHAMPION STAKES, BATH 1991

DOG WORLD'S TOP BROOD [1] BITCH 1998

Champion Ingledene First Love was a truly remarkable bitch being extremely successful both in the show ring and in the maternity stakes. As a youngster she gained her Junior Warrant, going on to win six Challenge Certificates. She whelped four litters to different dogs producing nine Collies gaining Stud Book recognition, including two Champions, Ingledene Cherish the Love and multi-titled Ingledene Power of Love, both with four Challenge Certificates. Interestingly her nine Stud Book-entry progeny equals those whelped by Champion Witchcraft of Rokeby (see page 74), albeit from less litters.

Cherry's first litter, to Champion Easy Come at Drenoss, produced Ingledene Love Comes Easy at Drenoss and Champion Ingledene Cherish the Love who, when mated to Sandiacre Stop 'n' Think, whelped siblings Ingledene Slave to Love, Ingledene Thinkin Bout Love and Champion Ingledene Penny Lover. Penny Lover, Britain's Top Rough Collie for 1997, won nine Challenge Certificates including the Best of Breed award at Crufts in 1998, her ninth Certificate coming from the Veteran class at the Collie Association Show in November 2000. Mated to 'grandma' Cherry, Slave to Love sired Ingledene Love is the Drug ('Chad') who, apart from being behind several of the Boughlee, Ynysybwl and Essenjay Collies, sired tricolour Challenge Certificate-winning puppy Rossavon Addicted to Love at Ingledene, and Karibuni Jezebel with Pampardour, winner of a Reserve Challenge Certificate. To Bhyllsacre Shades of Gold, Cherry whelped the tricolour multi-titled Ingledene Power of Love and his sable sister Ingledene Ria'ly a Love, who was initially owned in partnership with Rene Cozens. Ria'ly a Love was mated to Champion Drenoss Wannabe Famous in 1993, whelping sibling Champions Ria'ly Famous at Bhyllsacre for Rene and Wannabe Ria'ly Loved at Ingledene, the latter bitch being transferred to Crawford Taylor who campaigned her to her title. By the time Ria'ly a Love whelped her second litter she was in Rene's sole ownership and has whelped several successful Collies since, including Bhyllsacre Black Rose (by Champion Brilyn Rum'n Black).

Champion and International Champion Ingledene Power of Love, or 'Chato' as he is fondly known, is a useful sire in his own right producing Rene Cozens' bitch Bhyllsacre Golden Gem, winner of two Challenge Certificates including Best of Breed at Crufts in 1997. Power of Love is also the grandsire of Tony and Daphne Iley's Champion Deeohn Blue Devoted to Ileyda, winner of the 1999 Crufts Dog Challenge Certificate, and is behind several of the Stokedale, Shepatin, Ladnar and Clynelish Collies.

Sire Champion Karava Kornishman	Ch Geoffdon Law Maker	Ch Arranbrook Mr Chips of Aberhill	Sangreat Sorrocco of Arranbrook
			Brettonpark Burnished Gold of Arranbrook
		Geoffdon Isabella	Ch Duntiblae Dodgem of Geoffdon
			Franwyns Fascination of Geoffdon
	Karava Kastille	Laughan Larinka	Leecroft Lover Boy of Dunsinane
			Remlaw Royalist of Laughan
		Kidlaine Kamille	Ch Aberthorne Arrester
			Anlyn Alicia
Dam Champion Ingledene Summer Love	Ch Brilyn Supertramp	Ch Myberns Minstrel	Ch Aberthorne Arrester
			Myberns Mistibelle
		Brilyn Duchesse Lace	Sangreat Sorrocco of Arranbrook
			Brilyn Golden Girl
	Ingledene Spring Song	Sandiacre Softly Softly	Dazzler of Dunsinane
			Sandiacre String of Pearls
		Ingledene Black Sequin	Pattingham Premonition
			Leawyn Annabelle

See '(Milroy's) Florrie-family 3' in Appendix II, and 'Dazzler lines' in Appendix I.

Footnote:

1. *'Dog World's' Top Brood Bitch competition is run on similar lines to the Top Stud Dog competition, so that when a collie wins a first challenge certificate its dam is awarded five points. An additional point is awarded to the dam for each subsequent challenge certificate won by that offspring during the same year.*

Photo courtesy of Lene Halvorsen/Brian Hawkins

Champion Brilyn Rum'n Black

1989

Champion Brilyn Rum'n Black is one of Champion Jasand Young Winston's most influential offspring, from the same litter as International Champion Brilyn Dark Delight and Champion Brilyn Painted Lady.

Rum'n Black proved a most popular 'all round' dog, winning four Challenge Certificates and seven Reserve Challenge Certificates, as well as siring a total of thirty-one Rough Collies to gain entry to the Kennel Club Stud Book including six Champions. These were sables Brilyn Satin'n Silk at Carostar and Rusforth Sweet Cherie, with four Challenge Certificates; Chrisarion Cromwell, winner of five Challenge Certificates, all with Best of Breed including Crufts in 1996; and blue merle Champions, Mayd Welcome at Atendus and Jasand True Blue, both of whom won four Challenge Certificates; plus Phreelancer Phrosty Moon Over Corydon, the breed's current record-holder with twenty Challenge Certificates, including Best of Breed at Crufts in 2000 (see page 124).

Besides influencing numerous kennels such as the Stokedale, Samhaven, Anderleen, Eilroy, Collingvale and Bhyllsacre Collies, Champion Brilyn Rum'n Black continues his sire's influence through two grandsons in particular, blue merle Champion Jasand Going Places (ex Champion Jasand True Blue), winner of eleven Challenge Certificates, and tricolour Chrisarion Collier (by Champion Jasand Young Winston).

The following critiques give us some idea of Rum'n Black's quality. Following the West of England Ladies' Kennel Society Championship Show of 1991, judge Val Plimmer (Firestone) commented:

".....a tri with a masculine head and exceptional eye and expression. Good ear carriage, and firm body with nice bone and feet. A jet black coat which was in lovely condition."

The following year Iris Cummings (Altnareagh) judged at the South Wales Championship Show and awarded him the Open Dog class from an entry of fifteen. She wrote: *" Hawkins Brilyn Rum'n Black, caught my eye as he entered the ring, most appealing expression, good dark almond shaped eye, lovely wedge of head. Not big but very sound, good spring of rib, nicely boned. Well let down hocks, moved well, presentation excellent, just asked for the CC and got it."*

Sire Champion Jasand Young Winston	Ch Karava Kornishman	Ch Geoffdon Law Maker	Ch Arranbrook Mr Chips of Aberhill
			Geoffdon Isabella
		Karava Kastille	Laughan Larinka
			Kidlaine Kamille
	Jasand Tuppence Coloured	Ch Arranbrook Mr Chips of Aberhill	Sangreat Sorrocco of Arranbrook
			Brettonpark Burnished Gold of Arranbrook
		Aberhill Prima Donna of Jasand	Ch Pied Piper of Aberhill at Rixown
			Aberhill Carousel
Dam Champion Lanteague Black Magic at Brilyn	Ch Lanteague Harvest Moon at Silvermoor	Lanteague Golden Harvest	Ch Brilyn Supertramp
			Lanteague Shady Lady
		Lanteague Shady Lady	Ch Pelido Sparticus
			Princess Gypsy Gay
	Lanteague Magical Kiss of Narragansette	Glenvilley Lad at Treglenza	Ch Lowerpark Izafella
			Deloraine Dee Dee
		Lanteague Abracadabra at Treglenza	Lanteague Golden Harvest
			Lanteague Bewitched at Aaronwell

See 'Dazzler lines' in Appendix I, and '(Salter's) Mountshannon Mona-family 10' in Appendix II.

Breeder/Owner: Mr B Hawkins

K.C.Stud Book No. 421CA

Tricolour Dog

D.O.B. 20 June 1989

Sire: Champion Jasand Young Winston

Dam: Champion Lanteague Black Magic at Brilyn

4 CHALLENGE CERTIFICATES

OUR DOGS TOP SIRE 1997 [1]

DOG WORLD'S TOP STUD DOG 1998

Footnote:

1. *The 'Our Dogs' Top Sire competition is an annual points-based competition, the winner being the dog who sires the greatest number of championship show-winning progeny in a particular year.*

Chrisarion Collier

Photo courtesy of Margaret Ruston/Chris Black

Chrisarion Collier, or 'Nero' as he is known at home, is the second of Champion Jasand Young Winston's important offspring and is closely bred along Dazzler lines, being the result of a grandfather to granddaughter mating. Although he gained his Stud Book entry, by winning a third place in Limit Dog at the Working Breeds of Wales Championship Show in 1994, Nero never really enjoyed the show ring and is a dog who will be remembered for his prowess as a sire. In Chris Black's own words: *"Nero was only shown as a youngster as it was patently obvious from the onset that he hated the show ring. Therefore people who used him did so on the strength of his pedigree and his consistency in producing top flight offspring from their valuable bitches."*

Chrisarion Collier has a Champion sable and white brother, Chrisarion Carbon Copy for Jasand, but Collier is proving the more useful stud dog of the two, having sired five Champions covering all three colours. Collier's most prolific litter (ex Rum'n Black daughter Champion Jasand True Blue) produced four Collies which gained Stud Book numbers, and these included Jasand Panama Hatty, Jasand Blue Vein at Birkmyre, Jasand Tru't Form at Altnareagh and the sensational blue merle, Champion Jasand Going Places or 'Oscar' as he is affectionately known. Champion Sassari Big Bold 'n' Blue, another of Collier's sons, has a tricolour litter sister, Sassari Soul Singer, on one Challenge Certificate; and his sable and white siblings, Champions Myskveil Master Craftsman at Seriema and Myskveil Melisande of Sunnyhurst, have a litter sister Myskveil Prim and Proper for Seriema on one Challenge Certificate. The tricolour, Sundorne Spiritualist, is Collier's fifth Champion son.

1992

Chrisarion Collier's son, Champion Jasand Going Places
Photo courtesy of Jasmine Round

In 1998 Champion Jasand Going Places began his show career in style by winning the Ladypark Points trophy[1] with fifty one points, and the East Anglian Collie Association's 'Pup of the Year' trophy. He was also a finalist in the Dog World/ Beta 'Pup of the Year' competition where, having won his heat at the West of England Ladies' Kennel Society Championship Show from an entry of five hundred and seven puppies, he was short-listed to the final thirteen. In addition to being awarded the 'Our Dogs/ Pedigree Chum' Top Puppy, Oscar was also awarded the British Collie Club's 'Collie of the Year' in 1999. One of the first Rough Collies to achieve the Junior Warrant in its current form, his achievements in 1999 secured him 'Dog World's' top winning Rough Collie. He is currently the holder of eleven Challenge Certificates, ten with Best of Breed and five with Best in Show awards at sub-group Championship Shows.[2]

It remains to be seen what lasting impression Chrisarion Collier is set to have on the future of the breed but there are several more recent children and grandchildren in a position to further his influence. The young siblings Chrisarion Gabarello, Chrisarion Consuela at Rantara, and Chrisarion Conchita at Sassari are double grandchildren of Collier, each currently enjoying a spectacular run of show ring success for their respective owners. Gabarello won six Championship Show Puppy classes and Best Puppy Dog at the Working and Pastoral Breeds of Wales Championship Show; Consuela took eight Championship Show firsts, adding Best Puppy in Show at the East Anglian Collie Association's Championship Show in 2000. During the same year Conchita took Best Puppy in breed at the South Wales Kennel Association's Championship Show, Best Puppy Bitch at Windsor, and several Best Puppy in Show awards at Club Open Shows.

Breeders: Mesdames C Black & M Penwarne

Owner: Mrs C Black

K.C. Stud Book No. 623CE

Tricolour Dog

D.O.B. 8 August 1992

Sire: Champion Jasand Young Winston

Dam: Chrisarion Chanson

OUR DOGS/PEDIGREE CHUM TOP SIRE 1995

DOG WORLD'S TOP STUD DOG 1997 & 1999

Sire Champion Jasand Young Winston	Ch Karava Kornishman	Ch Geoffdon Law Maker	Ch Arranbrook Mr Chips of Aberhill
			Geoffdon Isabella
		Karava Kastille	Laughan Larinka
			Kidlaine Kamille
	Jasand Tuppence Coloured	Ch Arranbrook Mr Chips of Aberhill	Sangreat Sorrocco of Arranbrook
			Brettonpark Burnished Gold of Arranbrook
		Aberhill Prima Donna of Jasand	Ch Pied Piper of Aberhill at Rixown
			Aberhill Carousel
Dam Chrisarion Chanson	Ch Brilyn Rum'n Black	Ch Jasand Young Winston	Ch Karava Kornishman
			Jasand Tuppence Coloured
		Ch Lanteague Black Magic at Brilyn	Ch Lanteague Harvest Moon of Silvermoor
			Lanteague Magical Kiss of Narragansette
	Brilyn Cachet at Chrisarion	Ch Tashadon Tommy Tucker	Ch Aberthorne Arrester
			Tambourine Toetapper
		Ch Lanteague Black Magic at Brilyn	Ch Lanteague Harvest Moon of Silvermoor
			Lanteague Magical Kiss of Narragansette

See 'Dazzler lines' in Appendix I, and '(Salter's) Mountshannon Mona-family 10' in Appendix II.

Footnotes:

1. *The Ladypark Points Trophy is open to all Puppies (Minor Puppy and Puppy classes) who compete at Championship Shows where Challenge Certificates are on offer. At one time the Trophy was presented at Crufts but is now awarded annually at British Collie Club Championship Shows. Trophies are presented to the winner and runner-up, with rosettes being given to tenth place.*
2. *A 'Sub-Group' Show is for related breeds within the same Group, such as Rough and Smooth Collies.*

Champion Phreelancer Phrosty Moon Over Corydon

Head study by Miranda Blake

Lene Halvorsen, a young Norwegian breeder and exhibitor, based her Kennel on Corydon stock and on coming to England in 1988, spent several years with John, Barbara and Miranda Blake waiting for her work permit. Whilst there she made the brave and extremely successful decision to outcross her blue merle bitch, Corydon Silver Moon, to Champion Brilyn Rum'n Black and the elegant and beautifully coloured blue merle **Champion Phreelancer Phrosty Moon Over Corydon** resulted. In Lene's own words: *"I always considered Frosty's dam, Corydon Silver Moon, to be a very beautiful bitch and felt she had some qualities which I really wanted to preserve. It took a year before I finally decided to go ahead with what was simply a 'gut' feeling. Having noticed that many children of Ch Brilyn Rum'n Black had the exact qualities and type I wanted to keep I believed that, combined with Silver Moon's outstanding breeding, this could produce something quite special. Frosty's magical promise became evident at a very early age, his success has far exceeded any dreams I have ever had and I am immensely proud of him."* Unfortunately ill health temporarily took Lene back to Norway so Frosty was transferred into John and Barbara's ownership, whilst

1996

Frosty — *Photo courtesy of S Roos/B Blake*

still a small puppy, and he took the show-ring by storm winning eight Challenge Certificates at the first eight Shows he attended, all before his second birthday. His thirteenth ticket came at Crufts in 2000, his twentieth coming six months later at Richmond, awarded by Joan House (Lassina). Frosty has proved to be a great ambassador for the Rough Collie, not only by annexing twenty Challenge Certificates and six Group placings, but by being short-listed into the final six or eight exhibits at the Scottish Kennel Club's Show in May 1998 and 2000, as well as Crufts 2000.

Frosty's first major win came from an 'Open Dog' class of ten exhibits, at Birmingham National in May 1998, when he was just twenty-one months of age. Judge Ros Cartwright (Drenoss) had this to say: *"Blake's Phreelancer Phrosty Moon Over Corydon. Blue merle of the highest order. Soundly constructed and moving correctly. Well presented coat of glorious colour. Lovely head pattern with the slight stop the Standard calls for. Nicely shaped eye with sweet expression. Good ear carriage, shows well. Put together correctly-good shoulder placement, legs and feet. Just looked so right on the day, he justly deserved the CC and BOB."*

Frosty won his thirteenth Challenge Certificate at Crufts, in March 2000, from an 'Open Dog' class of twenty-two. Judge Joe Kirk's (Cregagh) critique reads: *"Blake's Ch Phreelancer Phrosty Moon over Corydon, b/m, best of heads, lovely expression, all male, balanced throughout, head excellent, good eye, correct ears, lovely in profile, correct dentition and pigmentation, first class front, good bone, well formed rib and angulated rear, good tailset, lovely coat which has good colour, moved with drive. CC and with agreement of co-judge, BOB. Pleased to see him in the final line-up of the group."*

To date Champion Phreelancer Phrosty Moon Over Corydon has been sparingly used at stud and it is too early to determine what influence he may exert on posterity.

Sire: Champion Brilyn Rum'n Black	Ch Jasand Young Winston	Ch Karava Kornishman	Ch Geoffdon Law Maker
			Karava Kastille
		Jasand Tuppence Coloured	Ch Arranbrook Mr Chips of Aberhill
			Aberhill Prima Donna at Jasand
	Ch Lanteague Black Magic at Brilyn	Ch Lanteague Harvest Moon at Silvermoor	Lanteague Golden Harvest
			Lanteague Shady Lady
		Lanteague Magical Kiss at Narragansette	Glenvilley Lad at Treglenza
			Lanteague Abracadabra at Treglenza
Dam: Corydon Silver Moon	Ch Lowerpark Moonlighter at Corydon	Ch & Aus Ch Corydon Tuck's Tiger	NZ Ch Corydon Hot Rod
			Corydon Polly Tucka
		Lowerpark Speckleberry	Ch Lowerpark Star Spangled
			Lowerpark Keepsake at Razda
	Corydon Glory Bee	Nu Ch[1] Corydon Augustus Caesar	Ch & Aus Ch Little Caesar at Corydon
			Corydon Polly Tucka
		Ch & Aus Ch Corydon Glory Hallelujah	Ch Rokeby the Radical
			Corydon Hannalara

See 'Dazzler lines' in Appendix I, and '(Claypole's) Curzon Jess-family 2' in Appendix II.

Footnote:

1. Nu Ch = Norwegian Champion

Breeder: Miss L Halvorsen
Owner: Mr & Mrs J J Blake
K.C.Stud Book No. 4007CH
Blue Merle Dog
D.O.B. 18 August 1996
Sire: Champion Brilyn Rum'n Black
Dam: Corydon Silver Moon

20 CHALLENGE CERTIFICATES

BORDER UNION 1998 – GROUP 4

NATIONAL WORKING BREEDS 1998 – GROUP 4

EAST ANGLIAN COLLIE ASSOCIATION 1998 & 2000 - BEST IN SHOW

WEST OF ENGLAND LADIES' KENNEL SOCIETY 1999 – GROUP 3

CRUFTS 2000 – BEST OF BREED & SHORT-LISTED IN THE PASTORAL GROUP

WINDSOR 2000 – GROUP 2

BORDER UNION 2000 – GROUP 3

PAIGNTON 2000 – GROUP 3

The Lassie Cup. Donated by Metro-Goldwyn Mayer Pictures Ltd and presented annually at Crufts to the Best of Breed Rough Collie.
Photo courtesy of M Blake

Appendices

INTRODUCTION TO APPENDICES I & II - Lines and Families

Appendix I includes a series of charts detailing the principal tail male 'lines', whilst Appendix II features principal tail female 'families'. For ease of reference the relevant 'lines' and 'families' are noted below the pedigrees of each 'Rough Collie of Distinction' in the main body of this book.

When studying pedigrees, the uppermost line is referred to as 'tail male' or 'line', whilst the extreme bottom line is known as the 'tail female' or 'family'. This terminology was devised by the equestrian world, which believed the forbears of these two outer lines exerted the greatest influence on progeny. Although such theories have long been discredited, this type of analysis is still valid for it remains the best way of appreciating the degree of influence any dog or bitch may have had over a breed's development.

Miss Margaret Osborne (Shiel) originally introduced this technique to the Collie world when she traced the 'lines' and 'families' of every post-war Challenge Certificate winner, publishing her findings in the Collie Association's Handbook of 1952. Fifty years on, Dareen Bridge has adopted the same technique to highlight principal male and female producers.

Because breeders have tended to use popular show-winning dogs in their breeding programmes, details of which are well documented in Kennel Club Stud Books, it is relatively easy to trace their tail male lines back to Trefoil in 1873.

Bitch families create greater problems because of the reluctance of early breeders to register stock not destined for the show ring. Early chroniclers gave some information on the breed's foundation bitches, and details published in the early Stud Books were useful if limited. As current families can rarely be traced back to these foundation bitches the important ones, not featuring in Margaret Osborne's original research, have now been designated as families a to d.

Miss Osborne originally isolated fourteen families, numbering them sequentially, as responsible for perpetuating the breed into modern times. Of this number only nine made significant contributions to the breed's development, most of which cannot be traced much beyond the beginning of the twentieth century. More recently two further families have been added to this total, both of which Miss Osborne declined to number, believing their origins would eventually become apparent. Despite modern technology and access to the Collie Association's considerable archives, additional information has not been forthcoming so Dareen has numbered these families 15 and 16.

It is highly improbable that major influential families of the nineteenth century such as those started by Digby's *Elsie,* Lacy's *Scott and Clyde* and Ashwin's *Lassie*, simply faded into obscurity. A more credible scenario is that bitches which later emerged, as the Kennel Club streamlined its system in 1896, were from unregistered descendants of these early families.

Key to Abbreviations:

B & T Black and Tan

B & W Black & White

BM Blue Merle – including grey & mottled

S & W Sable and White – including sable, red, mouse and all variations

Tri Tricolour – including Black, Tan & White

Footnote:
Only those dogs with UK titles are credited on the charts.

APPENDIX I -The Sire Lines

Early Collie Lines

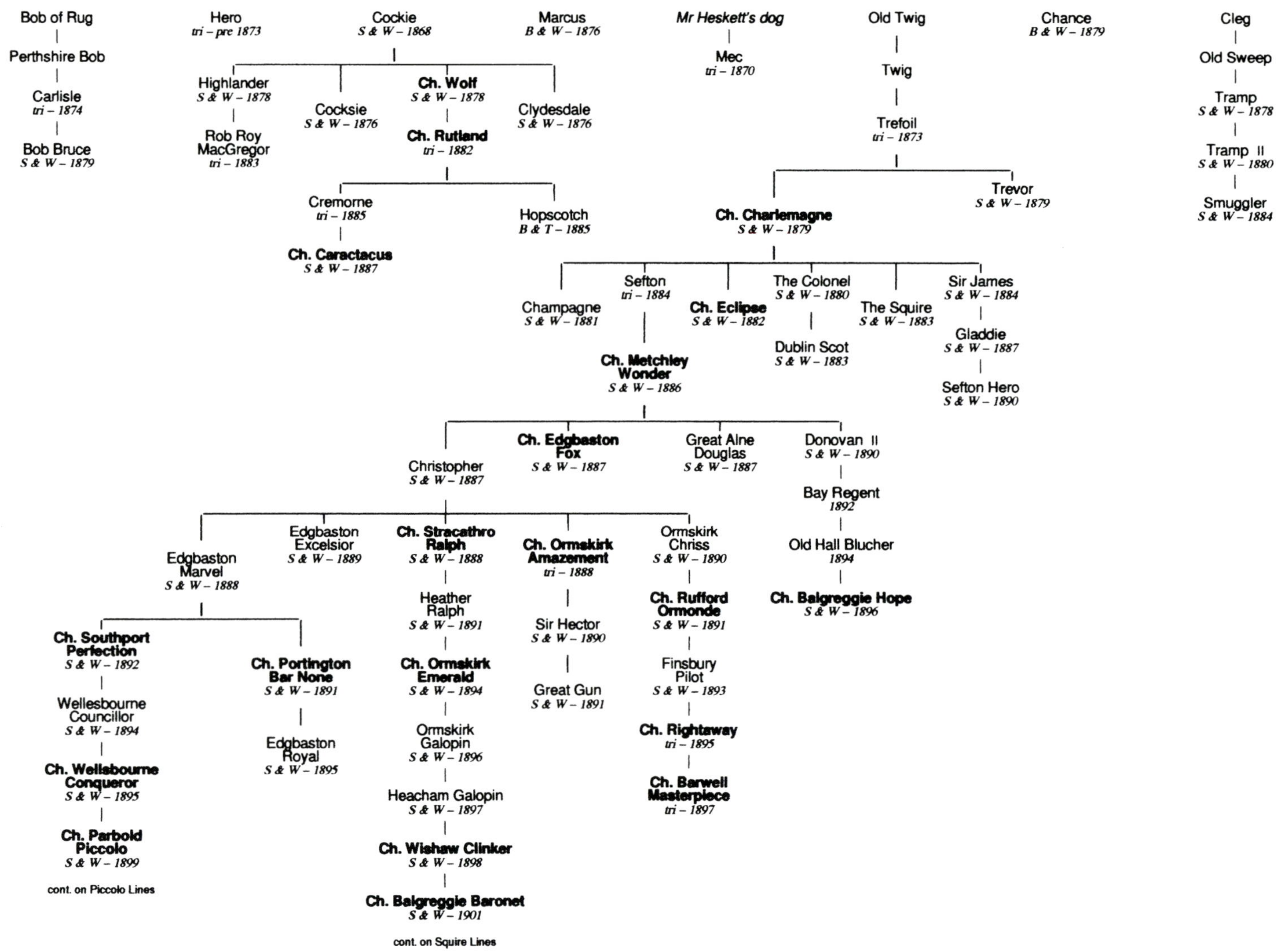

Piccolo Lines

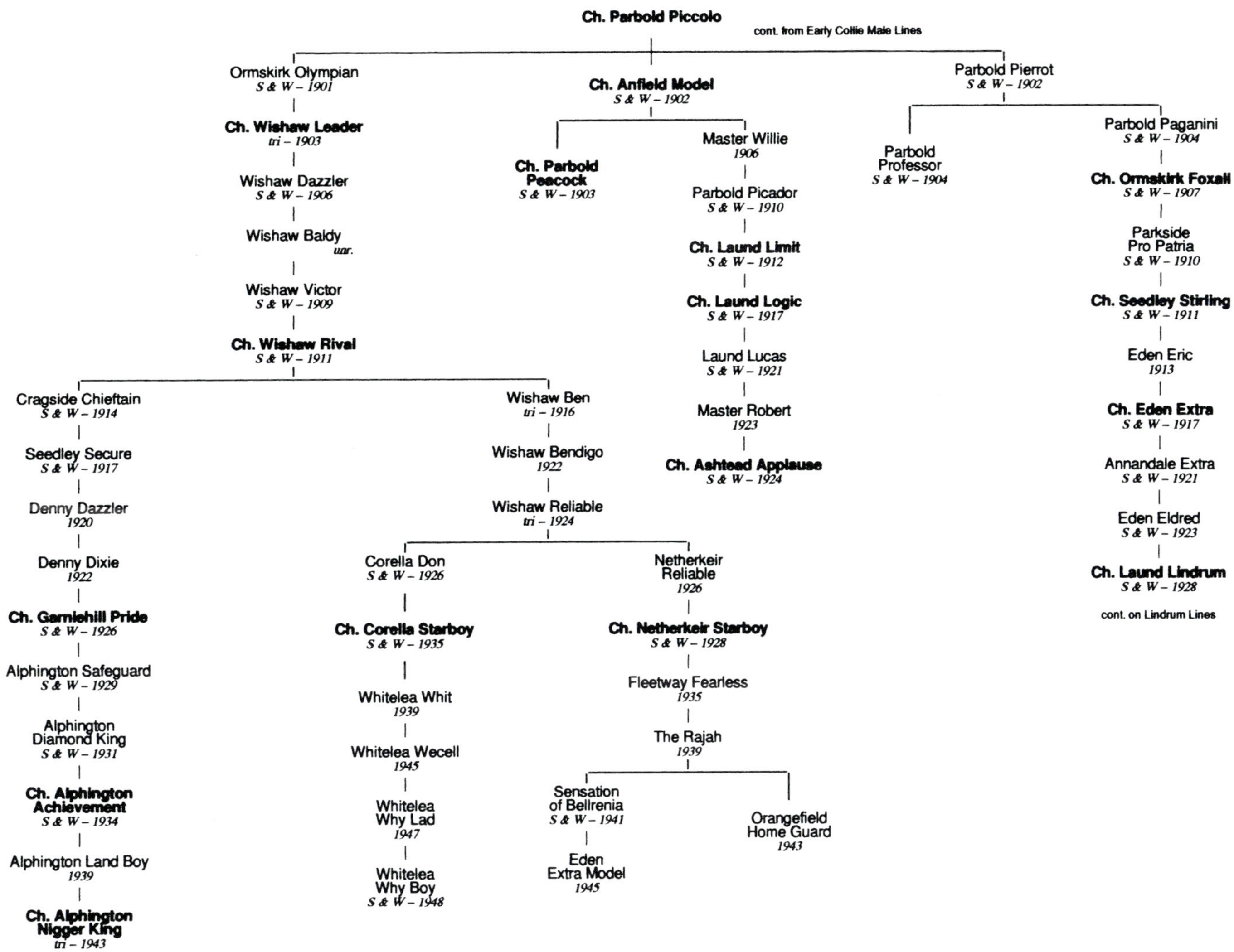

Lindrum Lines

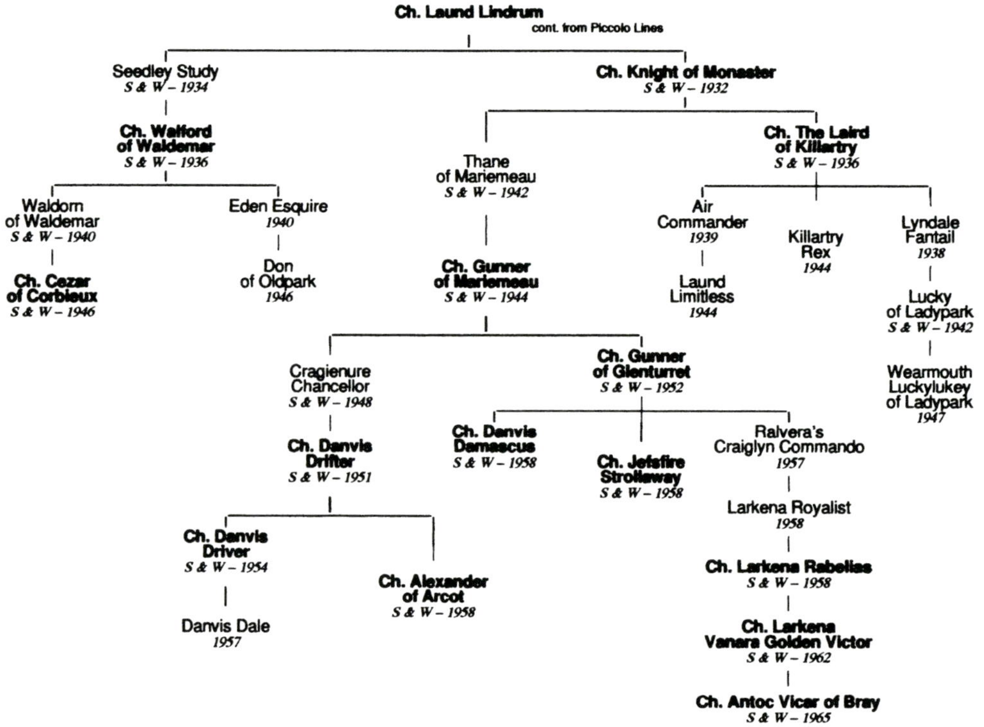

Squire Lines

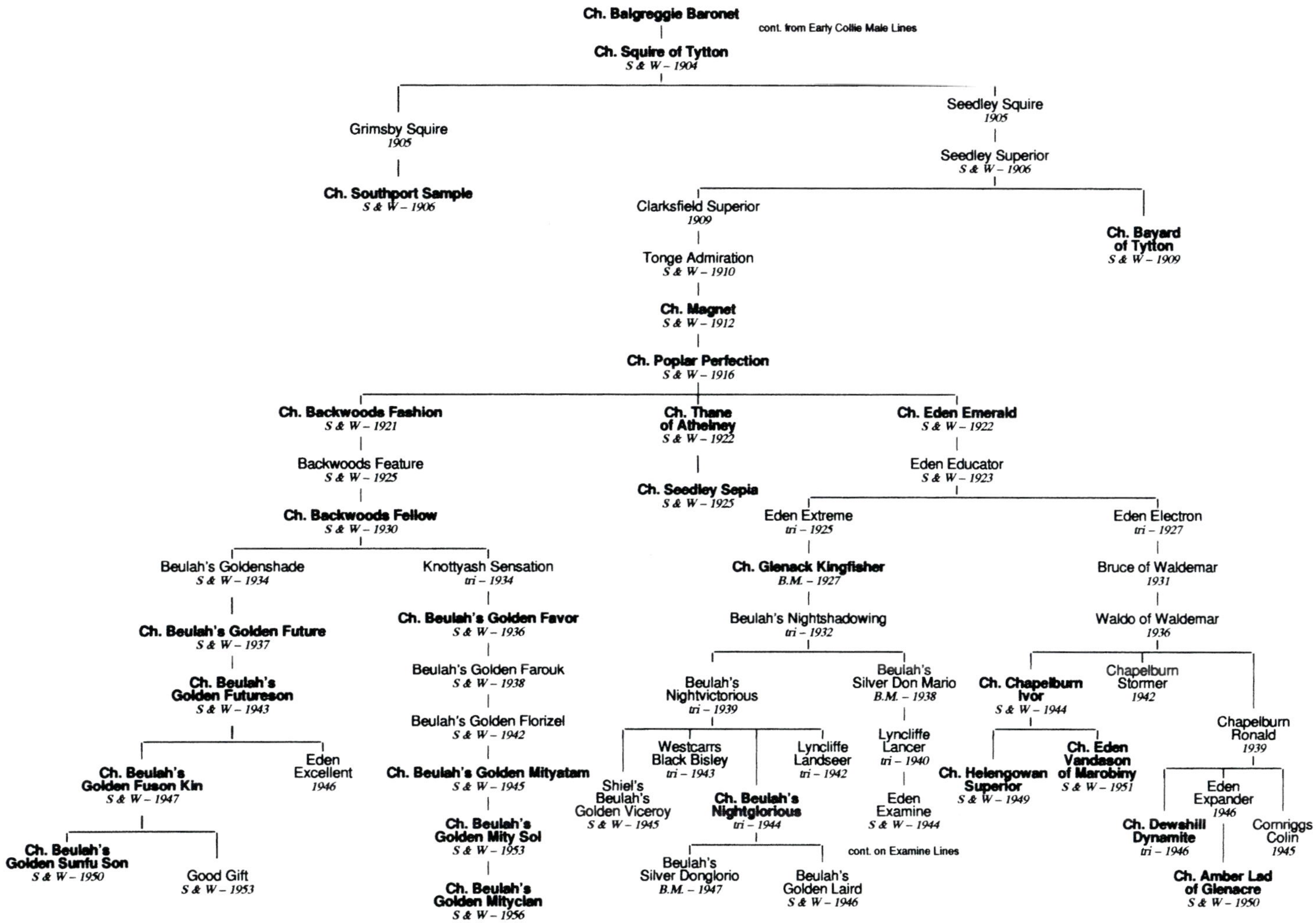

Examine Lines

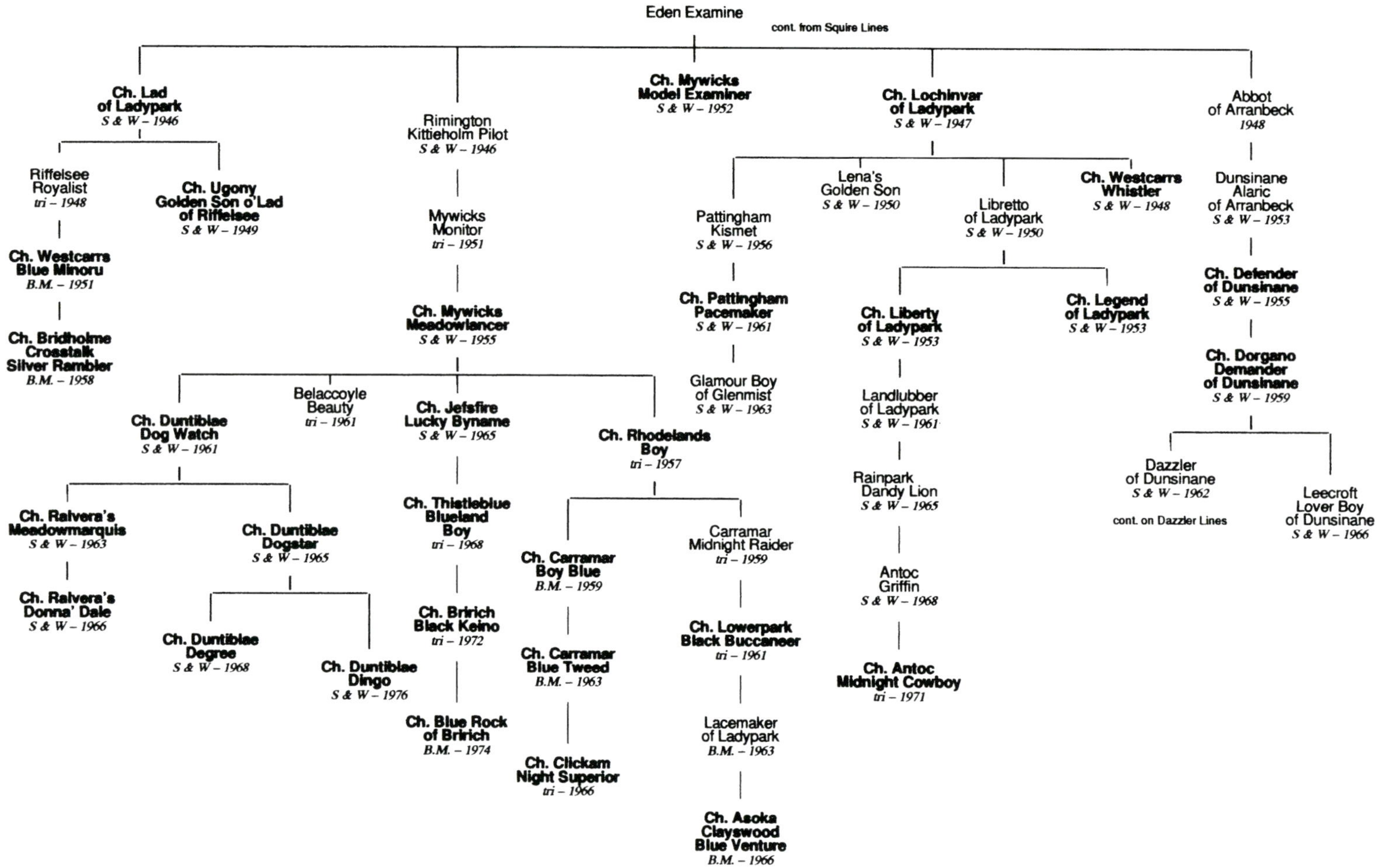

Dazzler Lines

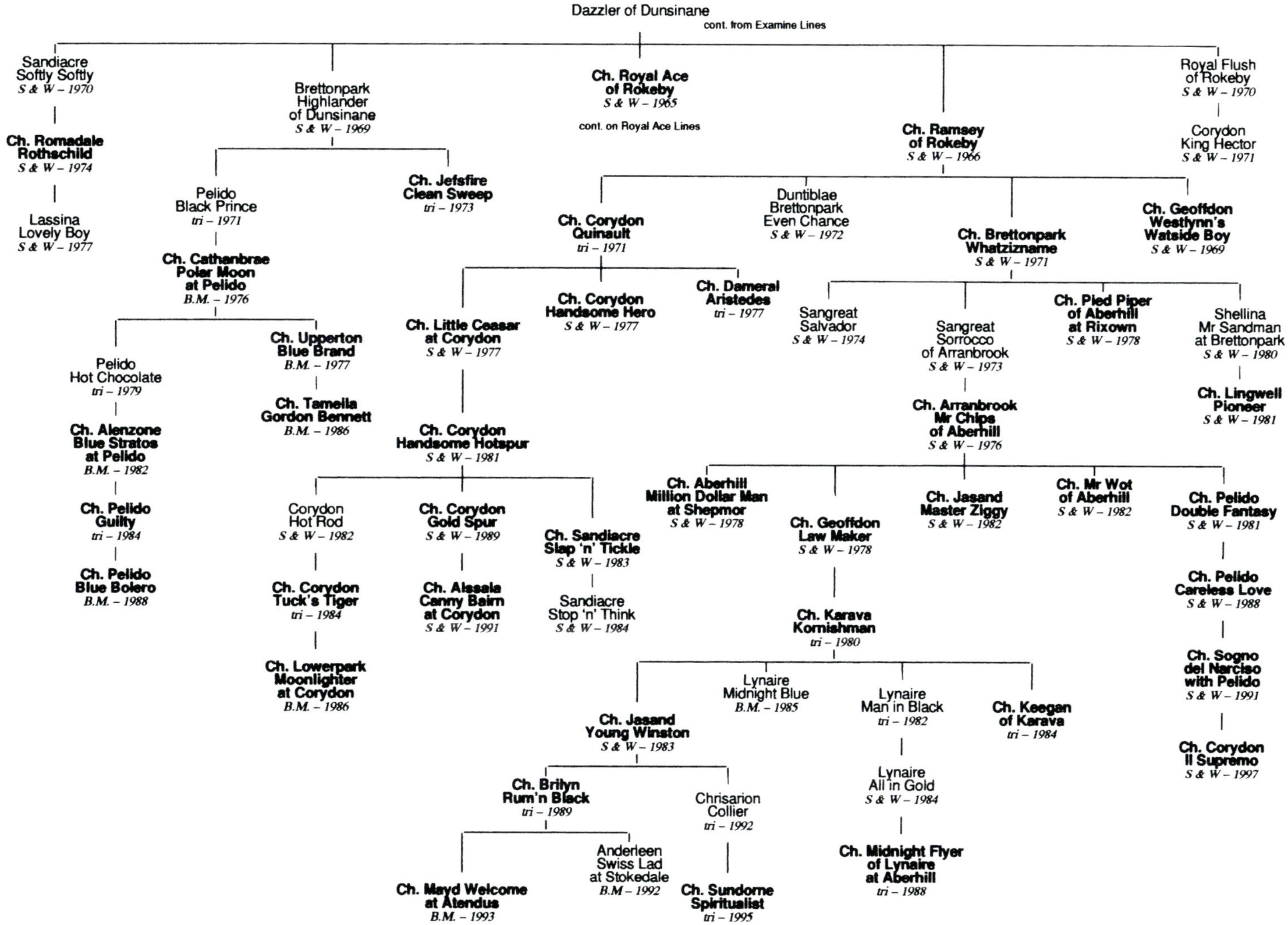

Royal Ace Lines

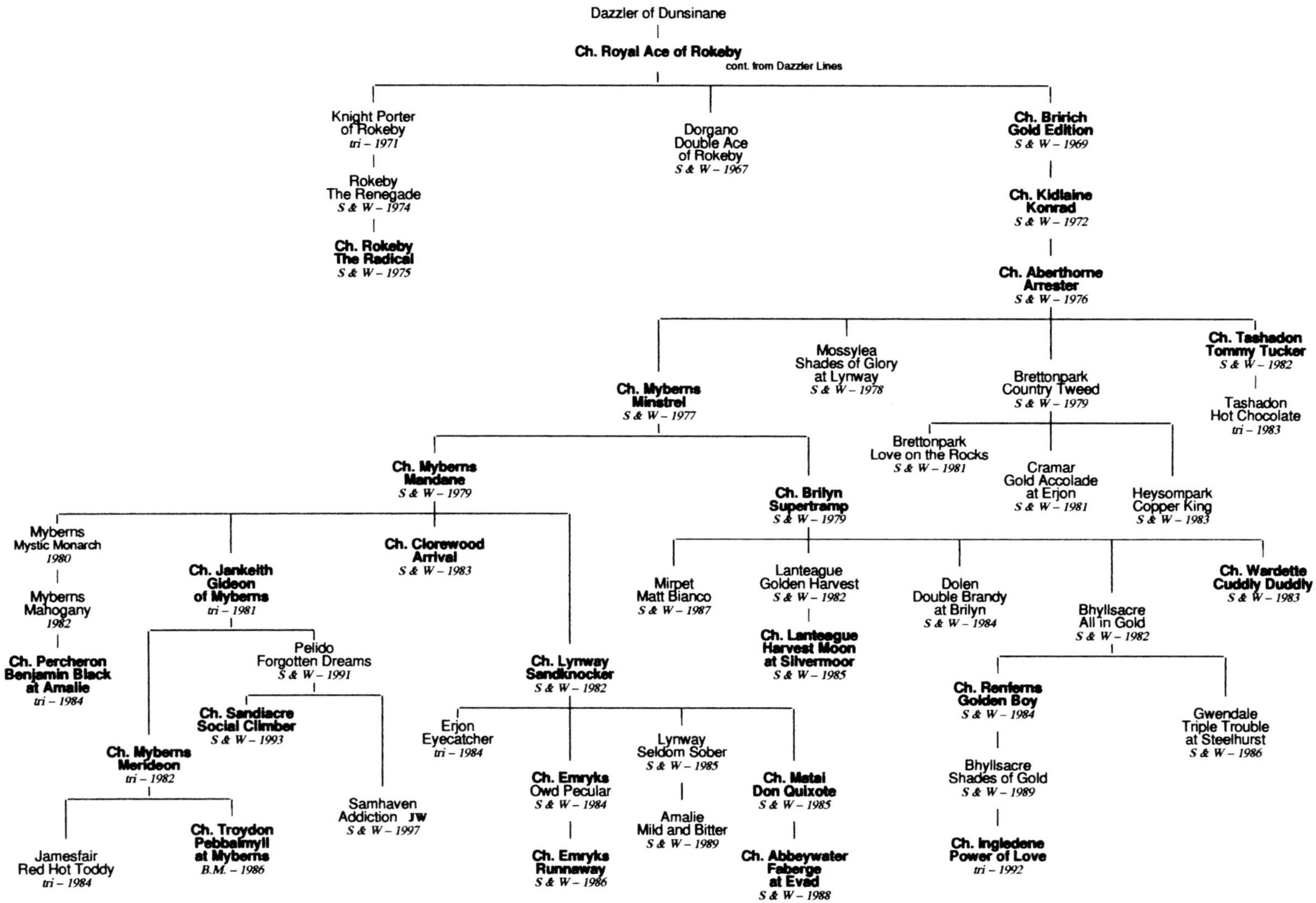

APPENDIX II -The Female Families

(Digby's) Elsie - family a

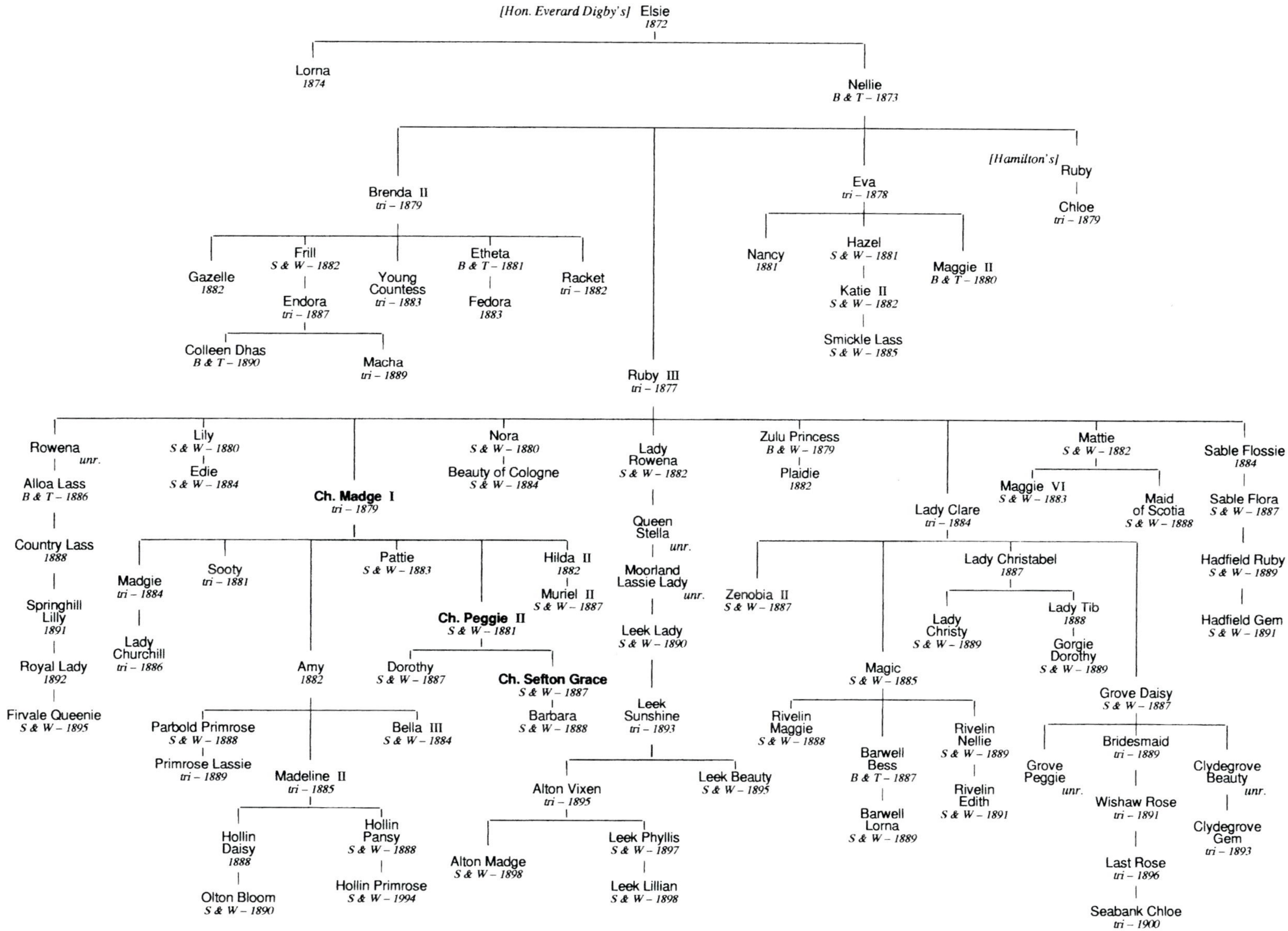

***Family a:** Starts with the Hon Everard Digby's Elsie born in 1872. This family was originally christened 'family 1a' by Margaret Osborne when she discovered Eve was not the dam of Eve II. At that time the family began with the Hon Digby's Nellie but it can now be extended one further generation to Elsie, which brings Tricolour II's dam Lorna into the same family. Destined to become one of the most important of the nineteenth century, this family includes such famous bitches as the Rev Hans Hamilton's Ruby III, Ch Madge I, Ch Peggie II, and Sefton Grace. It is therefore surprising that the family's influence hardly extended beyond the close of the nineteenth century.*

(Lacy's) Scott & Clyde - family b

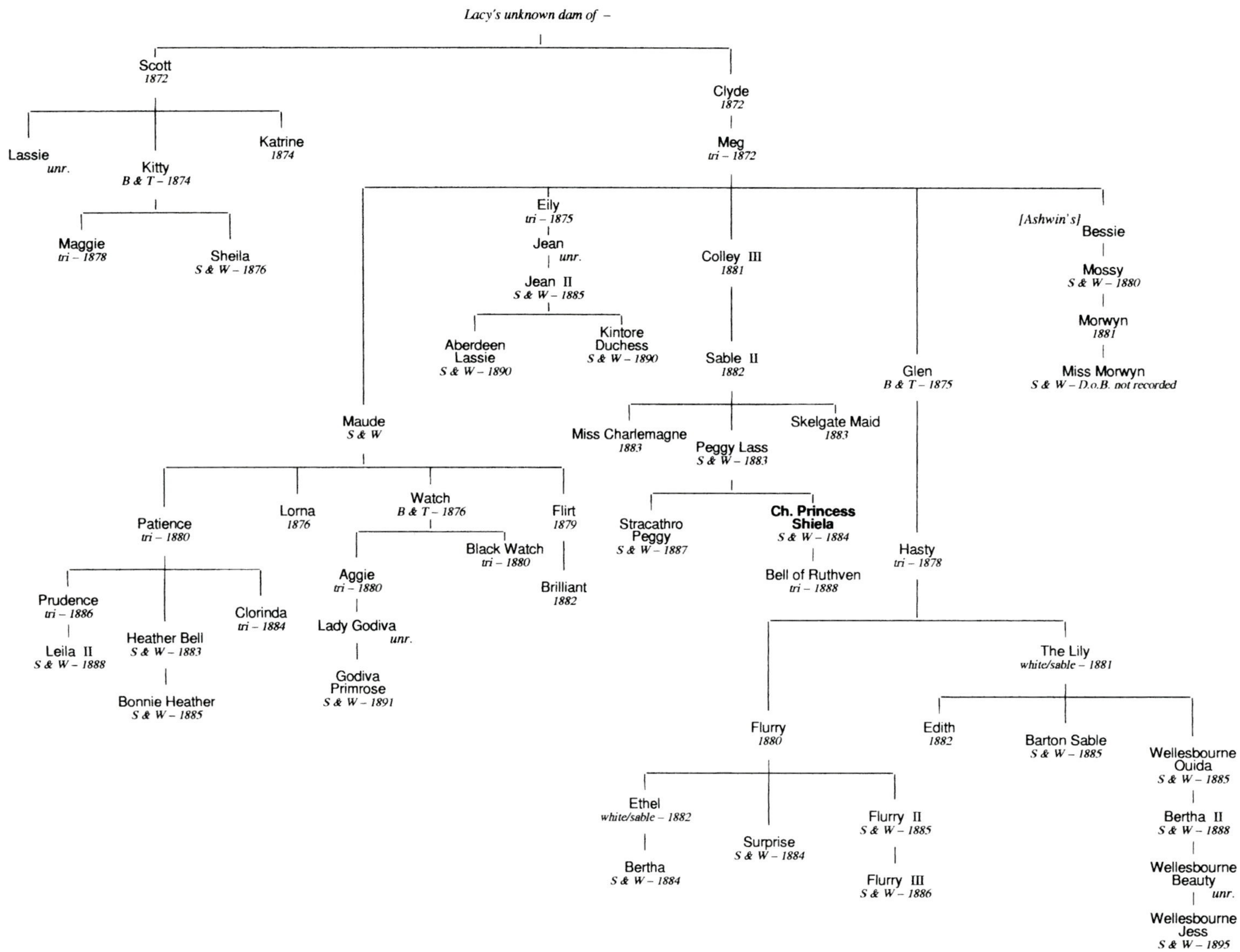

Family b: *Starts with the unknown dam of Scott and Clyde, litter sisters owned and possibly bred by H Lacy of Hebden Bridge. Scott's influence was short-lived although she earned her Stud Book number by winning a 1st prize in 1873. Glen's Stud Book entry extends her pedigree through Ashwin's Meg to Clyde (sister to Scott no. 2896, Vol I). From Clyde the family includes many famous bitches with Bissell's Maude and Lorna, Charles' Hasty, and Charlemagne's sister Flirt being the most important.*

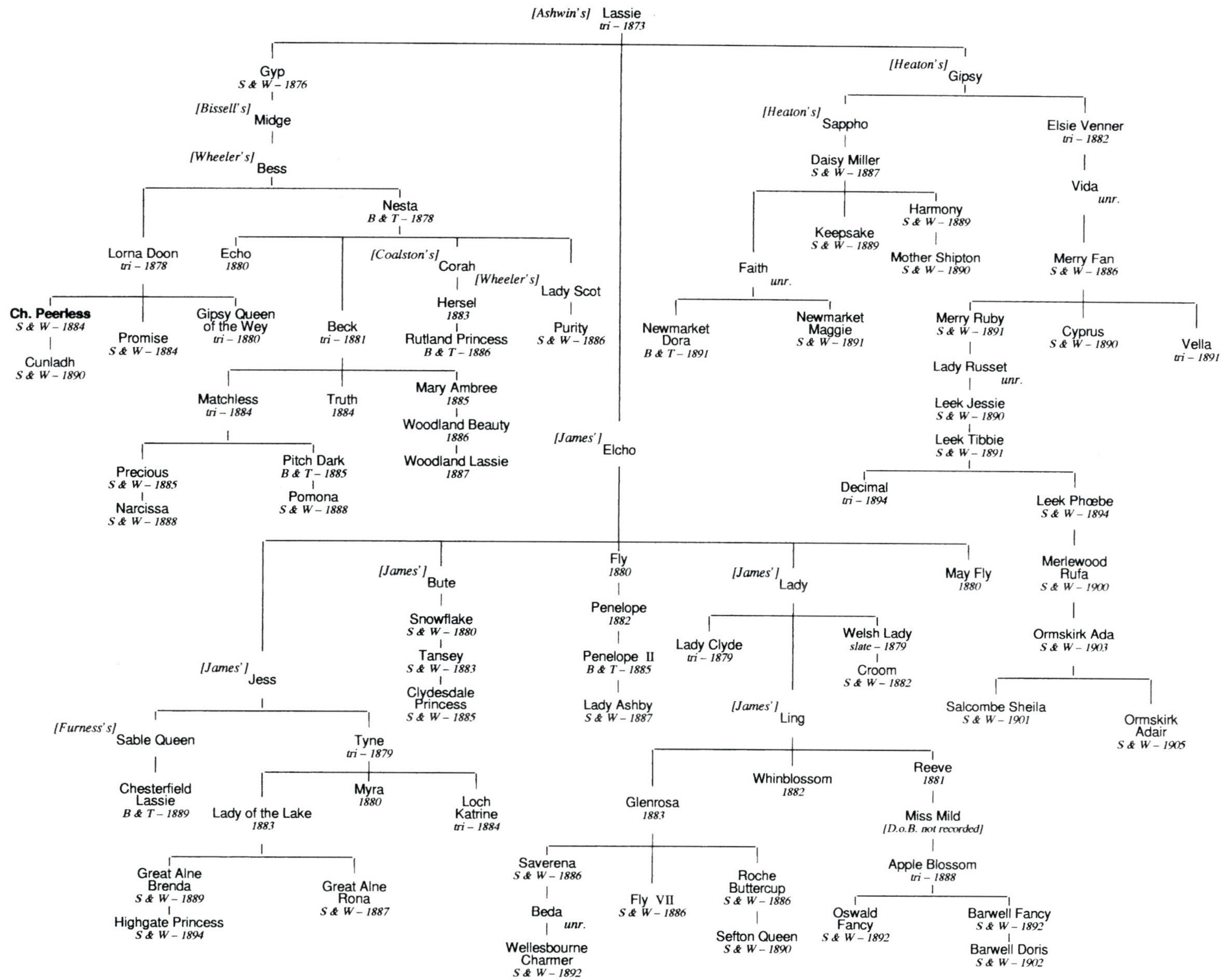

Family c: Starts with Ashwin's Lassie and, together with Digby's Elsie (family a), formed the backbone of nineteenth century breeding lines, being particularly influential with those breeders who formed part of the Birmingham school. Although few of the bitches became Champions, many not even exhibited, their influence over the period was extensive, with such well known breeders as the Charles brothers, Wheeler, Bissell, Boddington and Dr James basing their kennels on Ashwin's Lassie's descendants.

(Panmure-Gordon's) Hamish III - family d

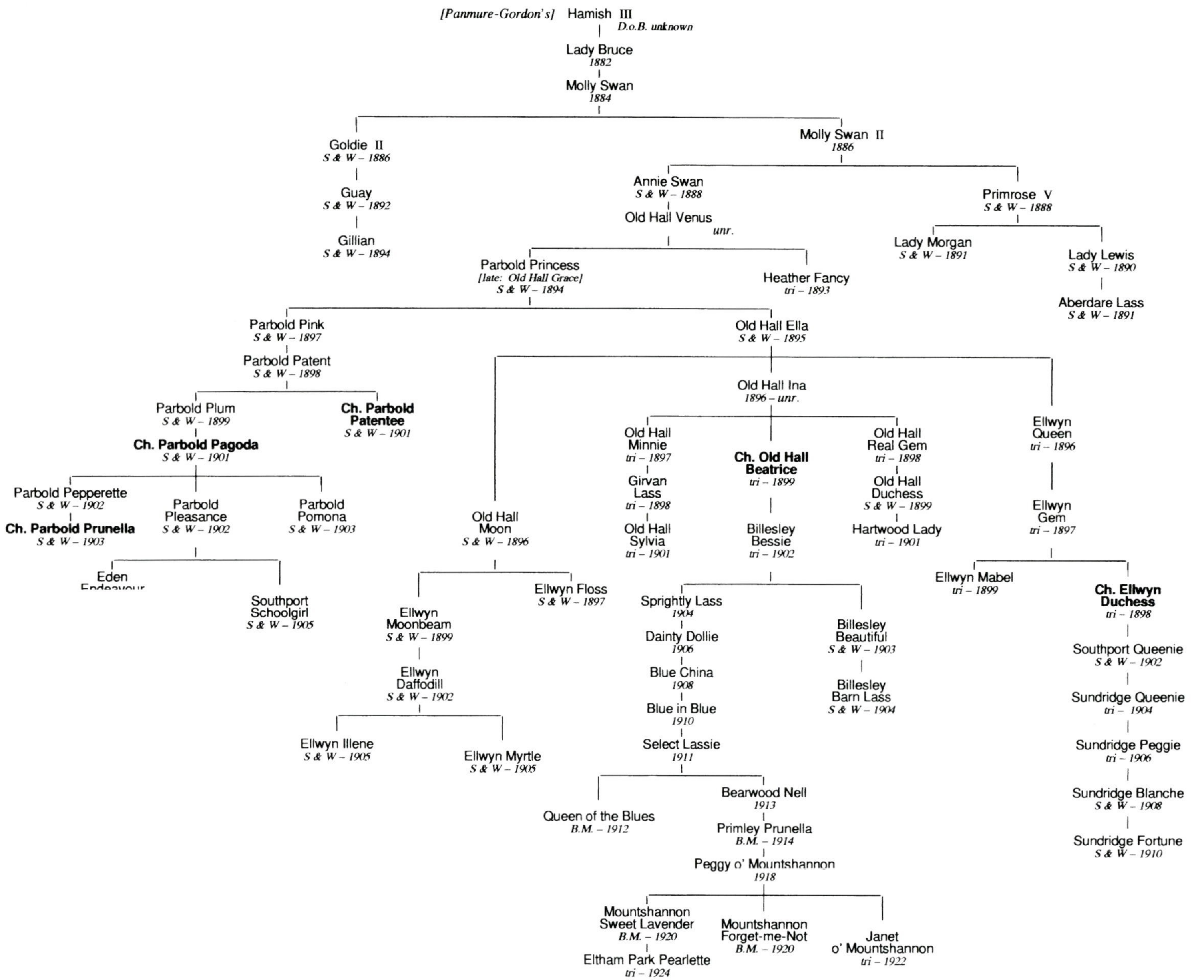

Family d: Starts with the unlikely named bitch, Hamish III. Of her we know only that she was owned by Mr Panmure-Gordon, and whelped Lady Bruce (by Bruce Boy, by Trevor ex Lorna Doon) in 1882. The family became particularly influential, with breeders from Scotland and the North of England, through Mr J Agnew's Old Hall Kennel which exerted a considerable influence over the foundation stock of Parbold, Ellwyn and to a lesser extent Southport. Unlike other early families the influence of this one is known to extend to the early 1920's, and includes stock owned or shown by the Rev T Salter's Mountshannon Kennel, which earned fame for its beautiful blue merle Collies.

(Roberts') Old Lassie - family 1

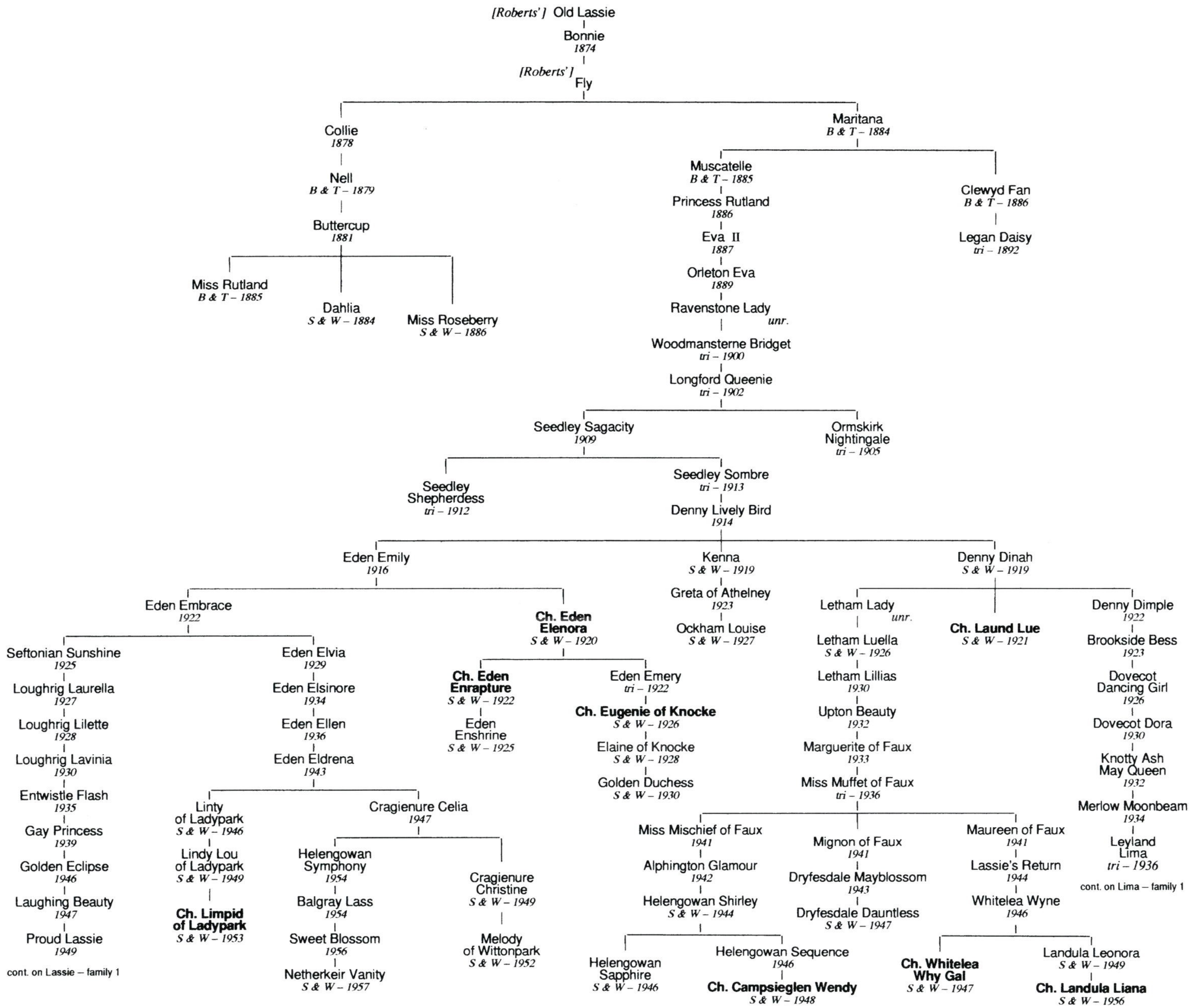

Family 1: Starts with Roberts' Old Lassie, born around 1873, and remains one of the few active families which can positively trace its ancestry back to the nineteenth century. On discovering that Eva II traced back to Mr E Roberts' Fly rather than the Hon Everard Digby's Nellie Margaret Osborne, acknowledging this in her updated 'Lines and Families 1965', designated this family 'family 1' and that headed by Nellie as 'family 1a' (now family a). Fly can now be traced back a further two generations to Old Lassie, dam of Carlyle (8505). More recent research confirms two further amendments to this family. Lethem Luella is now known to be out of the unregistered Letham Lady, daughter of Denny Dinah, which means that this branch of the family has moved sideways. More seriously Seedley Saville is out of Seedley Jessie, rather than Seedley Splash, which means her descendants have now migrated to family 14.

Lassie/Lima - family 1 (cont.)

Lassie

Proud Lassie
cont. from [Roberts'] Old Lassie – family 1

- Cathanbrae Enchantress *S & W – 1951*
- Danethorpe Laugh of Ladypark *S & W – 1951*
  - Pattingham Lovely Miss *1954*
    - Dena the Shepherdess *1961*
      - Amber the Shepherdess *1964*
        - Bess of Clovelly *1969*
          - Pers-Nality Girl of Glenalan *tri – 1972*
            - Glenalan's Blue Moon *B.M. – 1974*
            - Glenalan's Golden Karis *S & W – 1973*
              - Glenalan's Solitaire *1976*
                - Glenalan's Lucky Dream *1978*
                  - Kelron Sweet Talk at Glenalan *1980*
                    - Glenalan's Jazz Singer *1983*
                      - Glenalan Gold and Ivory *1985*
                        - Camanna Straitlaced at Lynway *tri – 1986*
                        - Camanna Chanel of Mystian *tri – 1986*
                          - Mystian Midnight Fantasy at Coarhabeg *S & W – 1990*
  - Pattingham Golden Lydia *S & W – 1953*
  - Pattingham Polka *1958*
    - **Ch. Deloraine Dinah-Mite** *S & W – 1961*
    - **Ch. Deloraine Distinctive** *S & W – 1961*
      - **Ch. Clanayre Chiffon Princess** *S & W – 1963*
    - **Ch. Deloraine Decorative** *S & W – 1961*
  - **Ch. Pattingham Lullaby** *S & W – 1953*
  - **Ch. Pattingham Prelude** *S & W – 1956*
    - **Ch. Pattingham Pheasant** *S & W – 1963*

Lima

Leyland Lima
cont. from [Roberts'] Old Lassie – family 1

- **Ch. Lyncliffe Blue Lady** *B.M. – 1940*
- Beulah's Nightblack and Beautiful *tri – 1940*
  - Beulah's Golden Kiska *S & W – 1943*
    - **Ch. Beulah's Golden Flora** *S & W – 1945*
      - Lenore of Ladypark *S & W – 1947*
        - Levity of Ladypark *1949*
          - Ladypark Cathanbrae Copyright *S & W – 1951*
            - Leonie of Ladypark *S & W – 1953*
              - Alphington White Girl *S & W – 1954*
              - **Ch. Ashcombe Annabella** *S & W – 1954*
                - Ashcombe's Airs and Graces *S & W – 1957*
    - Beulah's Golden Favorita *S & W – 1945*
  - Beulah's Nightglamorous *tri – 1944*
    - **Ch. Westcarrs Whitethroat** *S & W – 1947*
      - Westcarrs Black Ballet *tri – 1955*
        - Westcarrs What *S & W – 1958*
          - **Ch. Duntiblae Door Knocker** *S & W – 1960*
            - Duntiblae Dormouse *1965*
              - Beaublade Duntiblae Doch-n-Doris *S & W – 1966*

(Claypole's) Curzon Jess - family 2

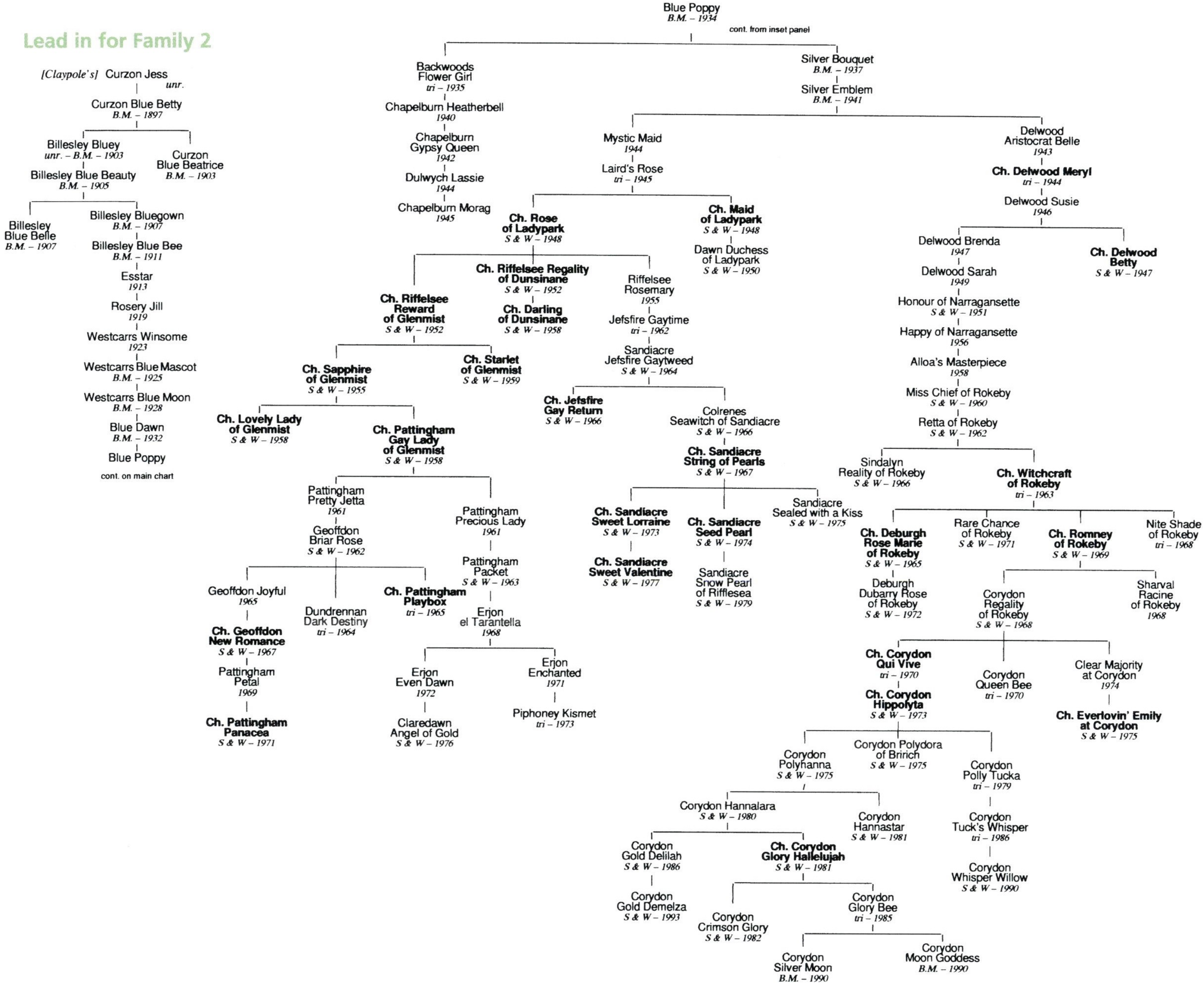

Family 2: Starts with Claypole's Curzon Jess, born about 1896. Miss Osborne never extended this important family beyond the unregistered bitch, Billesley Bluey. Archive material, loaned by the Collie Association, suggests her breeding is 'by Moreton Jason ex Curzon Blue Betty', making her a sister to Curzon Blue Beatrice and Curzon Blue Boy. As both these Collies gained their Stud Book numbers in 1904 it is possible to confirm the mating, in addition to tracing the family a further generation to the unregistered Curzon Jess. The Curzon affix appears to have been used by Mr W Claypole, who had strong ties with both Mr H E Packwood (Billesley) and Mr T W Coles, who owned the bitch Lady Curzon, in family 7. It is conceivable this bitch was both the inspiration for Mr Claypole's choice of kennel name, and the dam of Curzon Jess, possibly out of Lady Curzon's 1896 litter by Ch Metchley Wonder. It is unlikely that this will ever be confirmed but, if correct, it would both strengthen the otherwise weak family 7 and make it possible to trace family 2 to its source. The family has always been strong, including all Laird's Rose descendants, but this has now been further strengthened by the addition of Miss Chief of Rokeby's descendants which had previously been thought to fit into family 13.

(Milroy's) Florrie - family 3

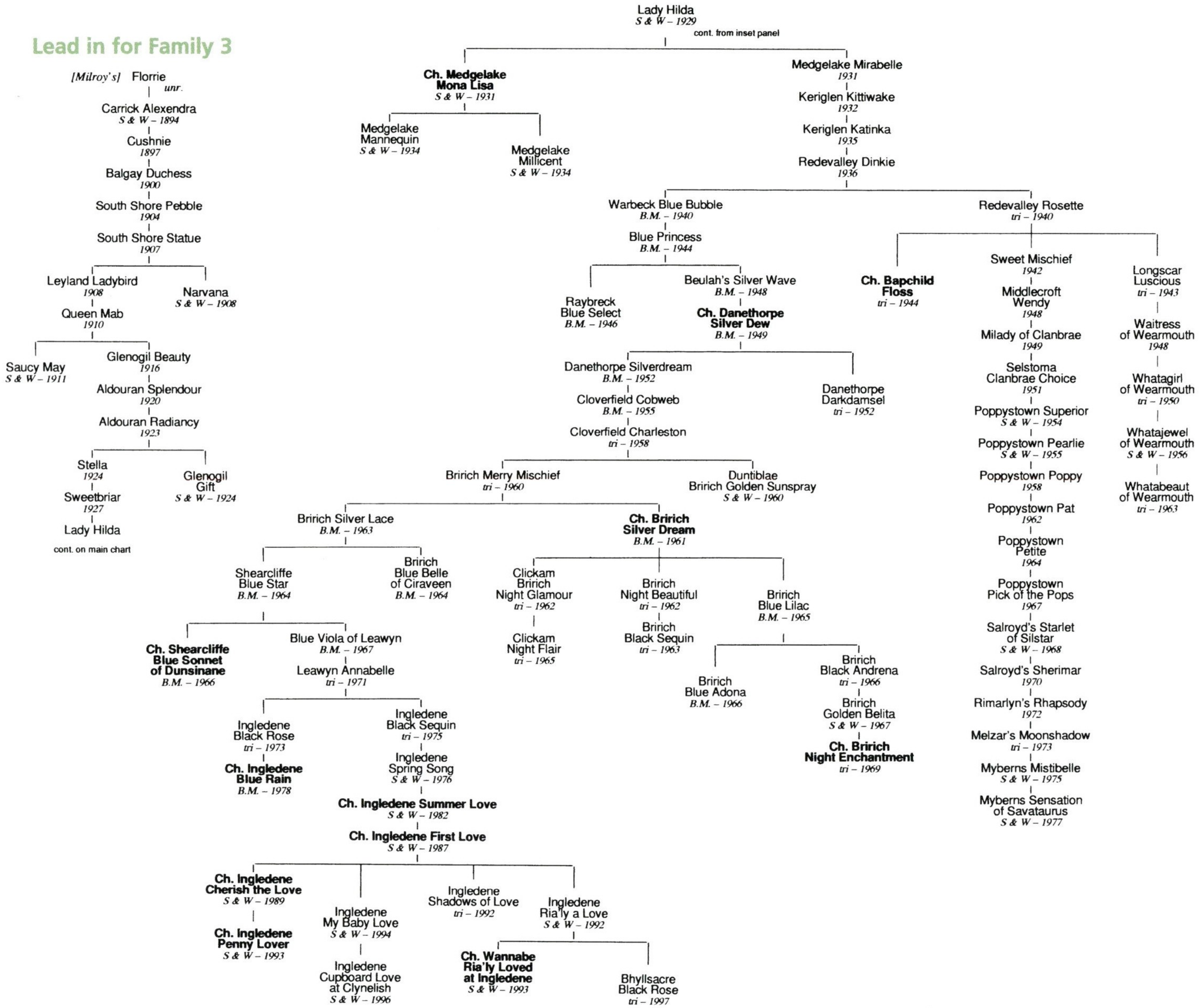

Family 3: Starts with Milroy's unregistered Florrie. The original research suggests this family started with the bitch Balgay Duchess, and this later extended through Cushine to Leila. Balgay Duchess' registration appears in the Kennel Gazette of April 1901 giving her breeding as 'by Hothfield Turk ex Cu-hine; born 17 June 1900, registered by Mr G Blake but no breeder is recorded. We now have two spelling variations for what must be the same bitch. A third spelling came to light with the registration of Panmure-Gordon's Perfection, in June 1901, obviously a litter brother to Balgay Duchess. As Perfection's registration gave the dam as Cushnie and the breeder as Mrs Panmure-Gordon, this latter spelling is now adopted because it is the one used by the bitch's owner/breeder. Cushnie was born some three years earlier, by Southport Perfection ex Carrick Alexandra, registered and bred by Mrs Panmure-Gordon. Carrick Alexandra (1449A) is out of the unregistered bitch Florrie. Leila's (family 7) recorded birth date makes it impossible for her to be Cushnie's dam, and whether Cushnie can be traced back to Leila remains a mystery. In view of her breeder's long term family interest in Collies it is just as likely that Cushnie can be traced to Mr Panmure-Gordon's Hamish III in family d.

(Baillie's) Yieldshields Beaute - family 4

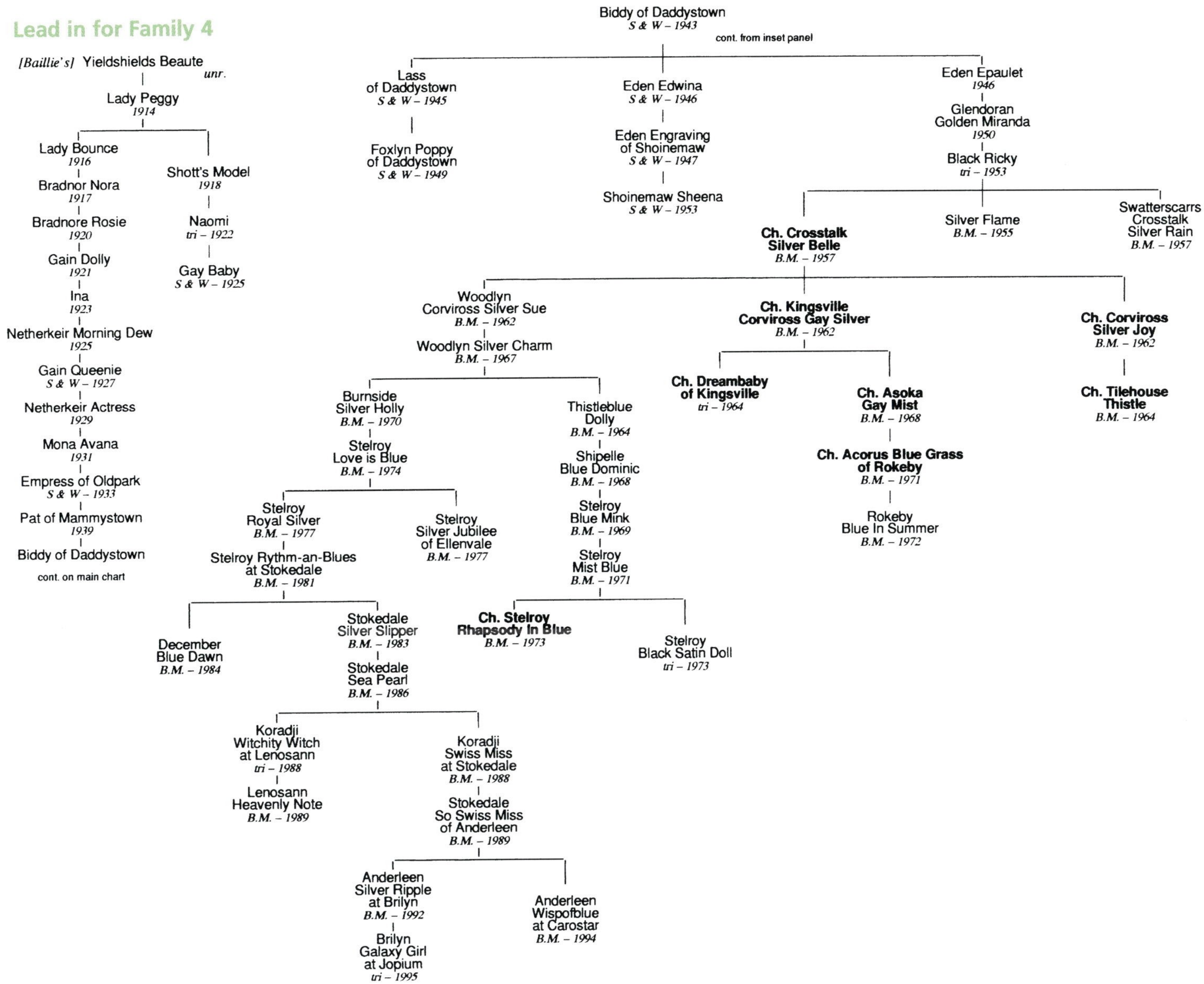

Family 4: Starts with Baillie's unregistered Yieldshields Beaute. The Yieldshields affix was used sparingly by a Mr J H Baillie, from 1905 until the beginning of the first world war and, with less than a dozen Collies registered with the name, the majority inevitably traced back to the unregistered bitch Ashgrove Kate. There is some dispute about the spelling of Beaute's name which Mr A Watt gave as Yieldshields Bute when he registered her daughter Lady Peggie. When registering stock prior to the first world war Mr Baillie always spelt it Beaute, so this form has been adopted.

(Lucas') Miss Perfection - family 6

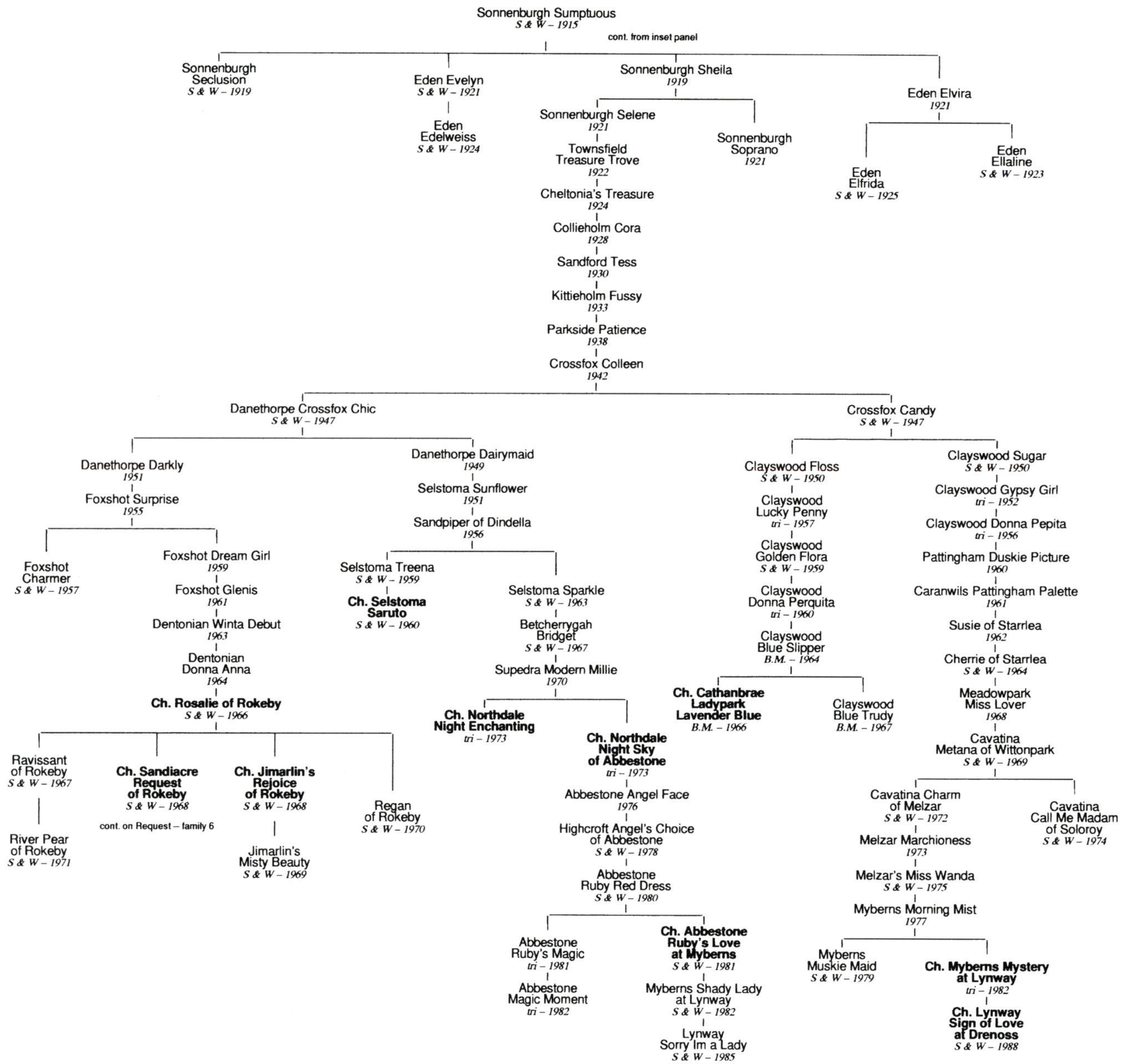

Family 6: Starts with Lucas' unregistered Miss Perfection. It is possible this bitch is out of Mera Mavoureen but no records of this bitch have been located. It should be noted, there is no spelling mistake in the name Edel Excellence – Edel was a kennel name long before Mr Rubmann/Robson chose Eden as his affix (see Eden Examine's footnote on page 53).

Lead in for Family 6

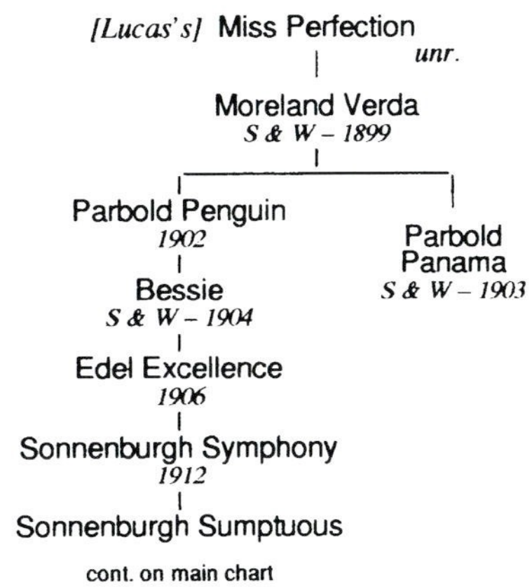

Request - family 6

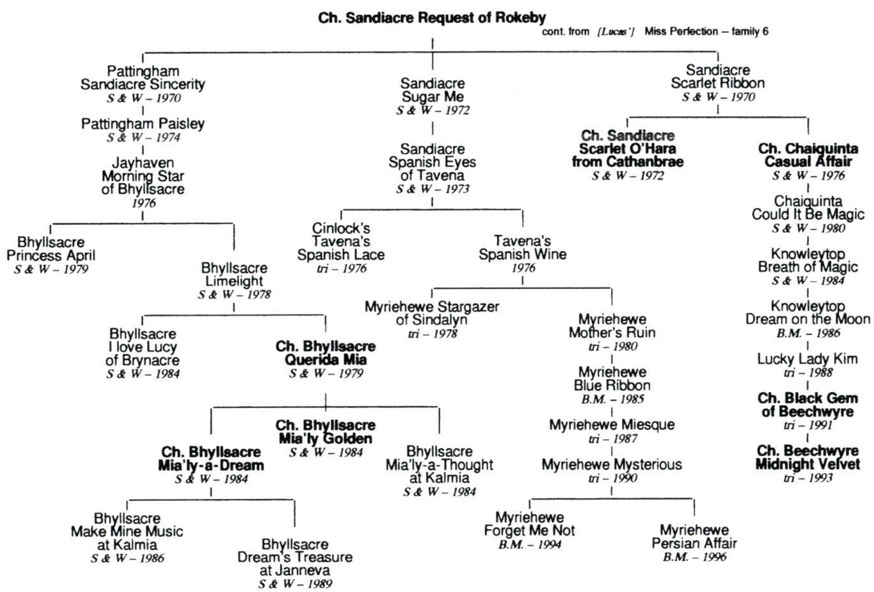

(Lamb's) Lassie - family 7

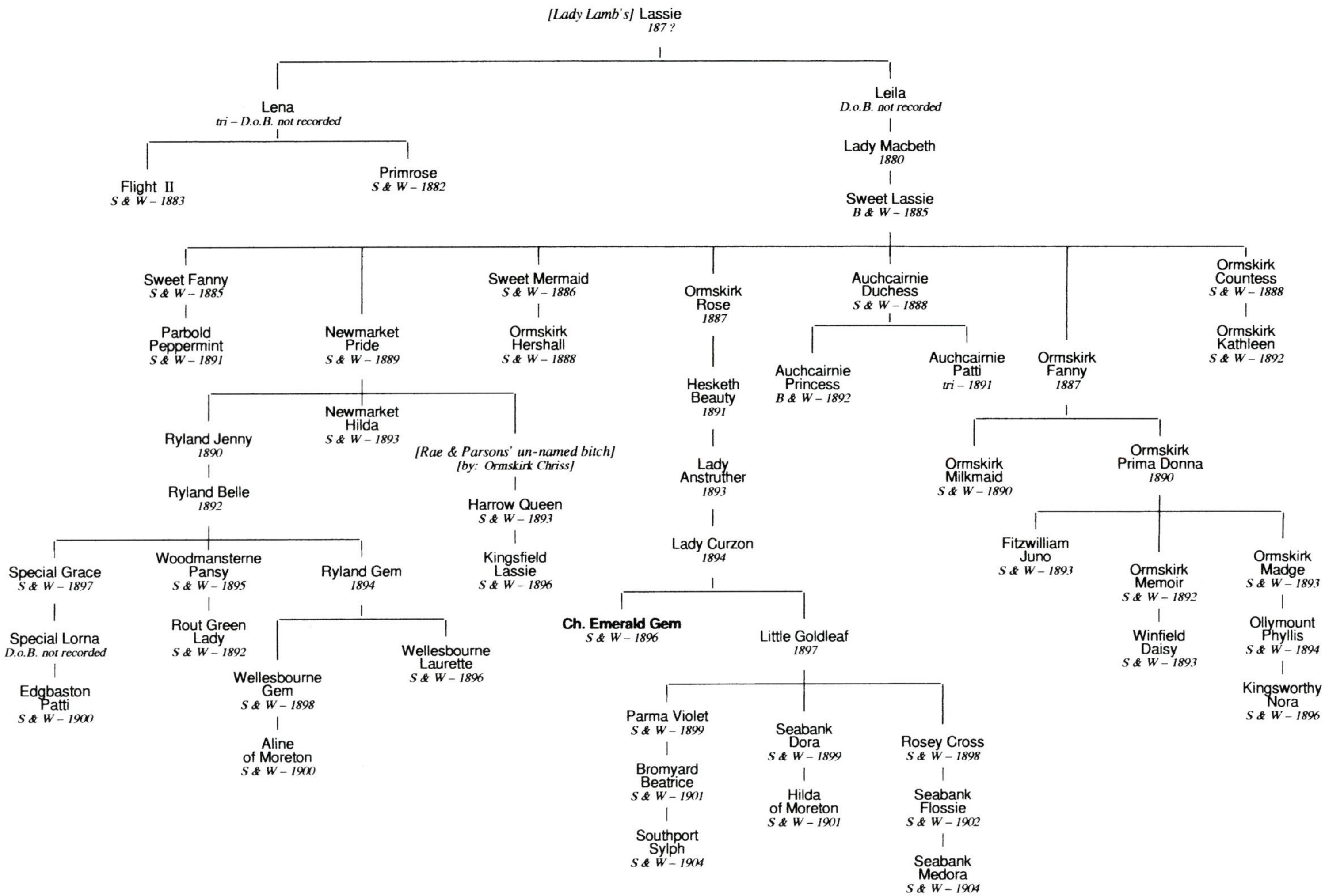

Family 7: Starting with Lady Lamb's Lassie this family was always a weak family which barely influences post-war Collies. Margaret Osborne's revised 'Lines and Families' (1965) extended the family backwards a further seven generations to the bitch Leila, dam of Lady Macbeth, who earned her Stud Book number in 1883, her registration published in the Kennel Gazette of August 1882. Neither entry records her breeder, and whilst both suggest Lady Macbeth was born in 1880 they are vague about the date, her breeding being given as by Wolf ex Leila. The Kennel Gazette of October 1880 records Lady Lamb's registration of a litter of seven Rough Collies, including bitches Leila and Lena - by Cheviot I ex Lassie, but *which* Lassie would have remained a mystery had two of Lena's daughters not gained Stud Book entry. Both Flight II and Primrose record their dam as Lena – by Cheviot I out of Lassie (5434). As Stud Book entries credit this number to the bitch Katrine (family b) it may be surmised that the dam of Lady Macbeth, and the Leila registered in late 1880, are one and the same bitch and that the dam is actually Katrine who became known as Lassie by new owners.

(Salter's) Mountshannon Mona - family 10

Lead in for Family 10

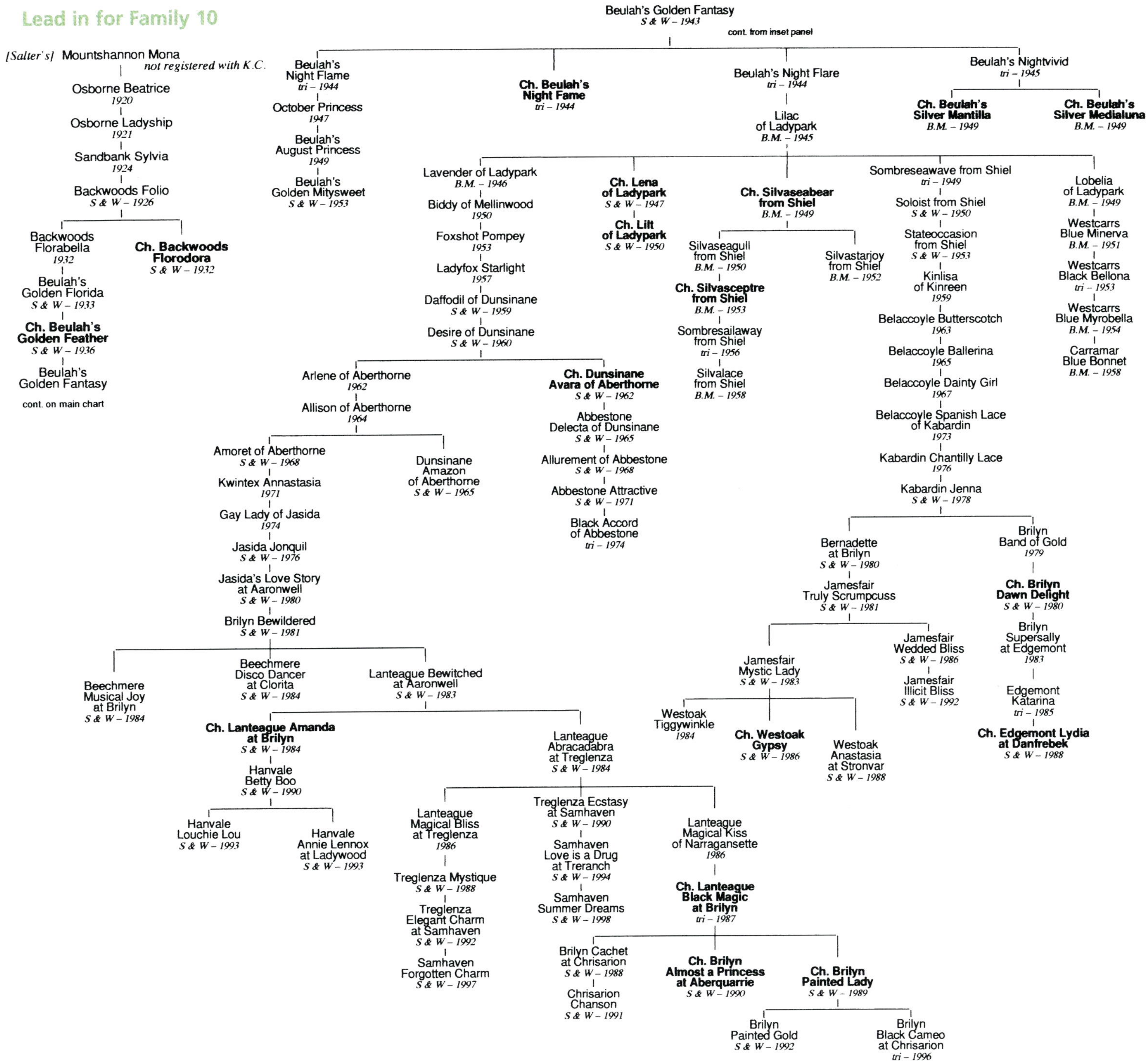

Family 10: Starts with Salter's Mountshannon Mona. The Rev T Salter was based in Ireland, which had established its independence around the time the untraceable Mountshannon Mona was born, sometime prior to 1920.

(Bell's) Stanhope Village Belle - family 13

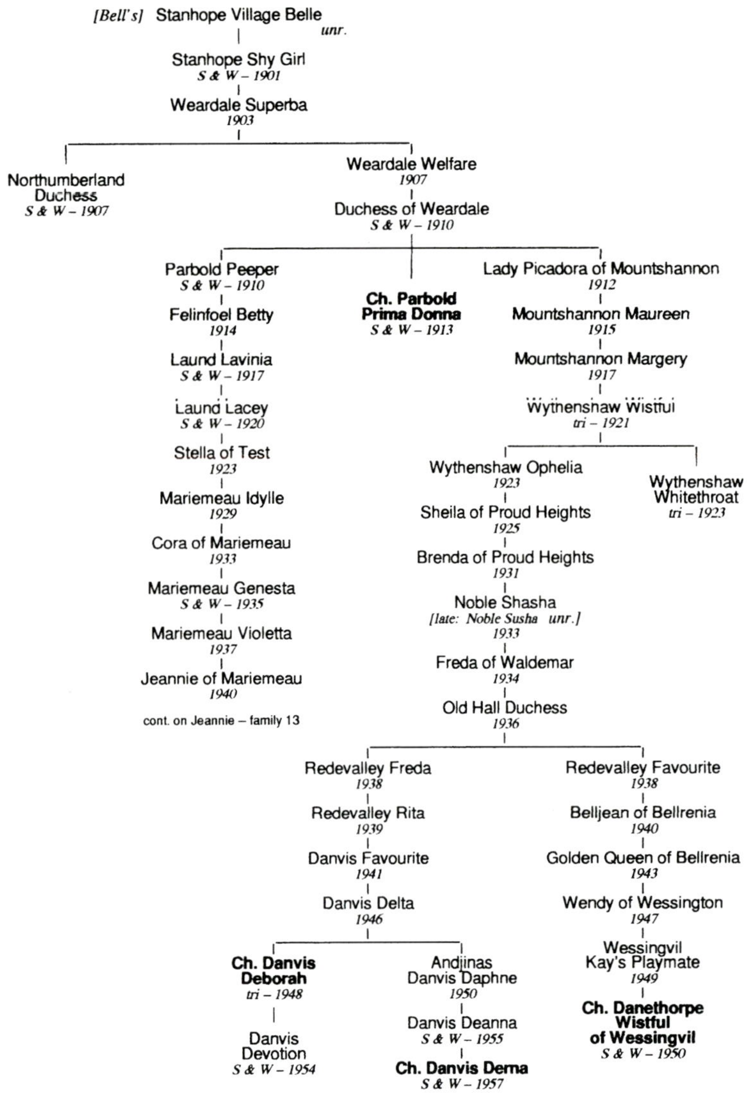

Family 13: Starts with Bell's unregistered Stanhope Village Belle, born in the last few weeks of the nineteenth century. Although the family no longer includes Ch Witchcraft of Rokeby and her descendants, as was previously thought, it has been strengthened by the inclusion of Sheila of Proud Heights and her descendants, which include many of the Redevalley and Danvis bitches.

Jeannie - family 13

Jeannie of Mariemeau
cont. from *[Bell's]* Stanhope Village Belle – family 13

- Grangefirth Biddy *1946*
  - Dorothy's Lassie *1952*
  - Bridholme Lightworth Sable Lady *S & W – 1954*
  - Selstoma Simonetta *1957*
  - Treasure of Audley *1958*
  - Dorgano Display *S & W – 1961*
  - Dorgano Darleen *S & W – 1962*
  - Truditown Dorgano Delishus *S & W – 1965*
  - Dorgano Devastate *S & W – 1967*
  - **Ch. Birich Idcam Amanda** *S & W – 1968*
    - Birich Gold Jeanette *S & W – 1972*
      - Birich Gold Pendant *S & W – 1974*
    - Birich Gold Refrain *S & W – 1975*
- Sandy of Mariemeau *1944*
  - Lassie of Courage *1946*
  - Lassie of Sudborough *1948*
  - **Ch. Sudborough Lochdorna** *S & W – 1949*
    - **Ch. Girley of Whitelea** *S & W – 1952*
    - Whitelea Watastra *tri – 1953*
      - Jefsfire Satin Sensation *S & W – 1956*
        - Jefsfire Duskie Dawn *tri – 1958*
          - **Ch. Jefsfire Joyous Jodie** *S & W – 1961*
            - Jefsfire Sheerjoy *1963*
            - Silvafox Shani *1966*
              - Silvafox Shuna *S & W – 1967*
                - Silvafox Sharla *S & W – 1971*
                  - Silvafox Sable Lady *S & W – 1972*
                  - Silvafox Sanella *1973*
                  - Sterndale Sweet Honey *S & W – 1975*
                  - Orbrie Sweet Abigail *S & W – 1976*
                    - Orbrie Angeline *S & W – 1978*
                    - Orbrie Sweet Ecstacy *S & W – 1978*
                      - Look Again of Jacabren *S & W – 1979*
                      - Jacabren Pride n'Joy *S & W – 1981*
                      - Templeview Juniper Girl at Paulador *S & W – 1983*
                      - Paulador Double Trouble of Westoak *S & W – 1987*
                        - Westoak Love-Bug *S & W – 1989*
                          - Corisian Sweet Saffron at Westoak *S & W – 1992*
                        - Westoak Angelina *S & W – 1991*
                - Silvafox Severine *S & W – 1971*
                  - **Ch. Lynaire Dancing Girl** *S & W – 1976*
                  - Lynaire Dancing Queen *S & W – 1976*
                - Silvafox Suvannah *S & W – 1968*
              - Silvafox Sweet Honey of Joywil *S & W – 1968*
              - Silvafox Serena *S & W – 1967*
                - Winrix Rosandra *S & W – 1969*
                - Winrix Brandy Snap *S & W – 1970*
                - Winrix Sweet Serenade *1976*
                - Aberhill Carousel *1977*
                  - Aberhill Prima Donna of Jasand *S & W – 1980*
                    - Jasand Tuppence Coloured *S & W – 1982*
                    - Jasand Tri Another at Sharich *tri – 1983*
                  - **Ch. Aberhill Personality Miss** *S & W – 1980*
                    - Aberhill Miss Personality of Woodwick *S & W – 1984*
                    - Aberhill Personality Plus *S & W – 1984*
                      - Aberhill Personality Madam *S & W – 1988*
                      - Aberhill Nosey But Nice *S & W – 1991*
                      - Aberhill Lady Luck at Takhisis *tri – 1995*
          - Jefsfire Melody *S & W – 1960*
            - Jefsfire Satin Symphony *S & W – 1962*
      - **Ch. Jefsfire Amberlinnet** *S & W – 1958*
        - Jefsfire Penny Black *tri – 1966*
          - Jefsfire Penny Edition *1968*
          - Altricia Crackling Rosie *S & W – 1971*
          - Altricia Over the Moon *1972*
          - Altricia Angie Babe of Geoffdon *S & W – 1976*
          - Geoffdon Joy Belle of Jayverly *S & W – 1977*
          - **Ch. Jayverly Yours Truly** *S & W – 1980*
        - Phares Golden Girl of Narragansette *S & W – 1963*
- Sirod Sirius *1946*
  - Runham Rowena *1947*
  - Sherry of Shencolne *S & W – 1951*
  - Antoc Tawny Token *S & W – 1953*
  - Antoc Tawny Lyric *S & W – 1959*
    - **Ch. Antoc Daydream** *S & W – 1963*
      - Antoc High Society *S & W – 1968*
        - Antoc Dearly Beloved *S & W – 1970*
          - Antoc Amazing Grace from Kinninvie *1971*
            - Antoc Antoinette of Soloroy *S & W – 1974*
              - **Ch. Soloroy's Saratoga Springs** *S & W – 1976*
              - Soloroy's Polly Perkins *S & W – 1977*
            - Kinninvie's Maid to Measure *1977*
              - Warjar Champagne Sparkle *1979*
              - Warjar Bubbles Galore *1981*
              - Warjar Diamond Dream *1982*
              - Warjar Hollyberry of Amalie *S & W – 1985*
                - Blossoms Black at Amalie *tri – 1987*
                  - Amalie Black Penny at Lewarne *tri – 1992*
                - Blackberry at Gayan with Rhodabern *1987*
                  - Gayan Irresistable to Amalie *S & W – 1989*
                  - Gayan Justa Sweet As Sugar at Rhodabern *S & W – 1989*
                    - Rhodabern Brown Sugar *S & W – 1990*
        - **Ch. Antoc April Love** *S & W – 1973*
        - Antoc Midnight Martini *tri – 1973*
          - Rubec Snow Flower *B.M. – 1977*
    - Antoc Rose Marie *S & W – 1961*

(Birkett & Walling's) Kendal/Lancaster - family 14

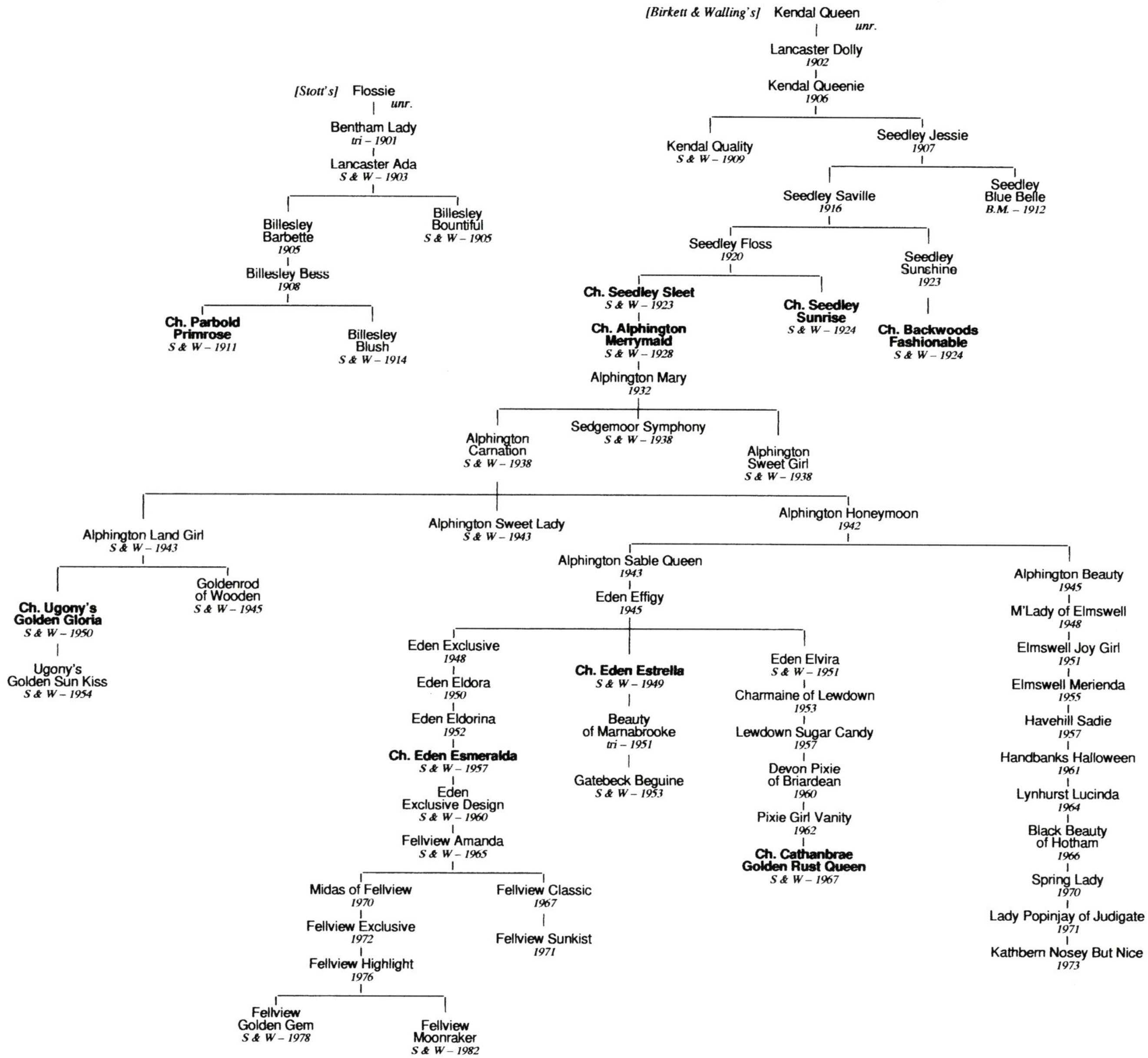

Family 14: Starts with the interchangeable Kendal and Lancaster Kennels of Walling and Birkett. Margaret Osborne originally started this family with Lancaster Ada who became an American Champion, and the family was later extended through Bentham Lady, Flossie, and Sweet Blossom to Leila (family 7). Recent research confirms Lancaster Ada's dam as Bentham Lady (Lancaster Victor ex Flossie), but it is impossible to trace the line further as Flossie was an unregistered bitch owned by Mr S Scott. However this information becomes academic as the family's influence traces through Lancaster Dolly, who was originally believed to be out of Lancaster Ada, but as Ada is younger than Dolly by some eight months, this is impossible. Lancaster Dolly's registration, published in the Kennel Gazette of June 1903, records her breeding as by Lancaster Rex ex Kendal Queen. Kendal Queen's breeding remains elusive. Surprisingly the family's principal influence comes through Seedley Jessie and her daughter Seedley Saville, who was originally considered to be out of Seedley Splash, putting her erroneously into family 1.

Lead in for Family 15

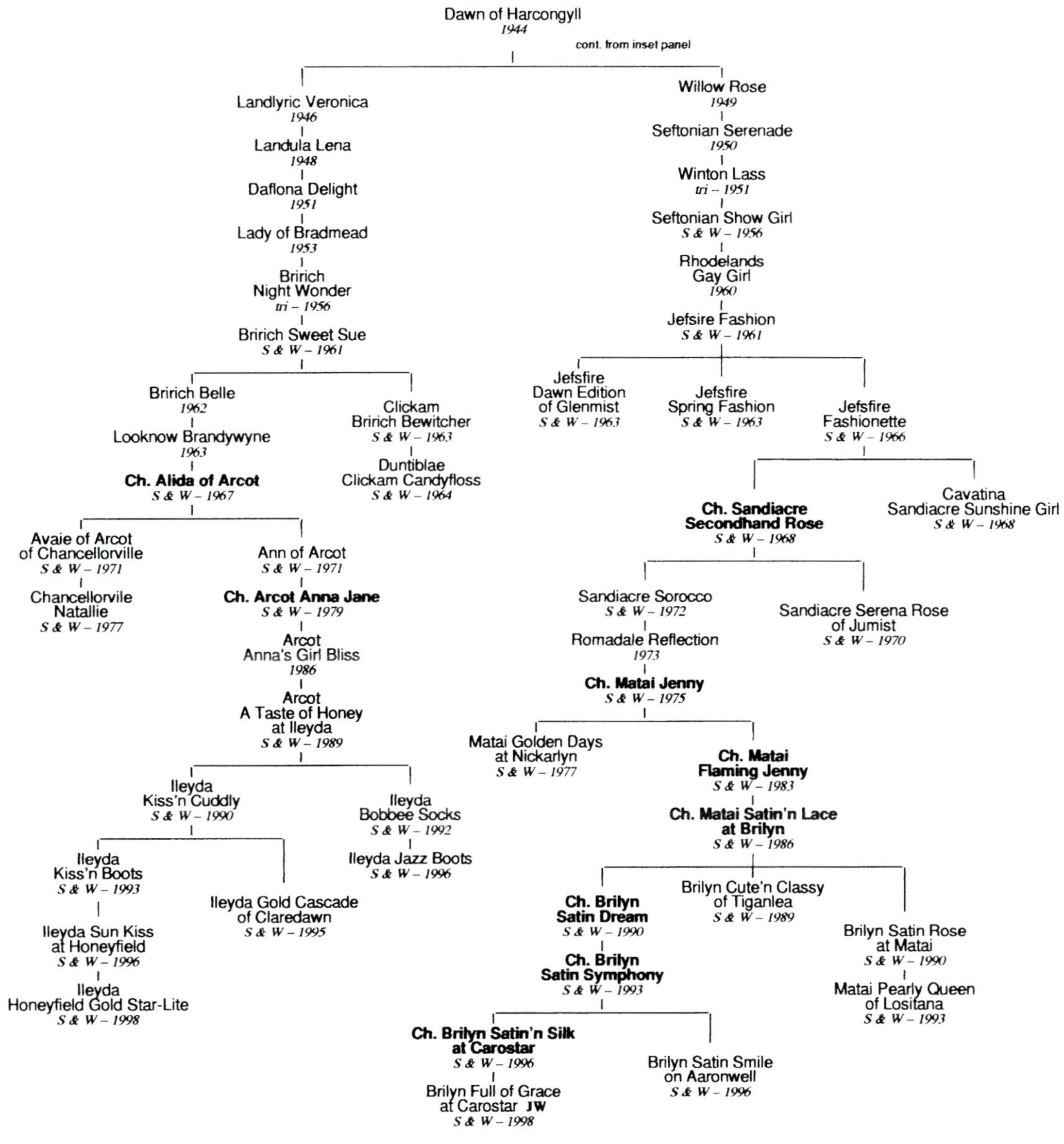

Family 15: Starts with Yellow Primrose, one of two families emerging in the early 1960's. Recent research has transferred Jefsfire Fashion and her many descendants from Seedley Lassie (family 16), whilst Bririch Sweet Sue and her descendants have been moved from family 2 thereby strengthening what had originally been considered to be a weak family.

(Lord's) Seedley Lassie - family 16

Lead in for Family 16

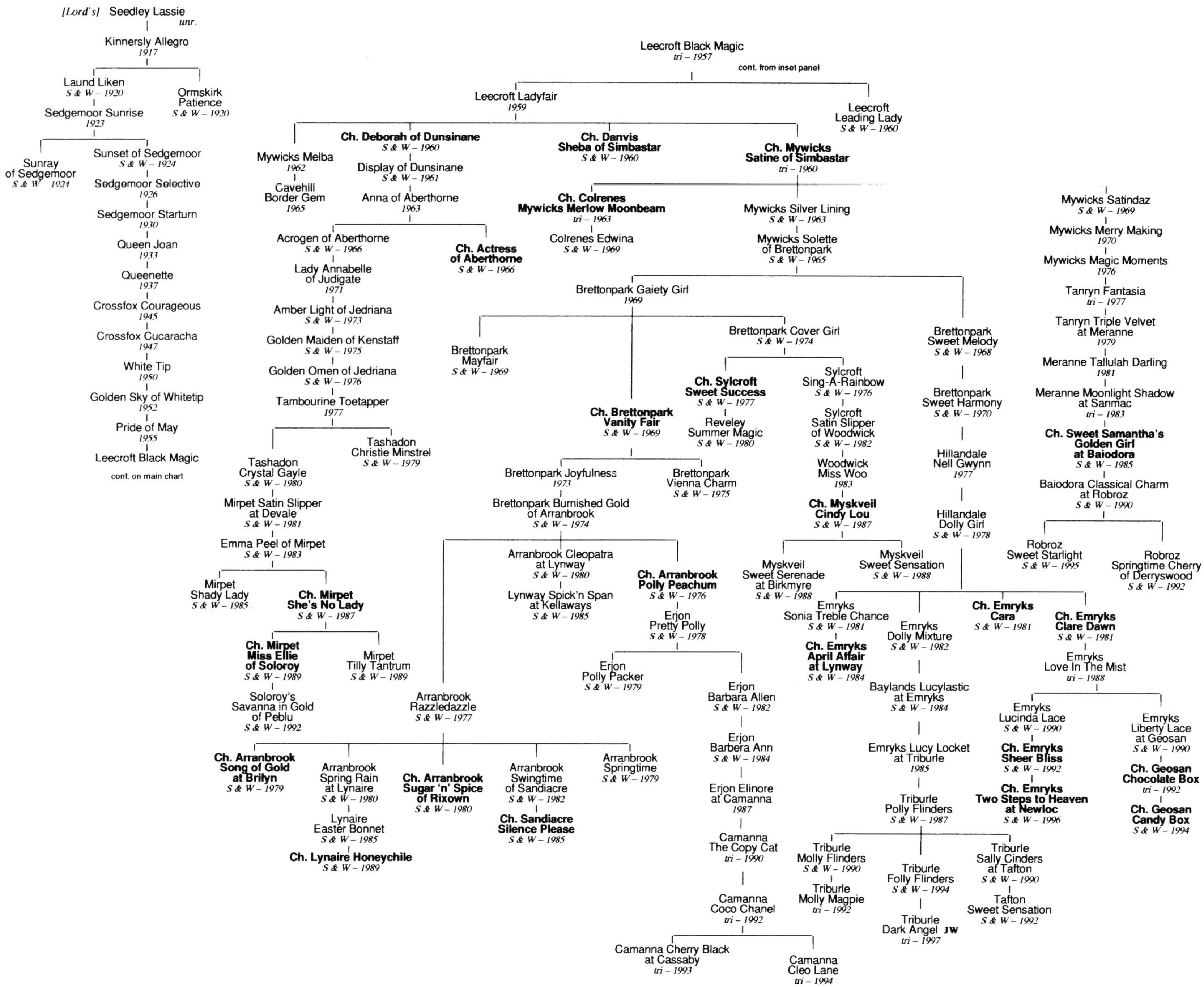

Family 16: Starting with Lord's unregistered Seedley Lassie this family first came to prominence with Champion litter sisters Danvis Sheba and Mywicks Satine, both of Simbastar, plus Deborah of Dunsinane.

APPENDIX III - Discussion on Rough Collie Breed Standards

When dogs first appeared in the show ring and were admired for their beauty rather than their working capabilities, guidelines were required by which breeders and exhibitors could recognise and evaluate

the qualities of specific breeds, as well as different types within the same breed. These guidelines formed a 'blue print' known as Breed Standards.

In 1881 the committee of the Collie Club drew up the inaugural Breed Standard for Rough and Smooth Collies, stating the essential features and qualities which distinguished them from all other breeds.

Besides describing the various anatomical aspects, a Scale of Points identifying the relative value given to each feature was also included to enable judges to evaluate the dogs more easily. The Scale of Points remained incorporated into the Standard until the Kennel Club took over the responsibility for Breed Standards in 1950, when it was removed as it was believed to encourage 'fault judging'.

The Breed Standard has been amended several times over the years, the first revision being in October 1898 when the Collie Club adopted a revised version of the Scottish Collie Club's Standard, which had been in existence for four years. Subsequent revisions were made in 1910, 1950, and 1969, the current version coming into operation in 1988 when the Kennel Club unified all Breed Standards and the Collie (Rough) and Collie (Smooth) were allocated separate Standards for the first time. Amendments must be approved by the Kennel Club, following a majority decision of Rough Collie Breed Council delegates representing the fourteen UK member Breed Clubs.

As a matter of interest, and to enable comparisons to be made between the various versions of the Breed Standard, the original version of 1881 is included here:

1881 The Collie Club's Standard and Scale of Points

"The SKULL: of the Collie should be quite flat and rather broad, with fine tapering muzzle of fair length, and mouth the least bit overshot; the EYES widely apart, almond shaped and obliquely set in the head; the skin of the head tightly drawn, with no folds at the corners of the mouth; the EARS as small as possible, semi-erect when surprised or listening, at other times thrown back and buried in the 'ruff'.

The NECK: should be long, arched and muscular; the SHOULDERS also long, sloping, and fine at withers; the CHEST to be deep and narrow at the front, but of fair breadth behind the shoulders.

The BACK; to be short and level, with the loin rather long, somewhat arched and powerful.

"BRUSH long, "wi' upward swirl"at the end and normally carried low.

The FORELEGS: should be perfectly straight with fair amount of flat bone; the pasterns rather long, springy and slightly lighter of bone than the rest of the leg; the FOOT with toes well arched and compact, soles very thick.

The HINDQUARTERS drooping slightly, should be very long from the hip bones to the hocks, which should be neither turned inwards, nor outwards, with stifles well bent. The hip bones should be wide and rather ragged.

The COAT: except on the legs and head, should be as abundant as possible; the outer coat straight, hard and rather stiff; the under coat furry and so dense that it would be difficult to find the skin. The 'ruff' and 'frill' especially should be very full. There should be but little 'feather' on the forelegs and none below the hocks on the hindlegs.

COLOUR: Immaterial.

SYMMETRY; The dog should be a fair length on the leg and his movements wiry and graceful. He should not be too small; height of dogs from 22in to 24in, of bitches from 20 in to 22in.

The Greyhound type is very objectionable, as there is no brain room in the skull and with this there are to be found a fatuous expression and a long, powerful jaw.

The Setter type is also to be avoided, with its pendulous ears, full soft eye, heavily-feathered legs and straight short flag.

The SMOOTH COLLIE only differs from the Rough in its coat, which should be hard, dense and quite smooth.

Scale of Points:		***Grand Total 100 points***	
Head and Expression	*15*	*Back and Loins*	*10*
Ears	*10*	*Brush*	*5*
Neck and Shoulders	*10*	*Coat with frill*	*20*
Legs and Feet	*15*	*Size*	*5*
Hindquarters	*10*		

In the 1888 edition of 'The Collie: Its History, Points and Breeding', Hugh Dalziel comments on this Standard as follows:

"I have few comments to make on the description of the Club, but will briefly point out where I differ from it. I consider the Club wrong in saying the eyes are set widely apart. If that were so they would not be in the position required by the dog, who has to look far and straight before him, and if wide apart he could not well do that. The form, too – "almond-shaped" – appears to me more fanciful and poetic than correct; and what almond had the Club in its eye when this description was agreed to; a Barbary, a Valencia, or a Jordan almond? – the three differ very greatly in shape. The ear is not constantly "thrown back and buried in the ruff" when it is not erect. In perfect repose the ear drops or falls down. The Collie is not short in the back. If so, he would be altogether a short dog, measured from nose to tail, or otherwise a deformity. He is a lengthy dog, and not shaped like a builder's trestle, with head and tail added. Many show dogs look short because they are overloaded with flesh, and the coat is cultivated and brushed and dressed to show its immense bulk. I do not know what is meant by the hip-bones being ragged. No Collie should be ragged anywhere, according to my idea of a good specimen. I fail to see the connection between a "fatuous" expression and a "long, powerful jaw". Terrier men demand in some varieties of their pets "a long, powerful jaw," and I must leave it to them to say whether such Terriers are feeble-minded and stupid curs. The note expressive of the opinion of the Club respecting judging by points, following on the heels of the scale of points, is the most "fatuous" expression I ever read. If the figures show comparative value of the different properties, why not use them for that purpose? and if they do not, why give them?"

It is interesting to note that 20 points from a total of 100 was allotted to 'coat with frill', whereas only 15 was awarded to 'head and expression'. Whilst Collie expression is deemed of great importance today, initially no guidelines were included in the description of the 'skull'. In the Scottish Collie Club's Standard of 1885 expression was only superficially covered under 'Eyes' with the statement *".....which gives that foxy expression so characteristic of the breed."* The 1898 revised version of the Scottish Standard makes more specific reference to expression as follows: *"Eyes: are a very important feature and give expression to the dog; .....expression full of intelligence, with a quick alert look when listening."*

In the first few versions of the Breed Standard colour was classified as either '*immaterial*' or '*any colour*' and, despite colour still being classified as 'immaterial', the 1910 version states *"a nice showily marked dog is preferred. All white or Red Setter colour is most objectionable."* These references remained in existence for forty years and were finally deleted from the official Standard in 1950. It was not until the 1969 version that a description of the three acceptable colours - sable and white, tricolour and blue merle - was included together with reference to the Collie's characteristic white markings.

Interestingly height variations have remained consistent whereas weight variations, originally introduced in the 1885 Scottish Standard stating *"45 – 60lb. for dogs and 40 – 50lb. for bitches"*, were increased by 5lb in the 1898 revised Standard and remained until 1988 when all reference to weight was omitted.

Under the sub-headings 'Symmetry' or 'General Appearance', Collie characteristics have been referred to in varying ways and to varying degrees. In the 1881 Standard, under 'Symmetry', the Collie *"should be a fair length on the leg and his movements wiry and graceful."* The Scottish version, under 'General Appearance', stated *"A lithe, active dog, with no useless timber about him, his deep chest showing strength, his sloping shoulders and well bent hocks speed, his 'bawsint'*[1] *face high intelligence. The face should bear a sharp, doubtful expression. As a whole, he should present an elegant and pleasing outline, quite distinct from any other domesticated breeds, and show great strength and activity."* The revised Scottish Standard referred to the Collie as a *"lithe, active dog, his deep chest showing lung power .... He should be a fair length on the leg, giving him more of a racy than a cloddy appearance. In a few words a Collie should show endurance, activity and intelligence, with free and true action."*

It was not until 1910 that reference was first made to the original purpose of the breed as follows *"To enable the Collie to fulfill his natural bent for sheepdog work .... free from cloddiness, without any trace of coarseness."* Unfortunately the current Standard, revised in 1988, has all reference to working abilities omitted whereas this clause still remains an important part of the Smooth Collie Standard.

All the early Standards refer, to a greater or lesser extent, to faults and many breeders feel that these should still be included although it can be argued that to do so encourages 'fault judging'. Under 'faults' the 1881 Standard refers only to *"Greyhound and Setter types"* as being objectionable, whereas subsequent versions cover an increasing number of faults with the 1969 version providing a comprehensive list. The current Breed Standard only covers faults with a rather sweeping statement *"Any departures from the foregoing points should be considered a fault and the seriousness with which the fault is regarded should be in exact proportion to its degree."* This Standard includes, for the first time, a reference to male dogs having two *"normal testicles fully descended into the scrotum."*

Footnotes:

1. *'Bawsint' is a poetic expression of Robbie Burns meaning a white blaze on the head, which gives an intelligent appearance! A white blaze is not a fault and is referred to in the 1988 Standard as "A white blaze may be carried on muzzle, skull or both." However it is not popular with breeders as many feel it gives the animal a common look and, unless it is symmetrically and centrally positioned, it detracts the judge's eye from the overall balance of the head.*
2. *For details of all versions of the Breed Standards please refer to:*
   London Collie Club's Handbook, 1992 - Frank Mitchell
   International Collie Handbook, 1998 - Dareen Bridge/Mary Farnes.
   For a copy of the current Breed Standard apply to the Kennel Club.

APPENDIX IV - The Junior Warrant

Love it or hate it, the **JUNIOR WARRANT** has been with us for over sixty years. It was originally introduced in the late 1930's with the intention of acknowledging those young dogs showing exceptional promise. From the outset a points system was selected and dogs between the ages of six and eighteen months had to achieve a minimum of twenty-five points to claim the award. One point was awarded for wins in breed classes at Open and Championship Shows with no Challenge Certificates on offer, and three points were allotted at Championship Shows with Challenge Certificates. An unusual feature of the Junior Warrant was the requirement for the dog's owner to claim the award from the Kennel Club, listing all Shows where points were gained. It is believed the first dog to win its J.W. was the tricolour Rough Collie, Eden Diadem, who became a Champion in 1938 before being exported to the Bellhaven Kennels in the United States of America where he also gained his American title.

It is probable that the Kennel Club never intended this award to be anything other than a transitionary one for, although recipients were published in the Kennel Gazette, no permanent record was included in the Stud Books until 1959. Even then they proved of short duration being discontinued in 1966 and not being re-introduced until 1971. Furthermore no rules governing the granting of the Junior Warrant appear to have been documented by the Kennel Club until further amendments were made in 1990.

Many established Kennel owners appeared unconcerned over the Junior Warrant as there is no acknowledgement of the award in the Collie Association's Handbook of 1952. This apathy continued for a further fifteen years until a single winner was advertised in the Yorkshire Collie Club's Handbook of 1967.

Little interest appears to have been generated until the late 1970's when two factors combined to alter the canine world in several ways. The previous decade saw a hasty decline in the larger, professional kennel, and this vacuum was filled with an influx of hobby exhibitors with differing attitudes to, and expectations of, the show scene. This was further exacerbated by the decline in Members' Limited and Sanction Shows which were replaced with large, multi-classed Open Shows scheduling several breed classes. This trend gained momentum during the eighties, with many owners advertising the rather meaningless title of 'Junior Warrant' after their dog's name.

With mounting concern over the concentration of showing that some puppies were expected to endure, the Kennel Club re-appraised the Junior Warrant award. The results were superficial, the only real change being a reduction of the period in which points could be earned. At this stage a Junior Warrant could only be claimed from wins gained by dogs between the ages of twelve and eighteen months. This amendment proved most unpopular because it seriously restricted the opportunities for coated breeds to achieve this accolade.

With the approach of the Millennium the Kennel Club set up a working party to review canine activities and one aspect included a significant enhancement to the importance of the Junior Warrant. These changes were introduced on 1st October 1997 and, for the first time in its history, the title of Junior Warrant gained official recognition. The award is now bestowed on dogs, between the age of six and eighteen months of age, which gain a minimum of twenty-five points, and upon application to the Kennel Club by the dog's owner. Points continue to be allocated to breed class wins as before but must now be gained from a combination of both Championship and Open Shows, with a minimum of twelve points gained at each type of Show. Furthermore it is only possible to claim from one show per day, and there must be three clear days between qualifying Shows. In addition, points can no longer be included from wins in classes where less than three dogs are present. These requirements mean that it is no longer possible for a dog to gain the award within the space of a few days, as has happened in the past.

Dogs gaining their Junior Warrant are now entitled to add the suffix JW to their names on all occasions, including show entries and advertisements. In addition JW holders gain automatic entry to the Kennel Club Stud Book, being issued with a Stud Number, therefore entitling them to permanent qualification for Crufts Dog Show.

APPENDIX V - The Kennel Club Stud Book

The Kennel Club's inaugural Stud Book was introduced to the public at the Birmingham Dog Show Society's National Exhibition, held between the 1st and 4th December 1874. Its contents included placed dogs at all shows held up to the end of 1873, with Rough Collies incorporated into Class XXV-Sheep Dogs and Scotch Collies. The second volume, issued one year later, was a more sophisticated publication with the sheep dog entry split into Rough and Smooth coats as well as by sex. Entry details in these early publications, compiled from old catalogues or by appeals to owners, were limited and of the seventy-seven sheep dog entries in the first volume only eleven record sire and dam, plus a further three providing extended breeding details.

In an effort to overcome these difficulties the Kennel Club introduced its 'Registry of Pedigree Dogs' in 1880. From this date owners were required to furnish a full description of all dogs they intended to show at licensed events, these details being published in the following month's Kennel Gazette.

Volume VIII of the Stud Book was the first to be compiled from records held by the Kennel Club, and gradually the information supplied became both more extensive and of greater value as a source of reference. Always dated for the year of its issue, it covered Shows and their winners for the preceding year, continuing to include every placed dog at all shows for a further fifteen years, thereby allowing today's researchers to verify or refute the exaggerated claims of the early fanciers.

As the Kennel Club's Silver Jubilee approached, a general appraisal of canine matters was undertaken, and 1896 saw the introduction of the Championship Show. Stud Book entries were then confined to those dogs awarded first to third in Limit or Open classes, in addition to those gaining the newly introduced Challenge Prize or Certificate at shows where such prizes were on offer for the breed. Volume XXIV introduced a system of annual numbering, each year's numbers bearing a suffix letter. A further refinement was the issuing of Stud Book Numbers as they were gained, rather than at the time Stud Book entries were compiled. Curtailment of breeding details to sire and dam was more surprising, but obviously this practise did not find favour, for extended pedigrees were reintroduced two years later. However, comprehensive entries were limited to registered ancestors, unregistered ones being designated *unr.* for the first time.

Almost from the Kennel Club's inception it had been possible to purchase a Stud Book entry for either the offspring of, or sire or dam of, any animal having won its way into the Stud Book. The introduction of restricted entries encouraged many serious breeders to take advantage of this facility, and the Stud Books of the early twentieth century contain countless such entries. Often these would be for important brood bitches whose achievements would be commemorated after their breeding worth had been assessed.

Apart from minor presentational alterations, such as the inclusion of Reserve Best of Sex, now referred to as Reserve Challenge Certificate or RCC, in the list of qualifying awards, few amendments were made either to the Stud Book or Kennel Gazette's registration of entries until February 1970 when the decision was taken to publish details in an independent periodical to be named the 'Breed Record Supplement to the Stud Book' (BRS) Today this is divided into groups and circulated quarterly, each issue listing all registrations, transfers, change of name, export pedigrees issued, awards etc in addition to the results of various health schemes received during the previous three month period.

The next change came as the Kennel Club completed its first centenary, when both the privilege of purchasing Stud Book entry, and the registering of stock from unregistered parents was withdrawn.

The latest amendment to Stud Book entry entitlement has proved significant. In 1992, with many voicing concerns over the ease in which the numerically smaller breeds could earn Stud Book entry, the Kennel Club proposed a system of differential qualification. For the first time the number of entries each breed attracted to its allocation of Championship Shows would determine the number of dogs eligible for Stud Book qualification. In all cases Challenge Certificate and Reserve Challenge Certificate winners would qualify, and since the end of 1997 Junior Warrant winners have been added. For class eligibility, however, breeds were to be divided into five bands ranging from 'A', which limits Stud Book entry to dogs winning 1st in the Open class, to 'E' which permits Stud Book entry to those placed first to third in both Limit and Open classes. Popular breeds like the Rough Collie, which draw large entries, are included in the latter band.

The Kennel Club Stud Books and Breed Record Supplements afford the serious breeder and researcher unique insights into a breed's development, from its original purpose to the role of show dog.

APPENDIX VI - The Development of Championship Entitlement

It was customary for early show organisers to set their own rules and classification. Frequently, in the stronger breeds, a Champions class would be scheduled and the prefix 'Champion' added to the winning dog's name at the whim of the owner.

In 1877, four years after the Kennel Club's formation, its committee stipulated that no title could be claimed until a dog had won three first prizes in a 'Champions' class. Three years later it became a requirement that a dog had first to qualify for a 'Champions' class, by winning three first prizes, and then to subsequently win a first in the 'Champions' class.

By 1885 the number of shows were rapidly increasing and qualifications for Champion entitlement required further amendment. Before a dog could claim the title of Champion it must win four first prizes to qualify for entry to a 'Champions' class, plus three wins from 'Champions' classes, one of which had to be gained at a show run by the Kennel Club or the Birmingham Dog Show Society. In this same year the 'Champions' class became known as the 'Challenge' class. This change of name caused confusion, not only among exhibitors at the time, but also among breed historians. Subsequent amendments enabled only Open class winners to qualify for entry to a 'Challenge' class.

In 1889 a two-tier system was introduced with wins at larger Shows counting as two points and others only one. To gain a title at this stage required a dog to win ten points before it was eligible to enter a 'Challenge' class and subsequently win six points from a 'Challenge' class, two of which had to be gained at a Premier Show.

Four years later, in 1893, the Kennel Club announced that selected shows would be granted Championship status and a Championship prize awarded to the Best of Breed. Once the dog had won three such prizes it earned the title of Champion. Apart from subsequent minor amendments, such as the renaming of the Championship Prize to the Challenge Certificate in 1902 and the announcement in 1920 that a Challenge Certificate would be awarded to the best of each sex, this is similar to the current system.

Currently, Challenge Certificates are automatically allocated to eligible breeds at the four representative Shows, that is Crufts, Birmingham Dog Show Society, and the Scottish and Welsh Kennel Club Shows. At the discretion of the Kennel Club, Challenge Certificates are allocated to specialist and general Show Societies, conditional upon them running previous events satisfactorily. They are awarded to the Best of Sex, providing the judge is of the opinion that the exhibit is 'worthy of the title of Champion'. To become a Champion a dog must win three Challenge Certificates, from three different judges, at least one of which must be won when the dog is over twelve months of age.

APPENDIX VII - Mr Sewallis Evelyn Shirley MP JP

Where it all began.......

Left: Mr Sewallis Evelyn Shirley MP JP, founder member of the Kennel Club and the first Collie Club.

Right: Lough Fea - Mr Shirley's Irish residence and the birth-place of Shamrock (1870) and Trefoil (1873).

Mr Sewallis Evelyn Shirley MP JP lived at Ettington Park, near Stratford-upon-Avon. His family owned a large Estate at Lough Fea near Carrickmacross in Ireland, and between 1868 and 1880 he was Member of Parliament for County Monaghan.

Mr Shirley's canine activities took up most of his leisure time and he was especially interested in Field Sports. On the death of his father, he took over the management of the 'Shirley Retrievers', a strain developed by his father that we know today as the Flatcoated Retriever. He was also very interested in the Collie breeds and owned and worked both Shamrock and Trefoil, the two dogs that all show Rough Collies descend from. In 1873 he became a founder member of the Kennel Club, and in 1880 helped establish the first Collie Club.

Whilst researching for an earlier book, " Herding Dogs - Their Origins and Development in Britain", Iris Combe corresponded with Mr Sewallis Evelyn Shirley's grandson, Major John Shirley, who provided the following profile of his grandfather:

"Mr S E Shirley   Born 1844   Died 1904

He lived at the family seat at Ettington Park, Stratford-upon-Avon, Warwickshire, and made frequent visits to the Irish Estate at Lough Fea, Carrickmacross, Co. Monaghan. He was an MP for the County of Monaghan from 1868-80.

He was always a great lover of dogs, and fond of all country pursuits, being a fine horseman, an excellent game shot and owned and hunted a pack of harriers in Ireland.

From an early age, he was not only a successful exhibitor, but also a very successful breeder of dogs. At one time he possessed the best kennel of small size bull terriers ever got together, but from 1874 he gave up exhibiting this breed of dogs.He also had for many years a very valuable breed of collies and his kennel took a very high position amongst the collied breed.

Apart from the flat coated retrievers, or Shirley Retrievers as they are still sometimes called to this day, his greatest service to the dog world has undoubtedly been the establishment of the Kennel Club.

Before the formation of the Club, he and a few others took keen interest in promoting the yearly dog shows at the Crystal Palace. There was no regular organisation, but a committee was appointed on each occasion to run the show. The first show was a heavy failure, the second was a loss but not so bad and in the end, seeing the inconvenience of organising a fresh Committee each year, conceived the idea of forming the Kennel Club. This could take in hand the organisation of the dog world so as to make exhibiting possible for all classes, to stamp out fraud, and generally to raise the tone all round. The Kennel Club was therefore started and held its first show at the Crystal Palace in June 1873.

It can be noted he was only 29 years of age then. In view of his early death, at the age of 60, in 1904 and the move to permanent residence in County Monaghan of his wife and children, the kennels at Ettington were not kept up and in due course the flat coated retrievers made way for black, and subsequently yellow, labradors as the sporting dogs of the Shirley family.

However, the splendid picture of him in his Kennel Club uniform and flat coated retriever by his side, painted by Stuart Wortly and presented to him by the Kennel Club, still hangs in Lough Fea.

J.E.S."

Appendix VIII - Champion Rutland (1882)

During the course of research the editors were loaned these two additional pictures of Champion Rutland which have been included here for readers' interest (see profile of Champion Rutland, page 24).

Watercolour by R H Moore from the 'Stock Keeper' Portrait collection. Note the incorrect Stud Book number, which should read 13894.

Reproduced by kind permission of Derek Smith/Anthony McKenna

Champion Rutland and an unknown sable, from an oil painting by John Emms, dated between 1880 and 1890.

Reproduced by kind permission of the Hamshere Gallery

John Hamshere, a London art dealer specialising in canine art, kindly provided this photograph of a portrait of Champion Rutland and an unknown sable, by John Emms, dated between 1880 and 1890. The sable Collie was originally considered to be Rutland's sire, Champion Wolf, but on closer examination of the Arthur Wardle portrait of Wolf (see page 9) he differs from this Emms sable with regard to his white feet and ankle markings. The dog is obviously related to Wolf and Rutland as they share similar head patterns, all having snipey muzzles, rounded eyes and wide set ears. It is believed that the sable dog was a son of Rutland, possibly Brighton (Breeder/owner Boddington) or Vulcan (Breeder/owner Megson). At some stage in Rutland's life he was owned by both Mr Boddington and Mr Megson, successful and wealthy businessmen either of whom could have known the artist John Emms - Mr Boddington through their joint Midlands connection, and Mr Megson through Sir H F de Trafford (Bart), who had commissioned John Emms to paint members of his Barton Kennel on several occasions.

For some unknown reason Maud Earl painted the same portrait, which experts believe to be a later version of the Emms original. The Earl is apparently not a copy of the Emms as her style differs and the brush strokes are more delicate. The suggestion is that this later painting was commissioned at the request of Rutland's breeder, the Reverend Hans Hamilton of Woodmansterne in Surrey, a close friend of Maud's from the neighbouring parish of Burgh Heath.

BIBLIOGRAPHY

Baskerville W ***Show Collies and Shetland Sheepdogs***
Bennett,Dr O P ***The Collie,*** 1917
Bishop, Ada ***All About the Collie,*** 2nd impression 1975
Bridge, Dareen ***Which is the Top Winning Rough Collie***, International Collie Handbook 1996
Bridge, Dareen ***Sires of Consequence***, International Collie Handbook 1998
Bridge, Dareen ***From Trefoil to the Present***, International Collie Handbook 1999
Chatfield, Audrey ***International Rough Collie Pedigrees***, 1886-1989
Catalogue of Livestock Exhibits at the Sandy Show, Beds. 28th August 1947
Clark, Stella ***Rough and Smooth Collies***, 1993
Collie Association's Handbook, edited by Margaret Osborne 1952
Collie Club of America Archives
Collie Club of America ***The Complete Collie***, 1962
Collie Club of America ***The New Collie*** 1988
Combe, Iris ***Collies Yesterday and Today,*** 1972
Combe, Iris ***Herding Dogs- Their Origins and Development in Britain***, 1987
Combe, Iris ***Rough Collie Records***, 1997
Dalziel, Hugh ***The Collie-Its History, Points and Breeding,*** 1888
Dog World ***Rough Collie Forum***, 24 July 1998
Hunt, Hazel ***Rough Collies- An Owner's Companion***, 1990
Hutchinson's ***Dog Encyclopaedia***, 1935
Jackson, Frank ***Crufts, The Official History***, 1990 (Pelham Books)
Jackson, Frank ***The Birmingham Dog Show Society- a History***, 1988
Johns, Rowland ***Our Friend the Collie***, 1934
Kennel Gazette ***The Judges' Choice***, 1994
Lee, Rawdon ***The Collie or Sheepdog; a history and description***, 1890
Mangles, Trudy B ***Evolution of the Collie***, 2nd edition 1971
Mason, W E ***The Collie Folio,*** Vol.9, no.94, December 1913
Osborne, Margaret ***The Collie***, 1st edition 1957 & 9th edition, 1978
Packwood, H E ***Show Collies Rough and Smooth,*** 1904
Roos, Mrs George H (Bobbee) ***Collie Concept*** 1982
Speding, Aileen ***The Collie***, revised edition 1986
Stansfield, Wm W ***The Collie Folio,*** Vol.11 no.117, November 1915
Sutton, Catherine G ***Dog Shows and Show Dogs,*** 1980
The British Fanciers' Annual Review for 1894
The Kennel Club Stud Books 1874-1999
The Kennel Club's ***Breed Record Supplements to the Stud Book***, February 1970-December 2000
The Kennel Club ***A Short History of the Kennel Club,*** Programme of the Centenary Banquet, 2 May 1973
The Kennel Club ***Year Book*** 1999/2000
The Kennel Gazette Breed Register, April 1880-January 1970 inclusive
Thomson, W W ***Pillars of the Stud Book – Collies***, Kennel Gazette December 1896
Various Contributors, ***Treasures of the Kennel Club,*** 2000
Watson, Sir William ***A Study of Contrasts***

Notes

Notes

Notes

Notes

Notes